MY BAD™

VOLUME ONE

IMPORTANT NEW SUPERHERO UNIVERSE

MARK RUSSELL

BRYCE INGMAN

PETER KRAUSE

KELLY FITZPATRICK

ROB STEEN

AHOY
COMICS

COMICSAHOY.COM 🐦 @ AHOYCOMICMAGS

HART SEELY - PUBLISHER
TOM PEYER - EDITOR-IN-CHIEF
FRANK CAMMUSO - CHIEF CREATIVE OFFICER
STUART MOORE - OPS
SARAH LITT - EDITOR-AT-LARGE
CORY SEDLMEIER - COLLECTIONS EDITOR

DAVID HYDE - PUBLICITY
DERON BENNETT - PRODUCTION COORDINATOR
KIT CAOAGAS - MARKETING ASSOCIATE
HANNA BAHEDRY - PUBLICITY COORDINATOR
LILLIAN LASERSON - LEGAL
RUSSELL NATHERSON SR. - BUSINESS

MY BAD

VOLUME ONE

IMPORTANT NEW SUPERHERO UNIVERSE

MARK RUSSELL & BRYCE INGMAN	WRITERS
PETER KRAUSE	ARTIST
JOE ORSAK	ARTIST (ONE-PAGE FEATURETTES)
MARK RUSSELL	ARTIST (PARODY MERCHANDISE ADS)
KELLY FITZPATRICK	COLOR (#1-4)
PAUL LITTLE	COLOR (#5 | ONE-PAGE FEATURETTES)
ROB STEEN	LETTERS
PETER KRAUSE	COVER ARTIST
TODD KLEIN	LOGO
JOHN J. HILL	DESIGN
DERON BENNETT	ASSOCIATE EDITOR
TOM PEYER	EDITOR
CORY SEDLMEIER	COLLECTION EDITOR

CREATED BY MARK RUSSELL, BRYCE INGMAN AND PETER KRAUSE

INTRODUCTION

There seem to be two paths when it comes to writing superhero comics—you either write them with a hefty helping of grimdark and "realistic" angst, or you lean into the nostalgia factor and go full retro. It's a spectrum, obviously, and there are myriad stories that fall between those two tentpoles, but few diverge from it. Or diverge from it well.

MY BAD, the collection you hold in your hands, is one such diversion—and a helluva fun one. Writers Mark Russell and Bryce Ingman, no strangers to comics and no strangers to subverting and tweaking the traps of the genre, team with industry legend Peter Krause to strike a mesmerizing balancing act—one that leans into the funny, with an absurdist bent, but is also loaded with heart and affection for the genre in a way that never feels cheesy or performative. This is a love letter to comics long gone, with a knowing grin and wink.

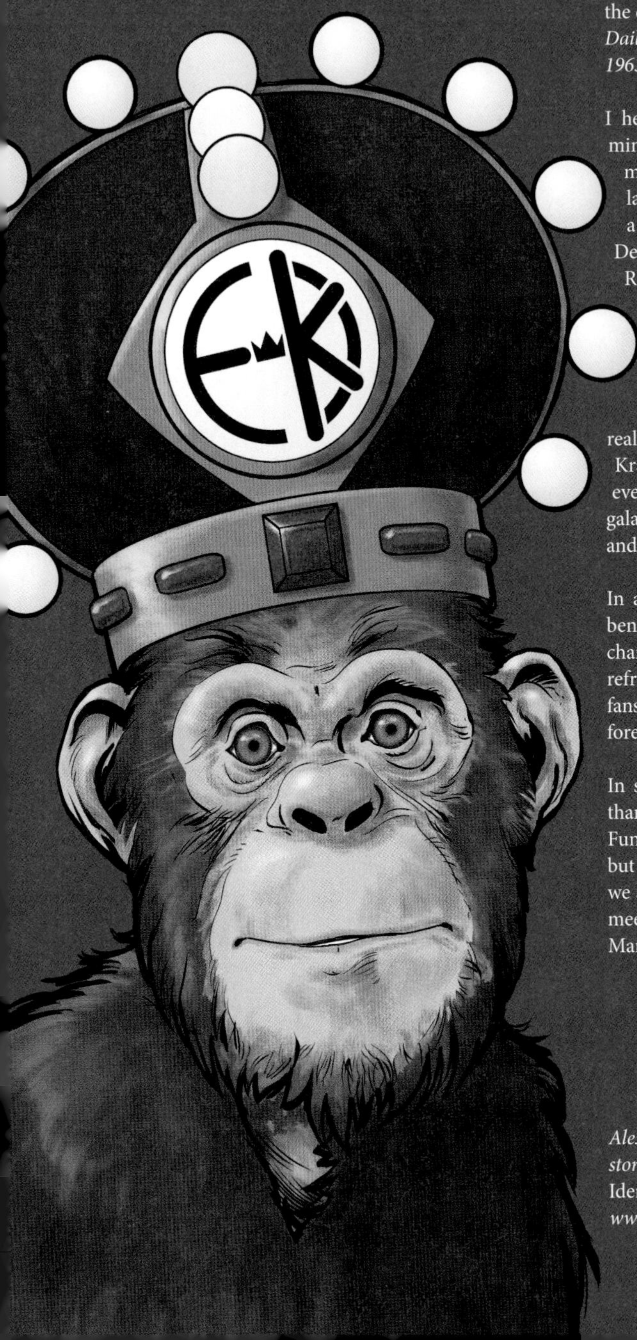

It's no surprise that this comic sprung from the publisher AHOY Comics, home to the fascinating, multiversal Batman riff, *THE WRONG EARTH*. But *MY BAD* levels things up in an impressive way—creating an entire universe that feels wholly new but eerily familiar. Russell is no stranger to cutting commentary, but it's blended with an unabashed love for superhero stories and the tropes we've all become comfortable with and love. *MY BAD* reads like a—well—*Who's Who* of heroic archetypes, pulled through the prism of the creative team's own affection for the Silver Age and their *Daily Show*-meets-*The Onion* humor. It's as if Alan Moore's *1963* series of one-shots were published by Bill Gaines.

I hesitate to even call *MY BAD* a spoof, because in my mind, a spoof implies some kind of dunking on the source material—and this book, while unafraid to sharply lampoon the traditions of superhero comics, does it with a joy and energy that evokes the early issues of Giffen/DeMatteis/Maguire's *Justice League International* and Russell's own *One-Star Squadron* with artist Steve Lieber. *MY BAD* is the heir-apparent to books like that, and more than earns its keep.

Krause's art, evocative and noir, brings a grit to the proceedings that balances the scales, adding a dose of realism to Russell and Ingman's absurdist universe-building. Krause is an artist's artist, the kind of illustrator who brings everything he's got to every panel, from the mundane to the galaxy shattering. And hey, his covers, and Jerry Ordway's and Jonathan Case's variants? Chef's kiss.

In a superhero comic book marketplace that often seems bent on doubling down on things like continuity and arcane character trivia coated with reheated nostalgia, *MY BAD* is a refreshing take on the timeless stories that made many of us fans — with the knowing zing of someone who can see the forest from the trees, and poke fun where it's needed.

In short: You're in for a treat, friend, and so much more than a "guess who this hero is" romp. *MY BAD* is a blast: Fun, engaging, and loaded with Easter eggs on every page, but also not short on the heart and characterization that we all love about the Silver Age of Comics. Hope you enjoy meeting heroes like The Chandelier, Accelerator, Rush Hour, Manchild and more; I certainly did.

Alex Segura
March 2022

Alex Segura is an acclaimed author of novels, comics, short stories, and more. His latest, the comic book noir Secret Identity, *is out now from Flatiron Books. Find out more at www.alexsegura.com*

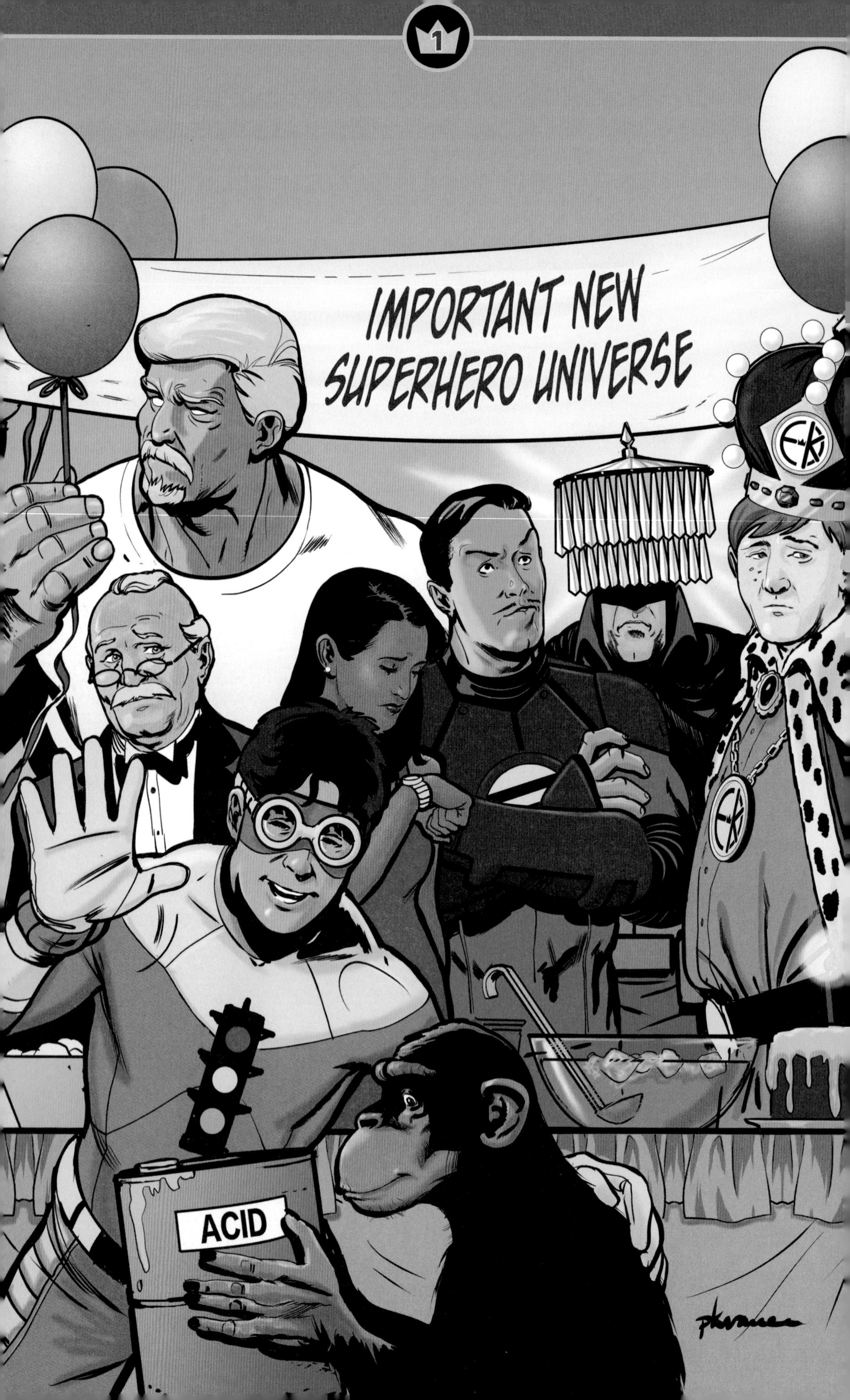
IMPORTANT NEW SUPERHERO UNIVERSE
ACID

"HE WAS A BRAVE MAN WHO FIRST ATE AN OYSTER."

-JONATHAN SWIFT

JUST ANOTHER NIGHT IN GRAVEL CITY.
A CITY WHICH DWELLS IN DARKNESS.
DUE, IN LARGE PART, TO BUDGET CUTS IN PUBLIC LIGHTING.
BUT ALSO, YOU KNOW, BECAUSE OF CRIME.
BUT THEN, I'VE ALWAYS BEEN ONE TO LIGHT A CANDLE...
FASTER, CHARLIE! I GOT A BAD FEELIN'...
AWW, GET OFF MY YAMS!
KAKLINK
...RATHER THAN CURSE THE DARKNESS!
IT'S... THE CHANDELIER!
NEED A LIGHT?
MY BAD
HAPPY BIRTHDAY

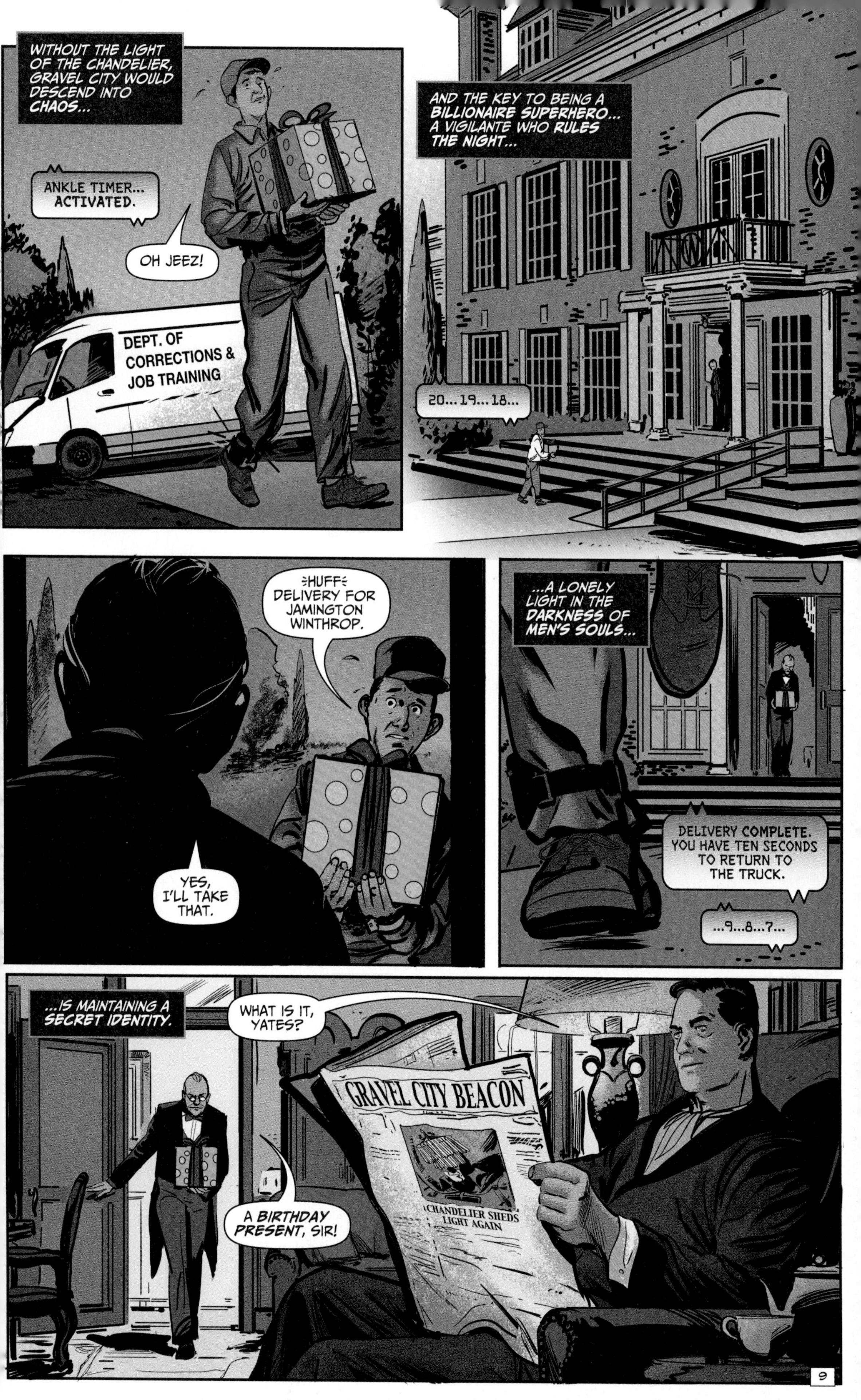
WITHOUT THE LIGHT OF THE CHANDELIER, GRAVEL CITY WOULD DESCEND INTO CHAOS...
ANKLE TIMER... ACTIVATED.
OH JEEZ!
DEPT. OF CORRECTIONS & JOB TRAINING
AND THE KEY TO BEING A BILLIONAIRE SUPERHERO... A VIGILANTE WHO RULES THE NIGHT...
20...19...18...
=HUFF= DELIVERY FOR JAMINGTON WINTHROP.
YES, I'LL TAKE THAT.
...A LONELY LIGHT IN THE DARKNESS OF MEN'S SOULS...
DELIVERY COMPLETE. YOU HAVE TEN SECONDS TO RETURN TO THE TRUCK.
...9...8...7...
...IS MAINTAINING A SECRET IDENTITY.
WHAT IS IT, YATES?
GRAVEL CITY BEACON
CHANDELIER SHEDS LIGHT AGAIN
A BIRTHDAY PRESENT, SIR!

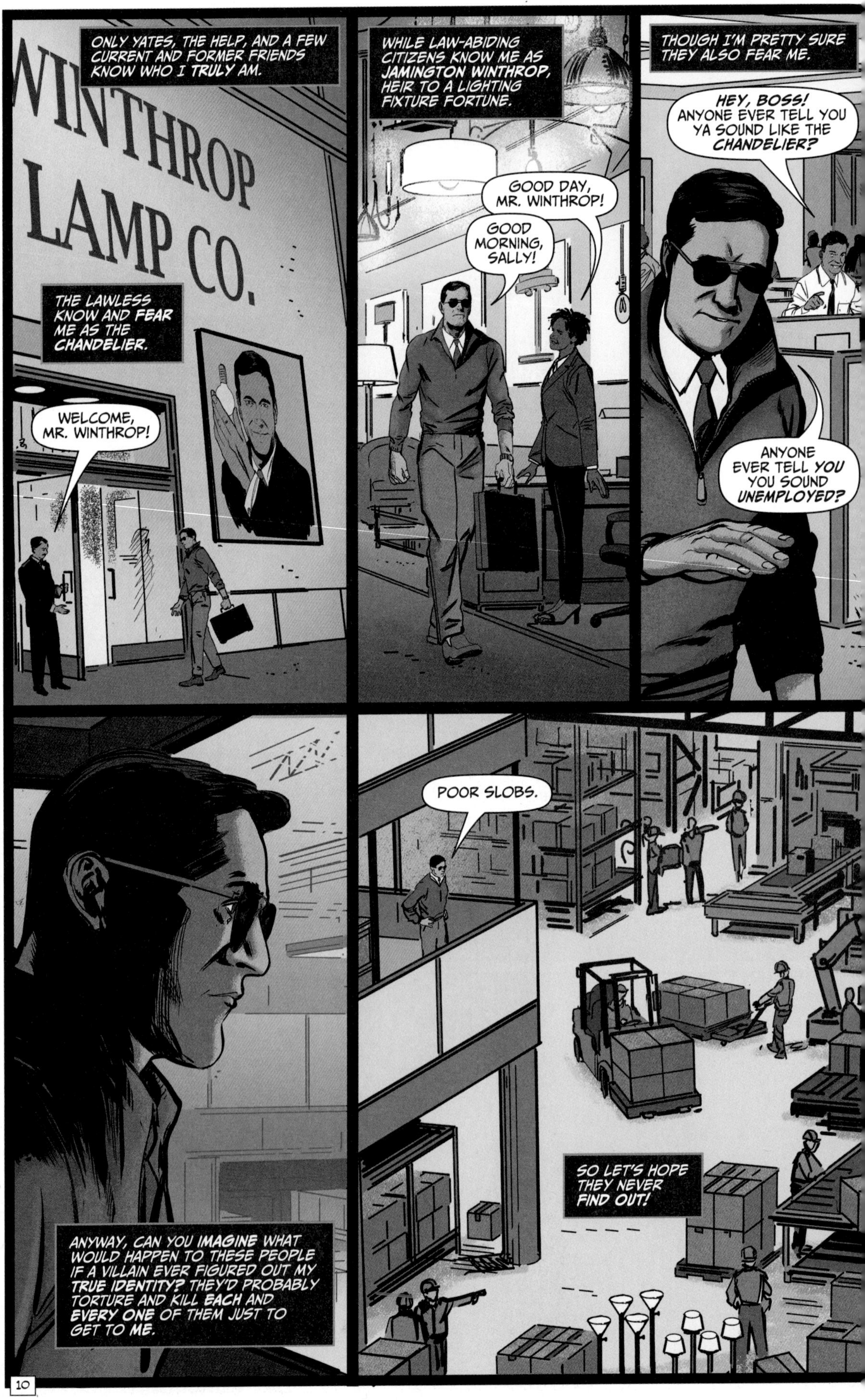
ONLY YATES, THE HELP, AND A FEW CURRENT AND FORMER FRIENDS KNOW WHO I TRULY AM.
WINTHROP LAMP CO.
THE LAWLESS KNOW AND FEAR ME AS THE CHANDELIER.
WELCOME, MR. WINTHROP!
WHILE LAW-ABIDING CITIZENS KNOW ME AS JAMINGTON WINTHROP, HEIR TO A LIGHTING FIXTURE FORTUNE.
GOOD DAY, MR. WINTHROP!
GOOD MORNING, SALLY!
THOUGH I'M PRETTY SURE THEY ALSO FEAR ME.
HEY, BOSS! ANYONE EVER TELL YOU YA SOUND LIKE THE CHANDELIER?
ANYONE EVER TELL YOU YOU SOUND UNEMPLOYED?
ANYWAY, CAN YOU IMAGINE WHAT WOULD HAPPEN TO THESE PEOPLE IF A VILLAIN EVER FIGURED OUT MY TRUE IDENTITY? THEY'D PROBABLY TORTURE AND KILL EACH AND EVERY ONE OF THEM JUST TO GET TO ME.
POOR SLOBS.
SO LET'S HOPE THEY NEVER FIND OUT!

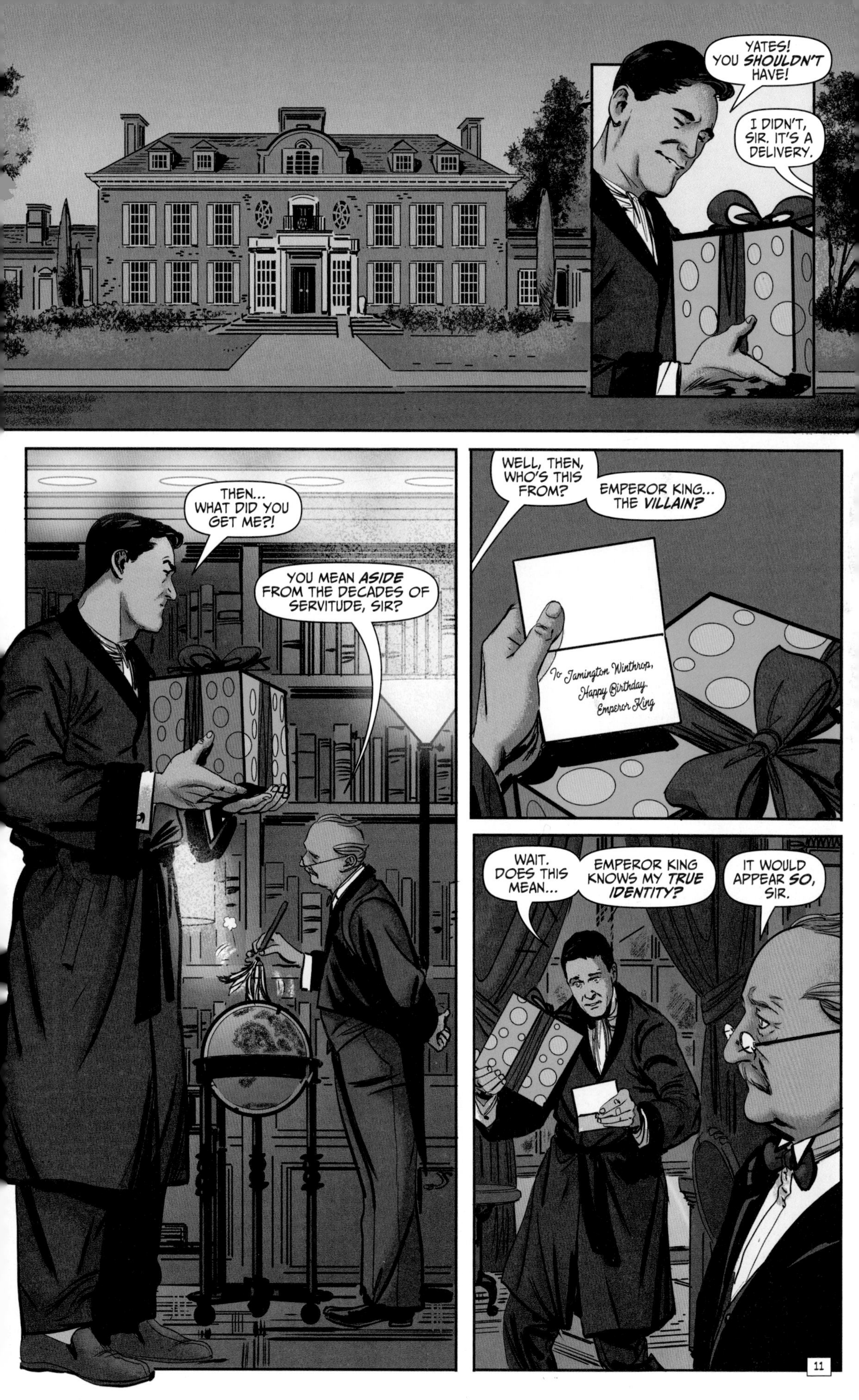
YATES! YOU SHOULDN'T HAVE!
I DIDN'T, SIR. IT'S A DELIVERY.
THEN... WHAT DID YOU GET ME?!
YOU MEAN ASIDE FROM THE DECADES OF SERVITUDE, SIR?
WELL, THEN, WHO'S THIS FROM?
EMPEROR KING... THE VILLAIN?
To Jamington Winthrop,
Happy Birthday.
Emperor King
WAIT. DOES THIS MEAN...
EMPEROR KING KNOWS MY TRUE IDENTITY?
IT WOULD APPEAR SO, SIR.

OH MY GOD! OH MY GOD!

HE'S COMING *HERE!* RAISE THE *BLAST SHIELDS*, YATES!

LOAD THE *LASER CANNONS!*

WE CAN'T LOAD THE LASER CANNONS.

WHAT?! WHY *NOT?!*

BECAUSE THEY DON'T *EXIST*, SIR.

HOLY CRAP.

THIS IS *BAD.* THIS IS *BAD!*

THIS LEAVES ONLY *ONE QUESTION,* YATES.

WHICH *IS*, SIR?

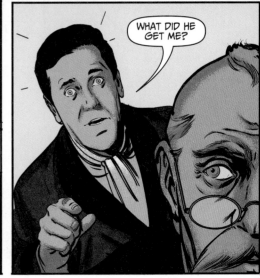

WHAT DID HE GET ME?

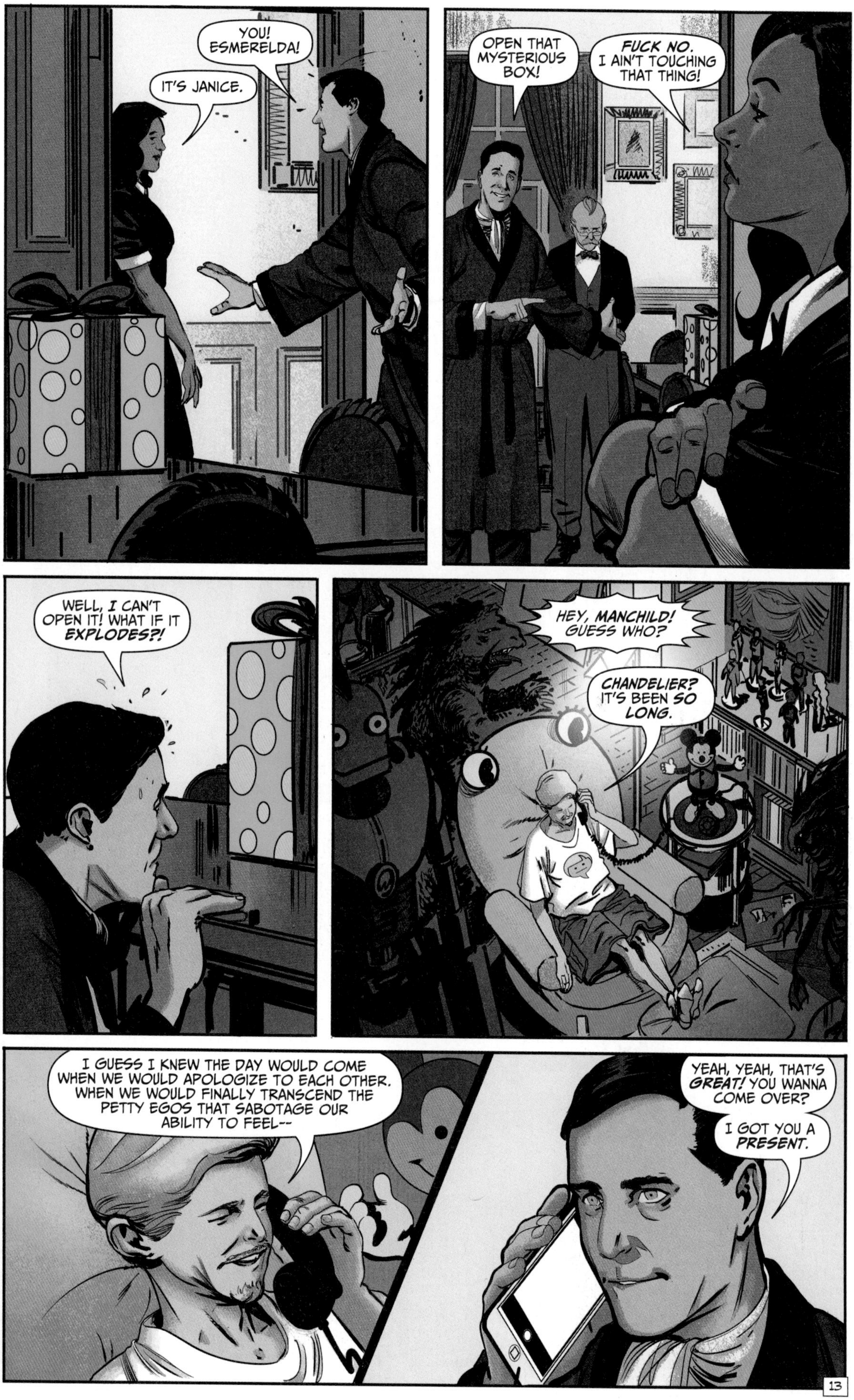
YOU! ESMERELDA!
IT'S JANICE.
OPEN THAT MYSTERIOUS BOX!
FUCK NO. I AIN'T TOUCHING THAT THING!
WELL, *I* CAN'T OPEN IT! WHAT IF IT *EXPLODES?!*
HEY, *MANCHILD!* GUESS WHO?
CHANDELIER? IT'S BEEN *SO LONG.*
I GUESS I KNEW THE DAY WOULD COME WHEN WE WOULD APOLOGIZE TO EACH OTHER. WHEN WE WOULD FINALLY TRANSCEND THE PETTY EGOS THAT SABOTAGE OUR ABILITY TO FEEL--
YEAH, YEAH, THAT'S *GREAT!* YOU WANNA COME OVER?
I GOT YOU A *PRESENT.*

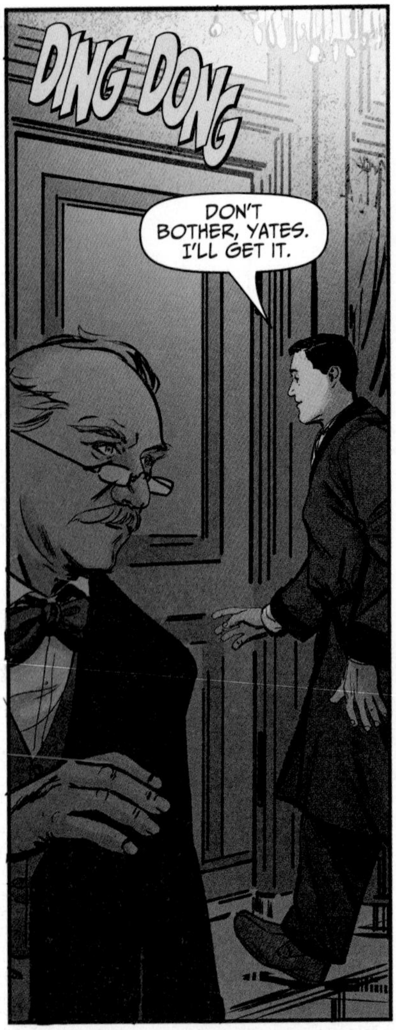
DING DONG
DON'T BOTHER, YATES. I'LL GET IT.
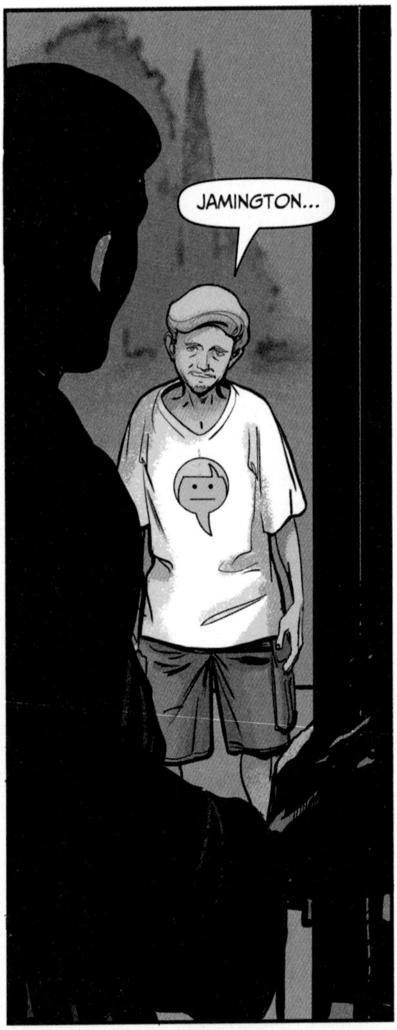
JAMINGTON...
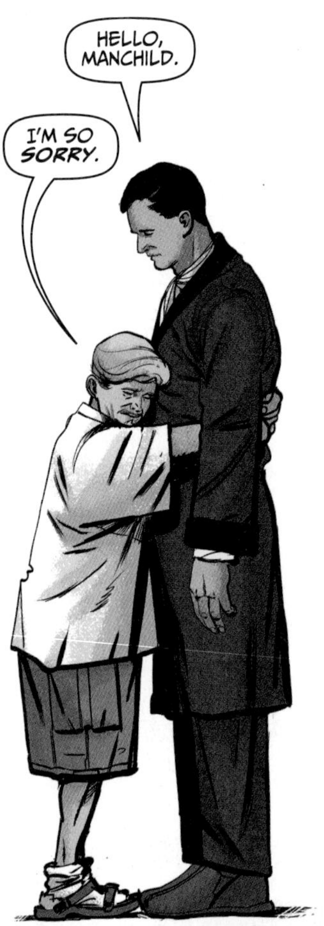
HELLO, MANCHILD.
I'M SO *SORRY*.
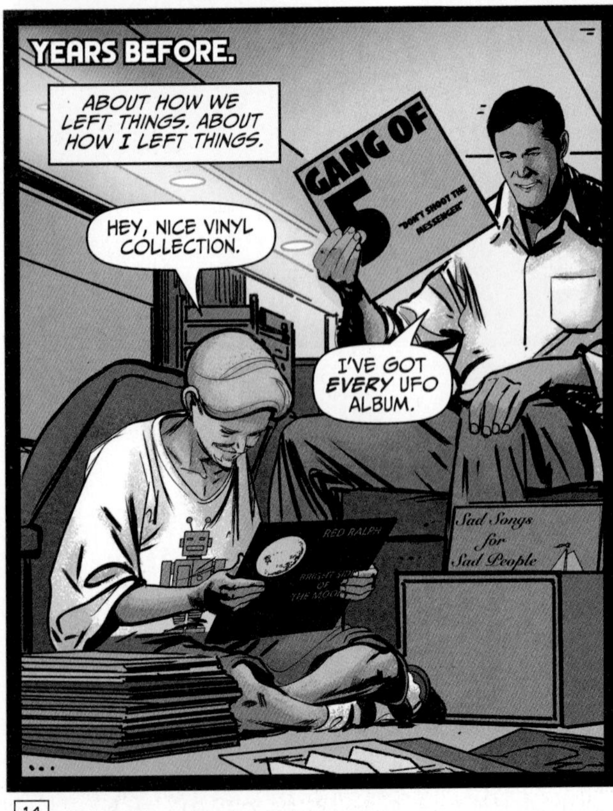
YEARS BEFORE.
*ABOUT HOW WE LEFT THINGS. ABOUT HOW **I** LEFT THINGS.*
GANG OF 5
"DON'T SHOOT THE MESSENGER"
HEY, NICE VINYL COLLECTION.
I'VE GOT ***EVERY*** UFO ALBUM.
RED RALPH
Sad Songs for Sad People
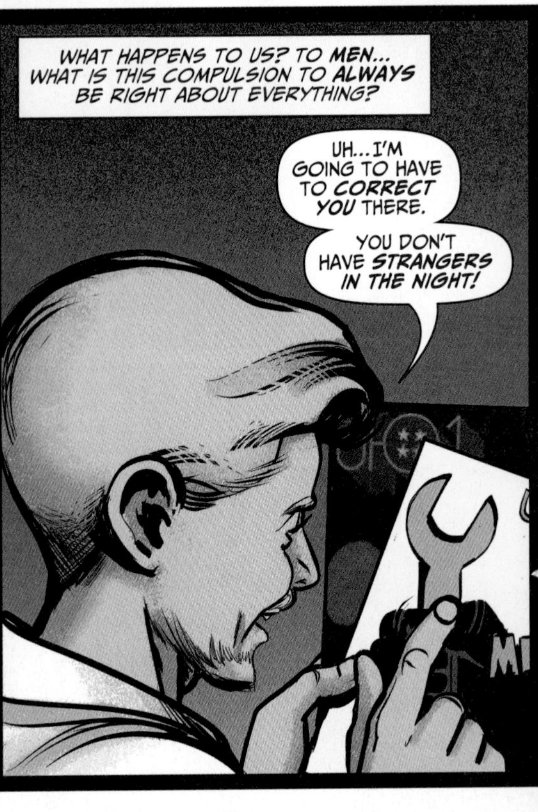
*WHAT HAPPENS TO US? TO **MEN**... WHAT IS THIS COMPULSION TO **ALWAYS** BE RIGHT ABOUT EVERYTHING?*
UH...I'M GOING TO HAVE TO ***CORRECT YOU*** THERE.
YOU DON'T HAVE ***STRANGERS IN THE NIGHT!***

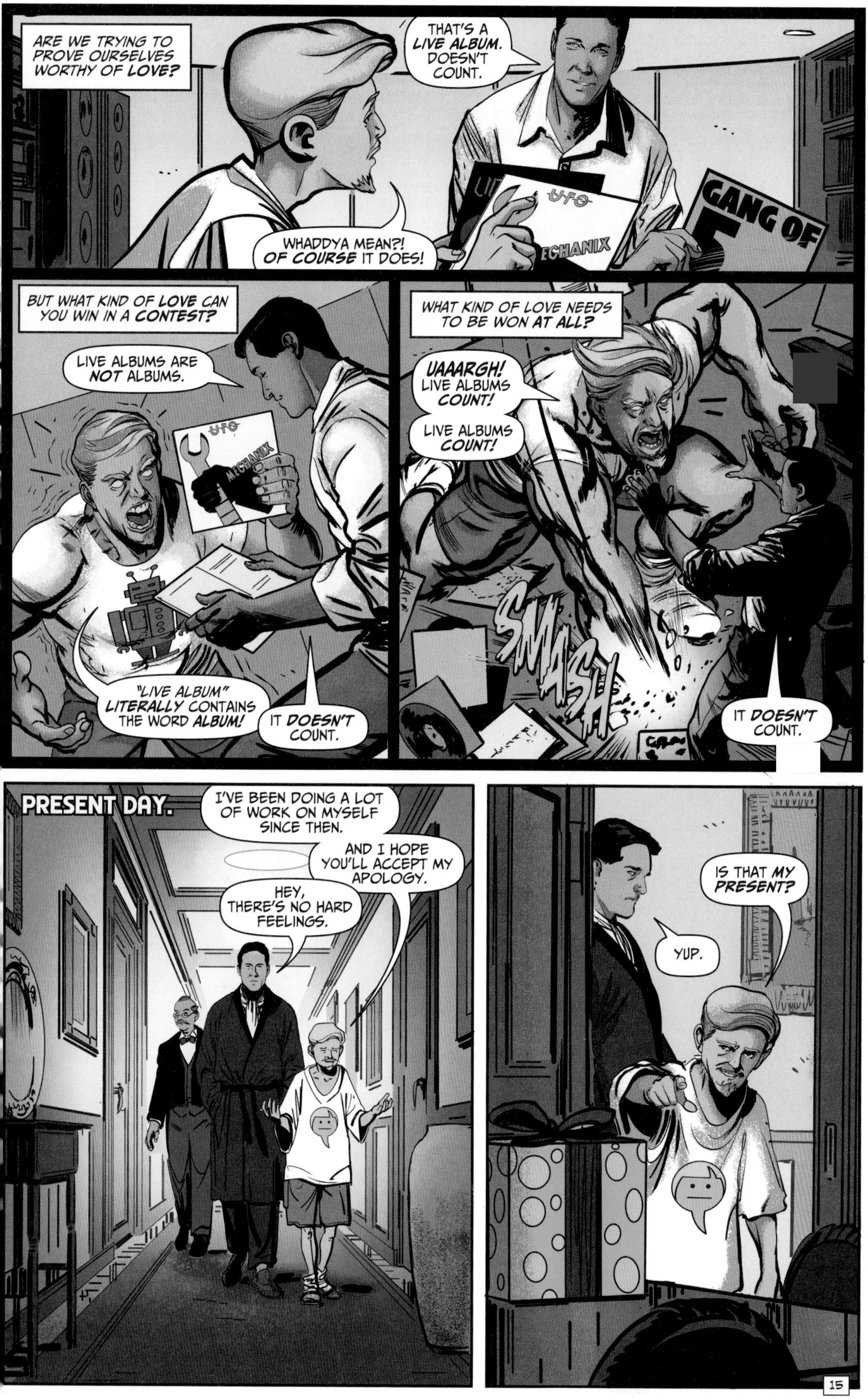
ARE WE TRYING TO PROVE OURSELVES WORTHY OF LOVE?
THAT'S A LIVE ALBUM. DOESN'T COUNT.
UFO
MECHANIX
GANG OF 5
WHADDYA MEAN?! OF COURSE IT DOES!
BUT WHAT KIND OF LOVE CAN YOU WIN IN A CONTEST?
LIVE ALBUMS ARE NOT ALBUMS.
UFO
MECHANIX
"LIVE ALBUM" LITERALLY CONTAINS THE WORD ALBUM!
IT DOESN'T COUNT.
WHAT KIND OF LOVE NEEDS TO BE WON AT ALL?
UAAARGH! LIVE ALBUMS COUNT!
LIVE ALBUMS COUNT!
SMASH
IT DOESN'T COUNT.
PRESENT DAY.
I'VE BEEN DOING A LOT OF WORK ON MYSELF SINCE THEN.
AND I HOPE YOU'LL ACCEPT MY APOLOGY.
HEY, THERE'S NO HARD FEELINGS.
IS THAT MY PRESENT?
YUP.

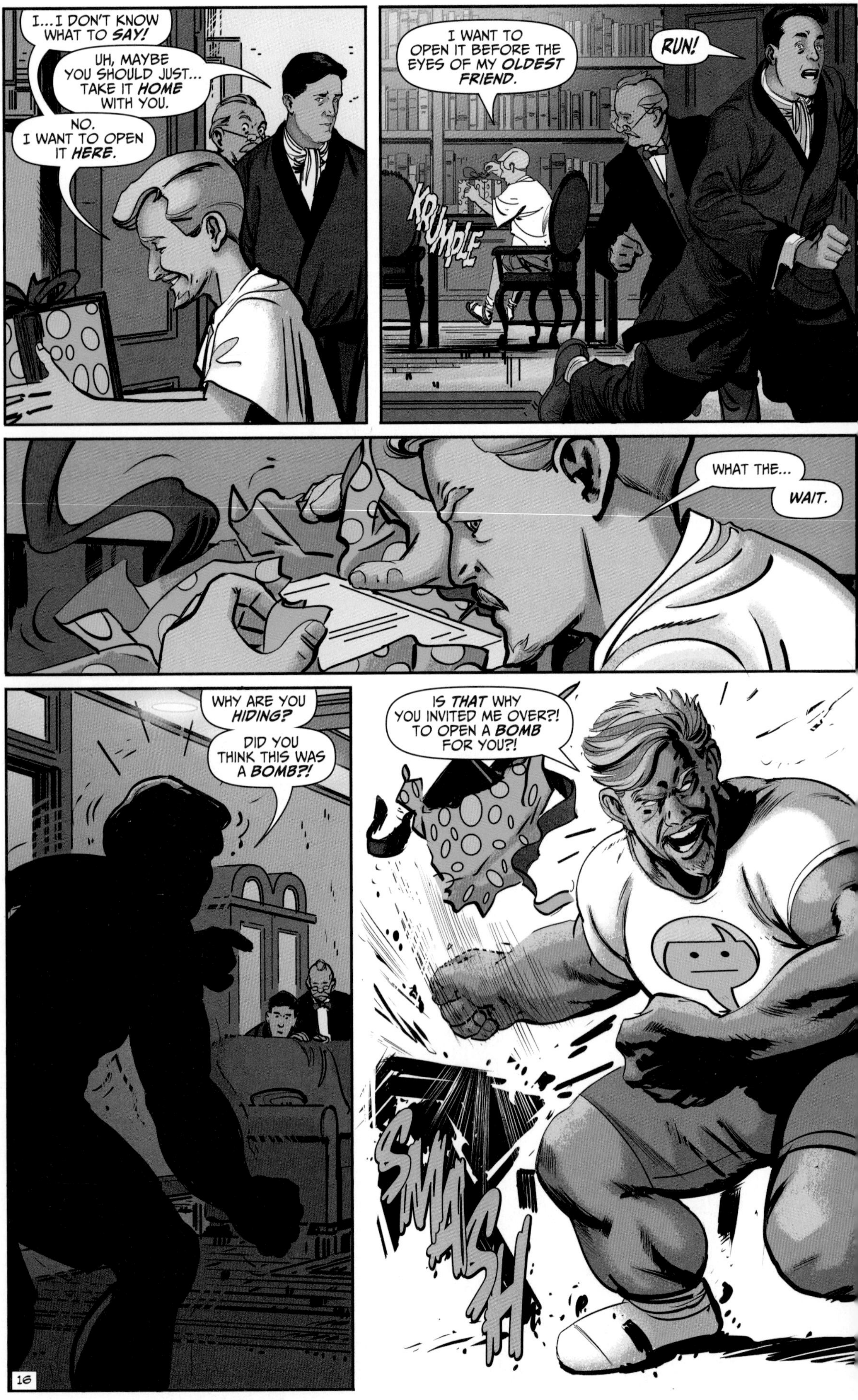

I...I DON'T KNOW WHAT TO SAY!
UH, MAYBE YOU SHOULD JUST... TAKE IT HOME WITH YOU.
NO. I WANT TO OPEN IT HERE.
I WANT TO OPEN IT BEFORE THE EYES OF MY OLDEST FRIEND.
RUN!
KRUMPLE
WHAT THE...
WAIT.
WHY ARE YOU HIDING?
DID YOU THINK THIS WAS A BOMB?!
IS THAT WHY YOU INVITED ME OVER?! TO OPEN A BOMB FOR YOU?!
SMASH

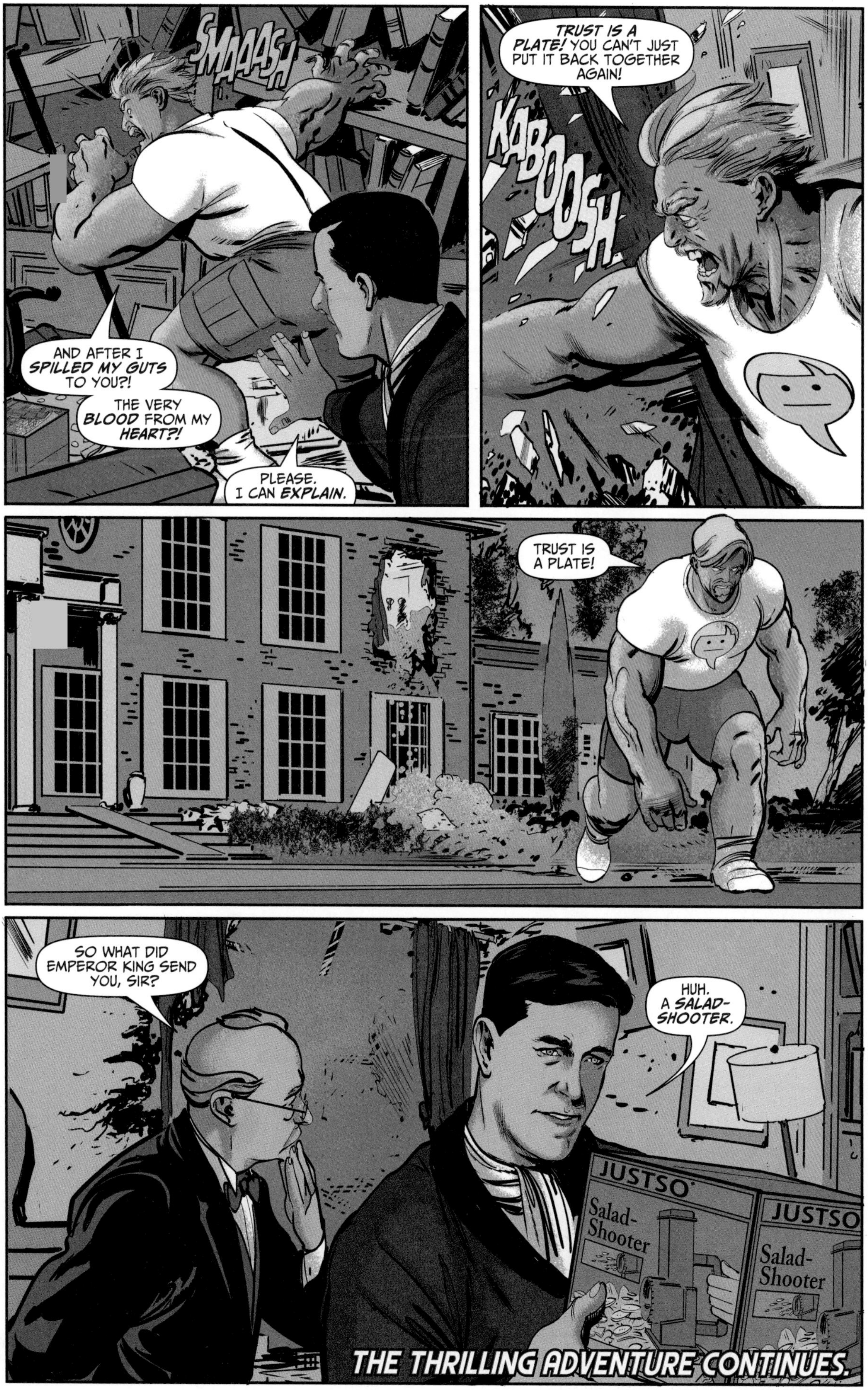
SMAAASH
AND AFTER I SPILLED MY GUTS TO YOU?!
THE VERY BLOOD FROM MY HEART?!
PLEASE. I CAN EXPLAIN.
TRUST IS A PLATE! YOU CAN'T JUST PUT IT BACK TOGETHER AGAIN!
KABOOSH
TRUST IS A PLATE!
SO WHAT DID EMPEROR KING SEND YOU, SIR?
HUH. A SALAD-SHOOTER.
JUSTSO
Salad-Shooter
JUSTSO
Salad-Shooter
THE THRILLING ADVENTURE CONTINUES.

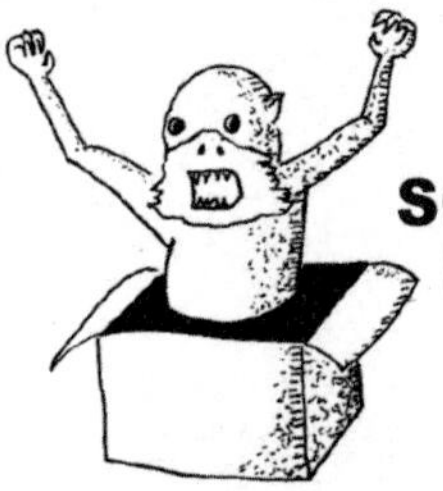

SQUIRREL MONKEY

America's #1 Pet! (No refunds). Send $20 to Texas Laboratory Surplus. El Paso, TX.

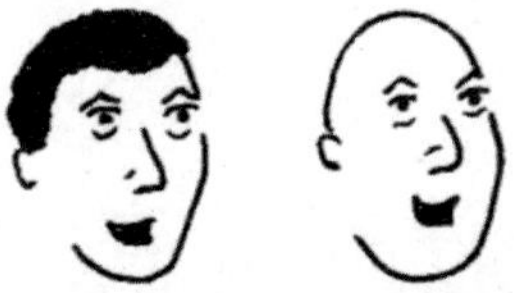

BALD CAP!

Run with skinheads or pretend to have cancer. We don't care. Ethics are a lie we tell others. Send $3 to Follicle Fraud. Pueblo, CO.

DOG CIGARETTES

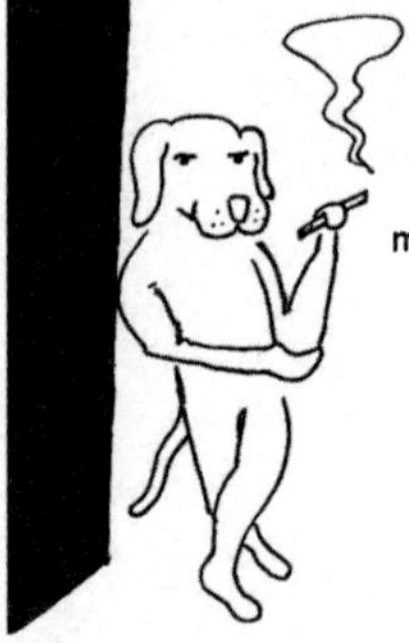

Specially formulated with the menthol flavor dogs love. Hours of sophisticated relaxation. Training manual not included.

Send $2 to French Pet. Saginaw, MI.

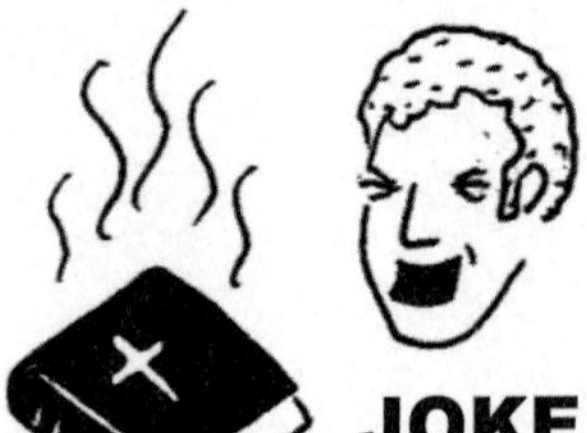

JOKE BIBLE.

Cause a stink in church. Literally! When people try to find where the smell is coming from, watch their faces when they realize it's coming from the Word of God! Christianity is just institutionalized paganism anyway. Send $8 to Creative Blasphemies. Gary, IN.

Do you have what it takes to make $$$ as a Hollywood writer? Find out! Send us a sample of your writing by writing us a check for $5.99! Our editors are waiting to discover their next big star! Dream On Studios. Hollywood, OK.

X-Ray Glasses!

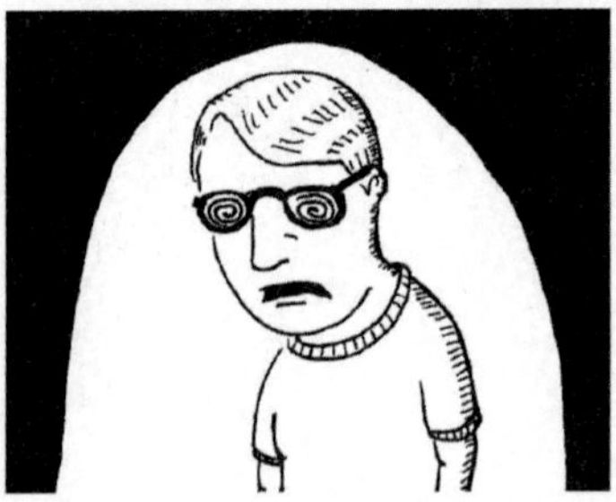

Powered by the occult! What is seen cannot be unseen. Throw off the veil and let the truth stand naked before you. Send $1 to Faustian Bargain, Des Moines, IA.

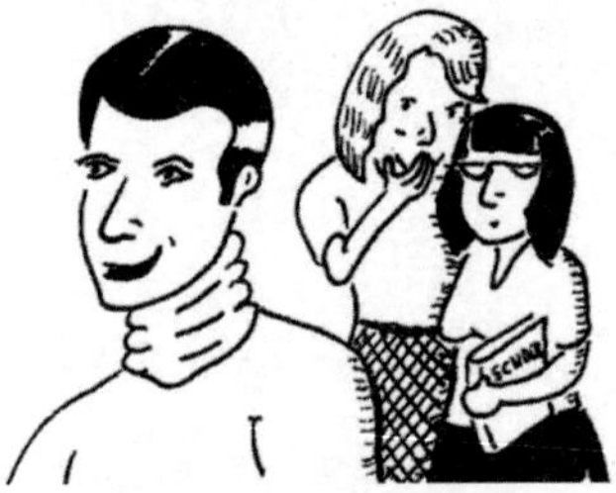

Turtlenecks!

Because there's always been something very special about you. Send $8 to Emerging Adonis Menswear. Independence, MO.

JOIN THE ORANGE BROTHERHOOD

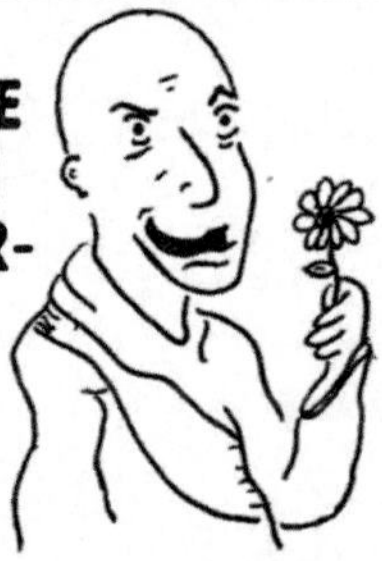

Possessions are vanities that mock your soul. Your parents died at birth. Don't let them kill you with their lies. Send any cash and credit cards in your father's wallet to the Orange Brotherhood today. Let the old world burn. Carmel, CA.

LI'L GENERAL BREAKFAST PLAY SET

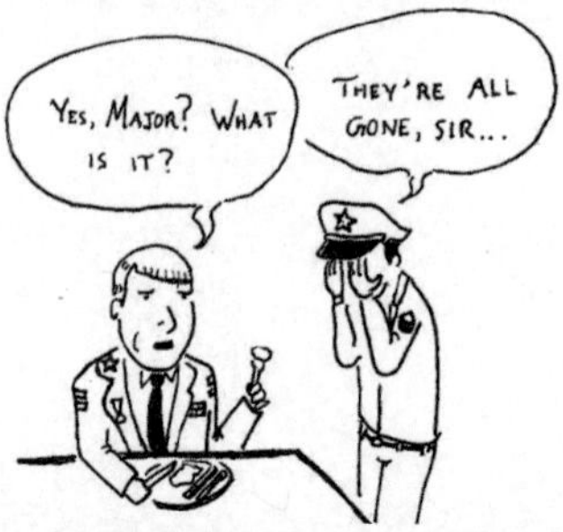
YES, MAJOR? WHAT IS IT?
THEY'RE ALL GONE, SIR...

Eat breakfast like a general! Just like they do in the real army! Send $10 to Art of War Costumes. Wilmington, VT.

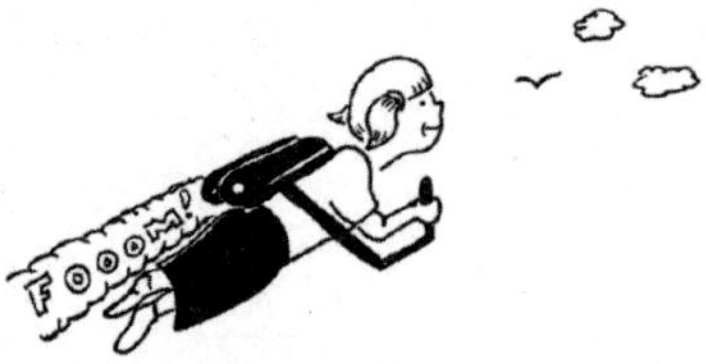
FOOOM!

STARTER JETPACK

Use only FAA-approved jetpack fuel (not included). Foam-of-life fire extinguisher and bone-setting kit sold separately. Send $19.99 to Big Bang Toys. Los Alamos, NM.

Make Big $ Running A Puppy Mill. Not as cute as it sounds. Apathetic personality and access to cheap hamburger a plus. Send for free brochure today.

Learn Karate

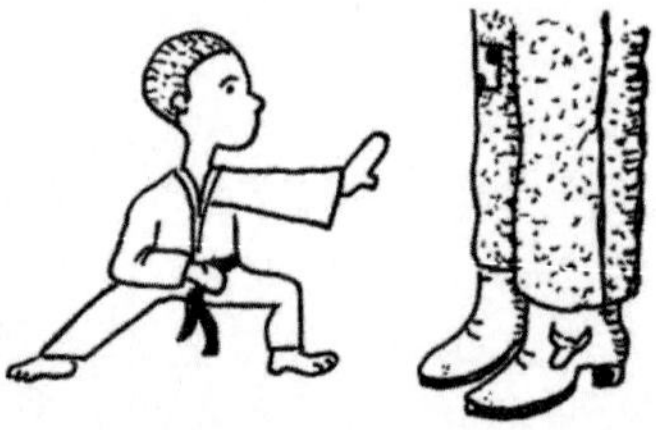

20 Page Booklet teaches you all you need to vanquish ANY opponent. Feast upon their humiliation. It works. Seriously. You don't even need to read the whole thing. Try it on anyone. You're a lion. Send $1 to The Combat Studio, Germantown, PA.

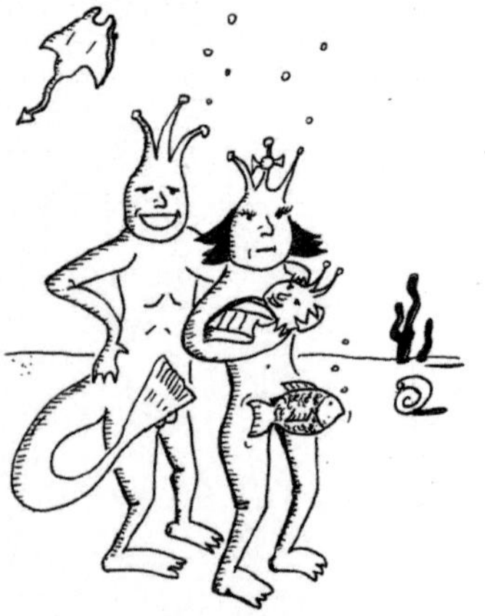

BRINE SHRIMP!

Now with genitalia! Put them in water. Maybe they'll be alive, maybe they won't. Your guess is as good as ours. Send $1.99 to Tainted Seafood Products. Clearwater, FL.

Exploit Comic Book Readers for Profit! Learn how! Send for our proven money-making methods and start bilking readers today! Send $8 to Place Your Own Comic Book Ads. Syracuse, NY.

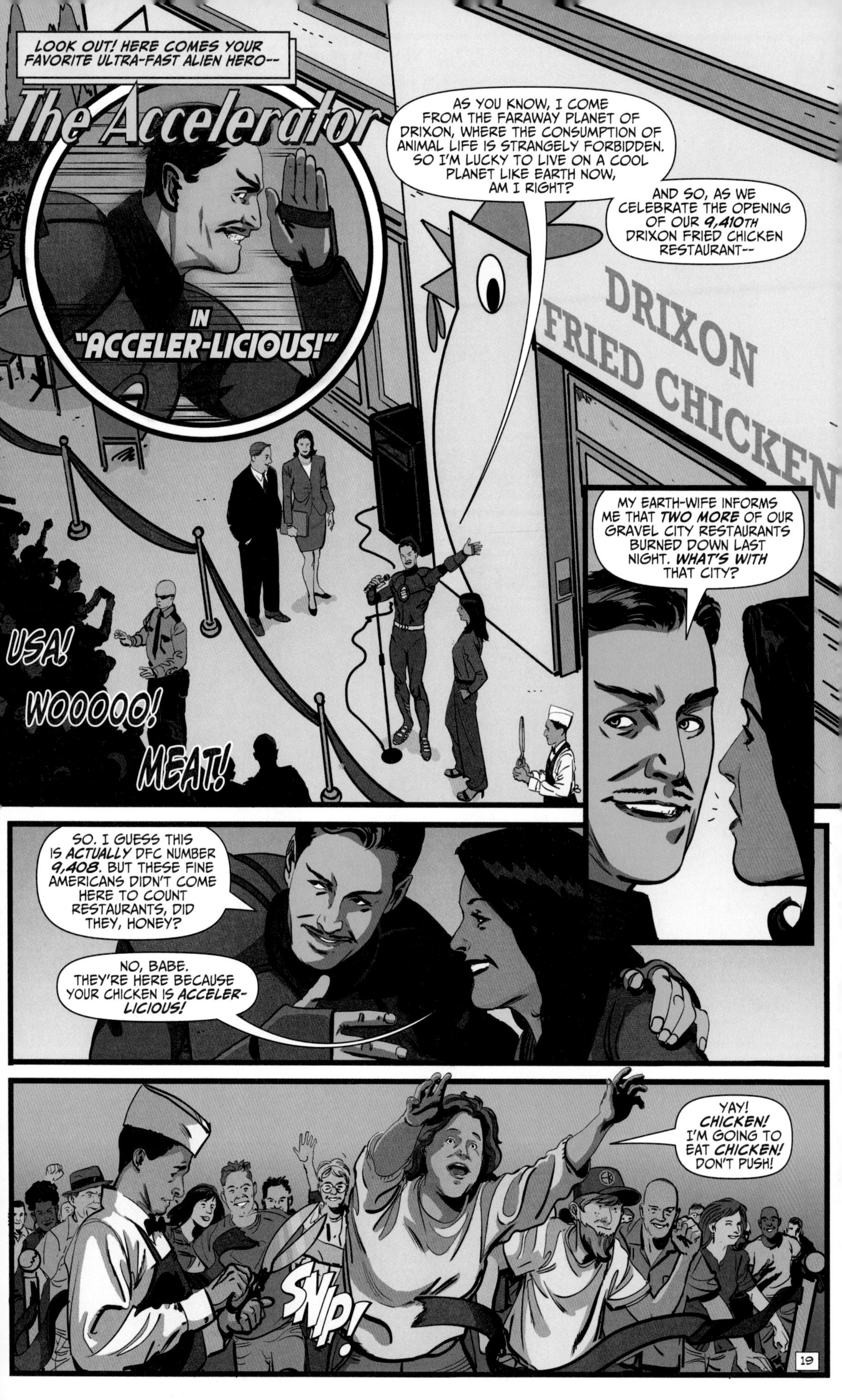

LOOK OUT! HERE COMES YOUR FAVORITE ULTRA-FAST ALIEN HERO--
The Accelerator
IN "ACCELER-LICIOUS!"
AS YOU KNOW, I COME FROM THE FARAWAY PLANET OF DRIXON, WHERE THE CONSUMPTION OF ANIMAL LIFE IS STRANGELY FORBIDDEN. SO I'M LUCKY TO LIVE ON A COOL PLANET LIKE EARTH NOW, AM I RIGHT?
AND SO, AS WE CELEBRATE THE OPENING OF OUR 9,410TH DRIXON FRIED CHICKEN RESTAURANT--
DRIXON FRIED CHICKEN
USA!
WOOOOO!
MEAT!
MY EARTH-WIFE INFORMS ME THAT TWO MORE OF OUR GRAVEL CITY RESTAURANTS BURNED DOWN LAST NIGHT. WHAT'S WITH THAT CITY?
SO. I GUESS THIS IS ACTUALLY DFC NUMBER 9,408. BUT THESE FINE AMERICANS DIDN'T COME HERE TO COUNT RESTAURANTS, DID THEY, HONEY?
NO, BABE. THEY'RE HERE BECAUSE YOUR CHICKEN IS ACCELER-LICIOUS!
YAY! CHICKEN! I'M GOING TO EAT CHICKEN! DON'T PUSH!
SNIP!

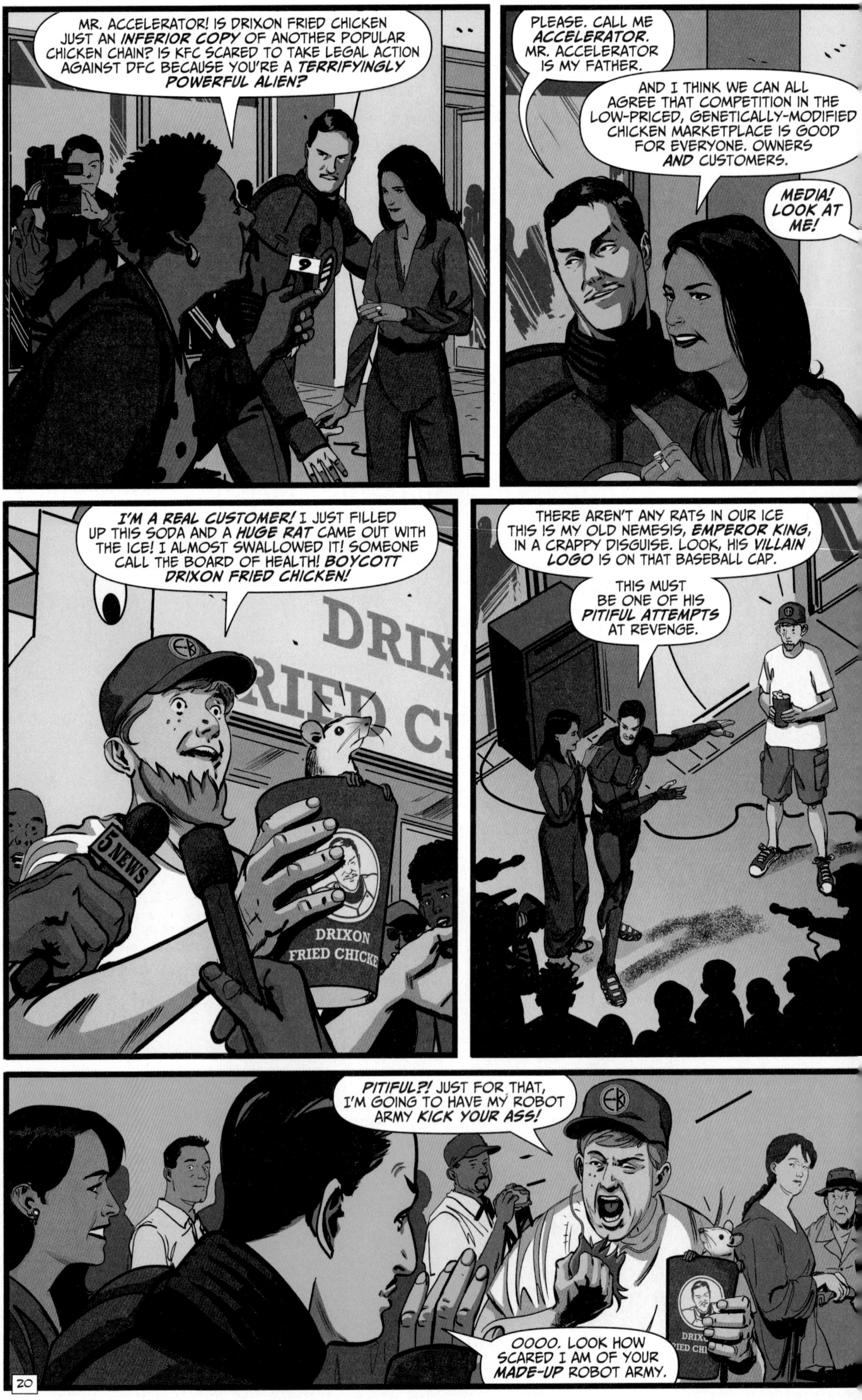
MR. ACCELERATOR! IS DRIXON FRIED CHICKEN JUST AN INFERIOR COPY OF ANOTHER POPULAR CHICKEN CHAIN? IS KFC SCARED TO TAKE LEGAL ACTION AGAINST DFC BECAUSE YOU'RE A TERRIFYINGLY POWERFUL ALIEN?
9
PLEASE. CALL ME ACCELERATOR. MR. ACCELERATOR IS MY FATHER.
AND I THINK WE CAN ALL AGREE THAT COMPETITION IN THE LOW-PRICED, GENETICALLY-MODIFIED CHICKEN MARKETPLACE IS GOOD FOR EVERYONE. OWNERS AND CUSTOMERS.
MEDIA! LOOK AT ME!
I'M A REAL CUSTOMER! I JUST FILLED UP THIS SODA AND A HUGE RAT CAME OUT WITH THE ICE! I ALMOST SWALLOWED IT! SOMEONE CALL THE BOARD OF HEALTH! BOYCOTT DRIXON FRIED CHICKEN!
5 NEWS
DRIXON
THERE AREN'T ANY RATS IN OUR ICE THIS IS MY OLD NEMESIS, EMPEROR KING, IN A CRAPPY DISGUISE. LOOK, HIS VILLAIN LOGO IS ON THAT BASEBALL CAP.
THIS MUST BE ONE OF HIS PITIFUL ATTEMPTS AT REVENGE.
PITIFUL?! JUST FOR THAT, I'M GOING TO HAVE MY ROBOT ARMY KICK YOUR ASS!
OOOO. LOOK HOW SCARED I AM OF YOUR MADE-UP ROBOT ARMY.

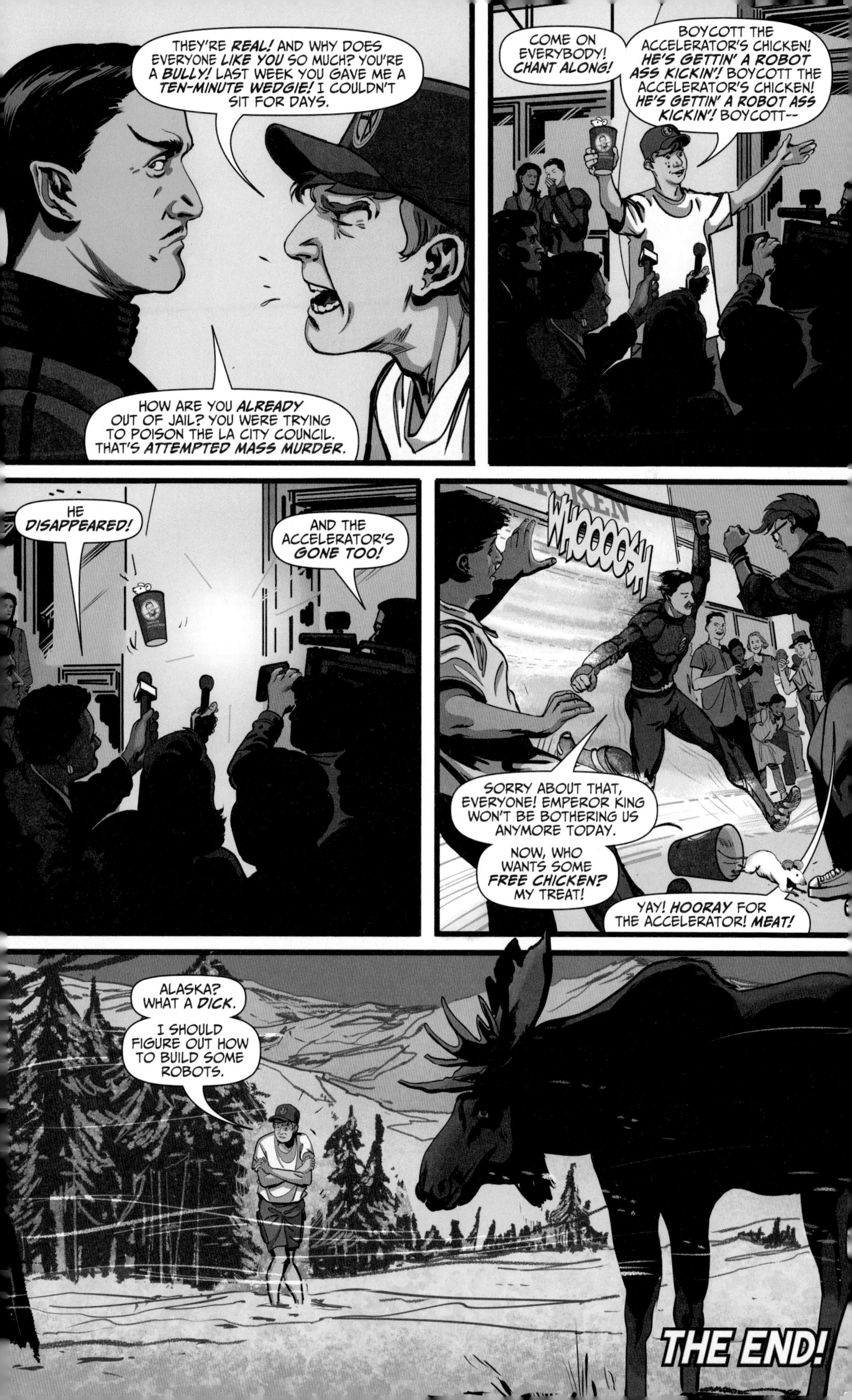
THEY'RE REAL! AND WHY DOES EVERYONE LIKE YOU SO MUCH? YOU'RE A BULLY! LAST WEEK YOU GAVE ME A TEN-MINUTE WEDGIE! I COULDN'T SIT FOR DAYS.
HOW ARE YOU ALREADY OUT OF JAIL? YOU WERE TRYING TO POISON THE LA CITY COUNCIL. THAT'S ATTEMPTED MASS MURDER.
COME ON EVERYBODY! CHANT ALONG!
BOYCOTT THE ACCELERATOR'S CHICKEN! HE'S GETTIN' A ROBOT ASS KICKIN'! BOYCOTT THE ACCELERATOR'S CHICKEN! HE'S GETTIN' A ROBOT ASS KICKIN'! BOYCOTT--
HE DISAPPEARED!
AND THE ACCELERATOR'S GONE TOO!
WHOOOOSH
SORRY ABOUT THAT, EVERYONE! EMPEROR KING WON'T BE BOTHERING US ANYMORE TODAY.
NOW, WHO WANTS SOME FREE CHICKEN? MY TREAT!
YAY! HOORAY FOR THE ACCELERATOR! MEAT!
ALASKA? WHAT A DICK.
I SHOULD FIGURE OUT HOW TO BUILD SOME ROBOTS.
THE END!

THE SOMEWHAT OFFICIAL HANDBOOK OF THE IMPORTANT NEW SUPERHERO UNIVERSE™ PRESENTS:

RUSH HOUR

Real Name: Aaron Maximus Lanebo

Occupation: Super-human adventurer, RV Salesman (weekends)

Known Relatives: Brad Lanebo (cousin)

Unknown Relatives: Half-sister in Kentucky

Group Affiliation: AAA Auto Club

Base of Operations: Half of a two-bedroom apartment, Los Angeles, CA

Wi-Fi Password: AaronDaBadass97

First Appearance: MY BAD #1

Height: 6′

Weight: 155 lbs (160 after the holidays)

Hips: Shapely

Facial Hair: Comes in patchy

Tips: 15%

Origin Story: A man and a woman had sexual intercourse in the missionary position conceiving a child. Choosing the first name listed at NameYourBaby.com, they christened him "Aaron."

History: Recently, Aaron Lanebo's car ran out of gas on a deserted California highway. A wizard appeared and granted him superhuman powers. Subsequently, this wizard may or may not have hypnotized Lanebo into believing he must use these powers to improve LA traffic.

Mission: "To improve Los Angeles traffic or die trying!"

Strength Level: Combined strength of two average 25-year-old men

Known Powers: Lanebo is capable of flying through the air under his own power. Additionally, he can generate "breath blasts" with his lungs that are powerful enough to knock over a car or light truck. Lanebo is also pretty good at Air Hockey and once tied a cherry stem into a knot with his tongue.

Promo Code: LOYALTY75

Secret Fear: Bug crawling into ear while sleeping

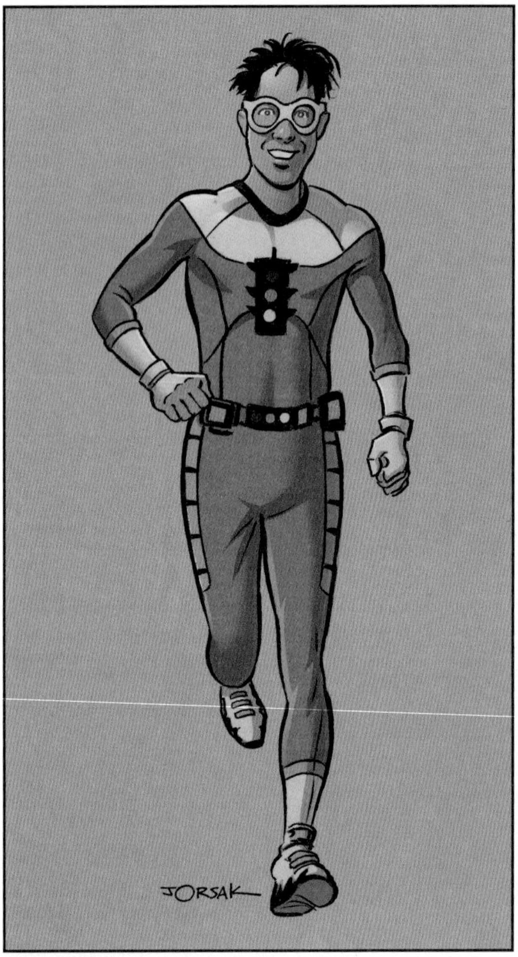
JORSAK

Turn-Ons: A nice smile

Turn-Offs: A murderous smile

Something he'd be embarrassed to see on his Handbook page: Pasta makes him gassy

Collects: Novelty spoons

Is it important to read all of this crap: Your life may depend on it

Food sensitivities: Allergic to sweet pickles, breaks out in hives if exposed

Doctor's statement on Mr. Lanebo's sweet pickle allergy: "Likely psychosomatic. Kind of funny."

Dream vacation: Riding a unicorn around Epcot

Why we do not serve burgers before 11am: To avoid grill cross contamination with breakfast foods

Why not add more grills to avoid cross contamination: Don't be a smart-ass

Final thought: Frogs have more in common with butterflies than you may realize

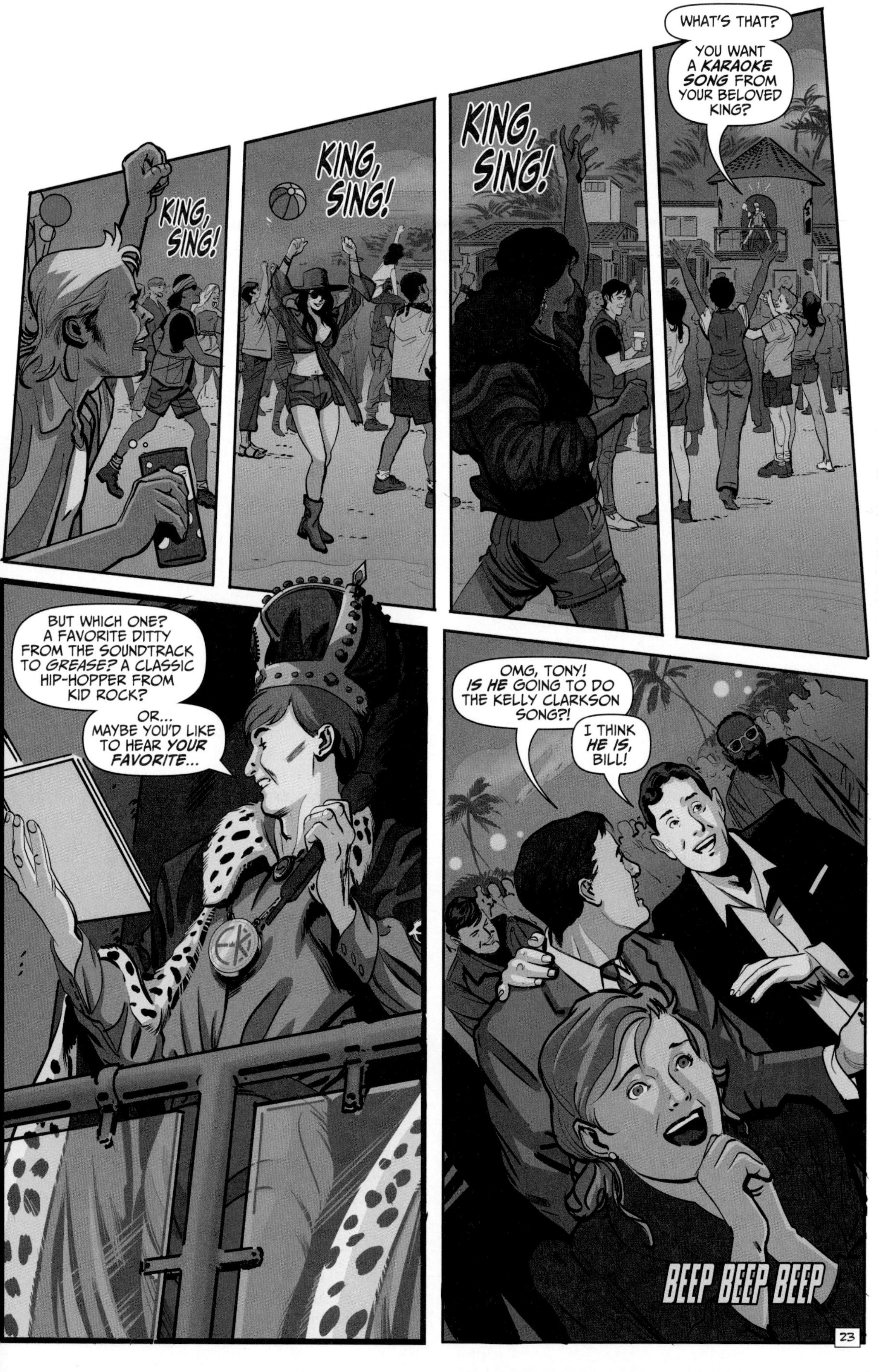
KING, SING!
KING, SING!
KING, SING!
WHAT'S THAT?
YOU WANT A *KARAOKE SONG* FROM YOUR BELOVED KING?
BUT WHICH ONE? A FAVORITE DITTY FROM THE SOUNDTRACK TO *GREASE?* A CLASSIC HIP-HOPPER FROM KID ROCK?
OR... MAYBE YOU'D LIKE TO HEAR *YOUR FAVORITE...*
OMG, TONY! *IS HE* GOING TO DO THE KELLY CLARKSON SONG?!
I THINK *HE IS,* BILL!
BEEP BEEP BEEP

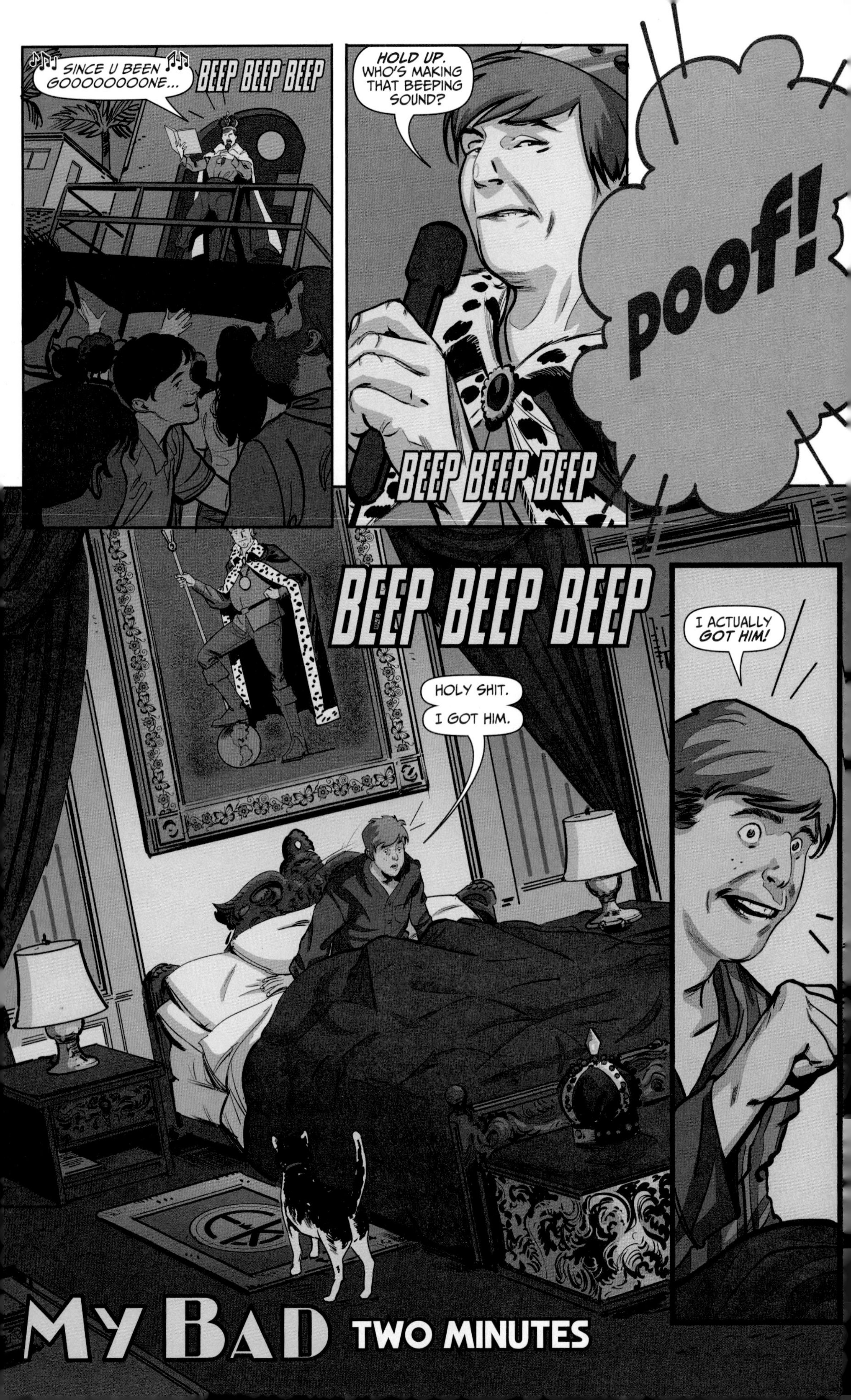
SINCE U BEEN GOOOOOOOONE...
BEEP BEEP BEEP
HOLD UP. WHO'S MAKING THAT BEEPING SOUND?
BEEP BEEP BEEP
POOF!
BEEP BEEP BEEP
HOLY SHIT.
I GOT HIM.
I ACTUALLY GOT HIM!
MY BAD TWO MINUTES

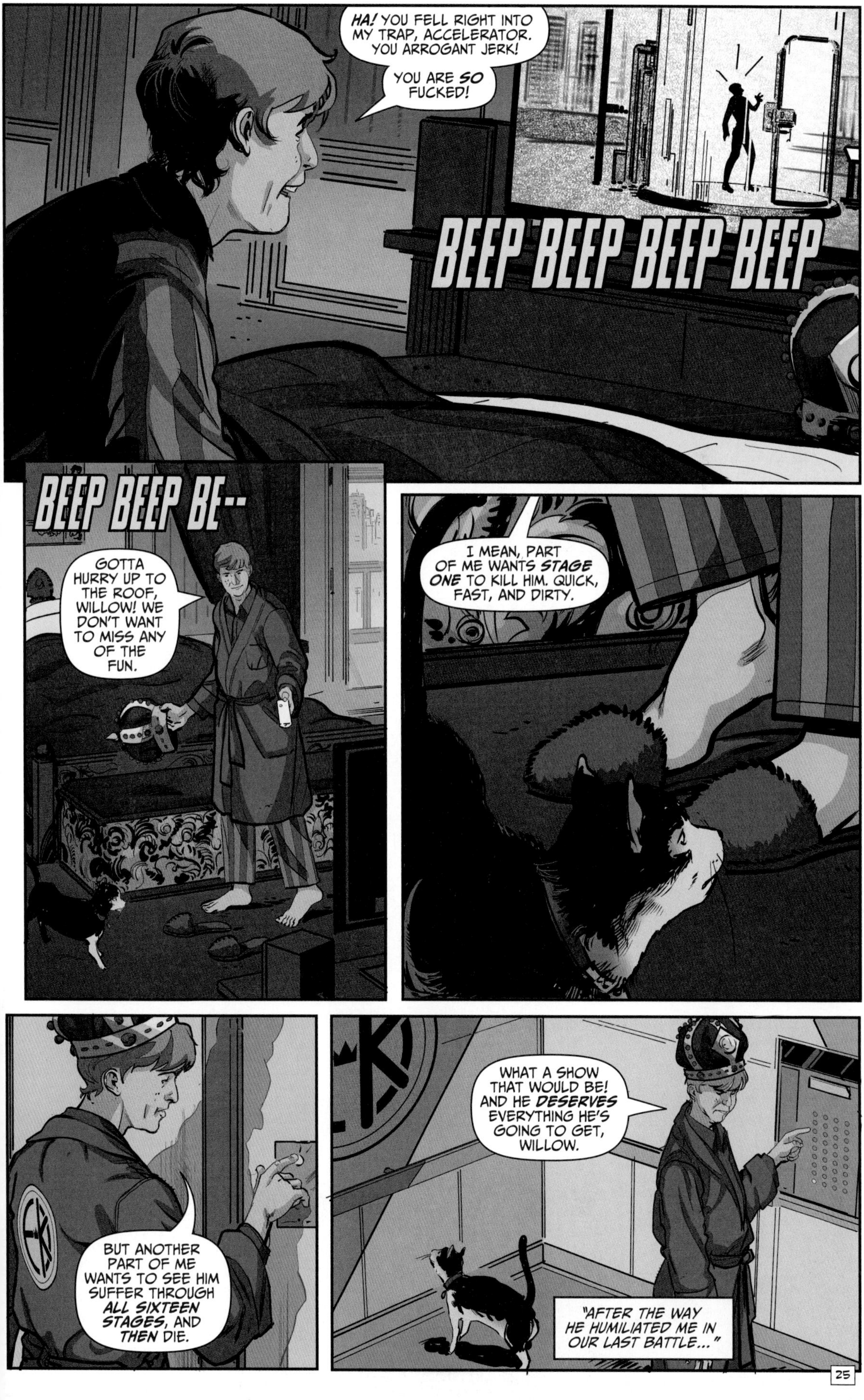

HA! YOU FELL RIGHT INTO MY TRAP, ACCELERATOR. YOU ARROGANT JERK!
YOU ARE SO FUCKED!
BEEP BEEP BEEP BEEP
BEEP BEEP BE--
GOTTA HURRY UP TO THE ROOF, WILLOW! WE DON'T WANT TO MISS ANY OF THE FUN.
I MEAN, PART OF ME WANTS STAGE ONE TO KILL HIM. QUICK, FAST, AND DIRTY.
BUT ANOTHER PART OF ME WANTS TO SEE HIM SUFFER THROUGH ALL SIXTEEN STAGES, AND THEN DIE.
WHAT A SHOW THAT WOULD BE! AND HE DESERVES EVERYTHING HE'S GOING TO GET, WILLOW.
"AFTER THE WAY HE HUMILIATED ME IN OUR LAST BATTLE..."

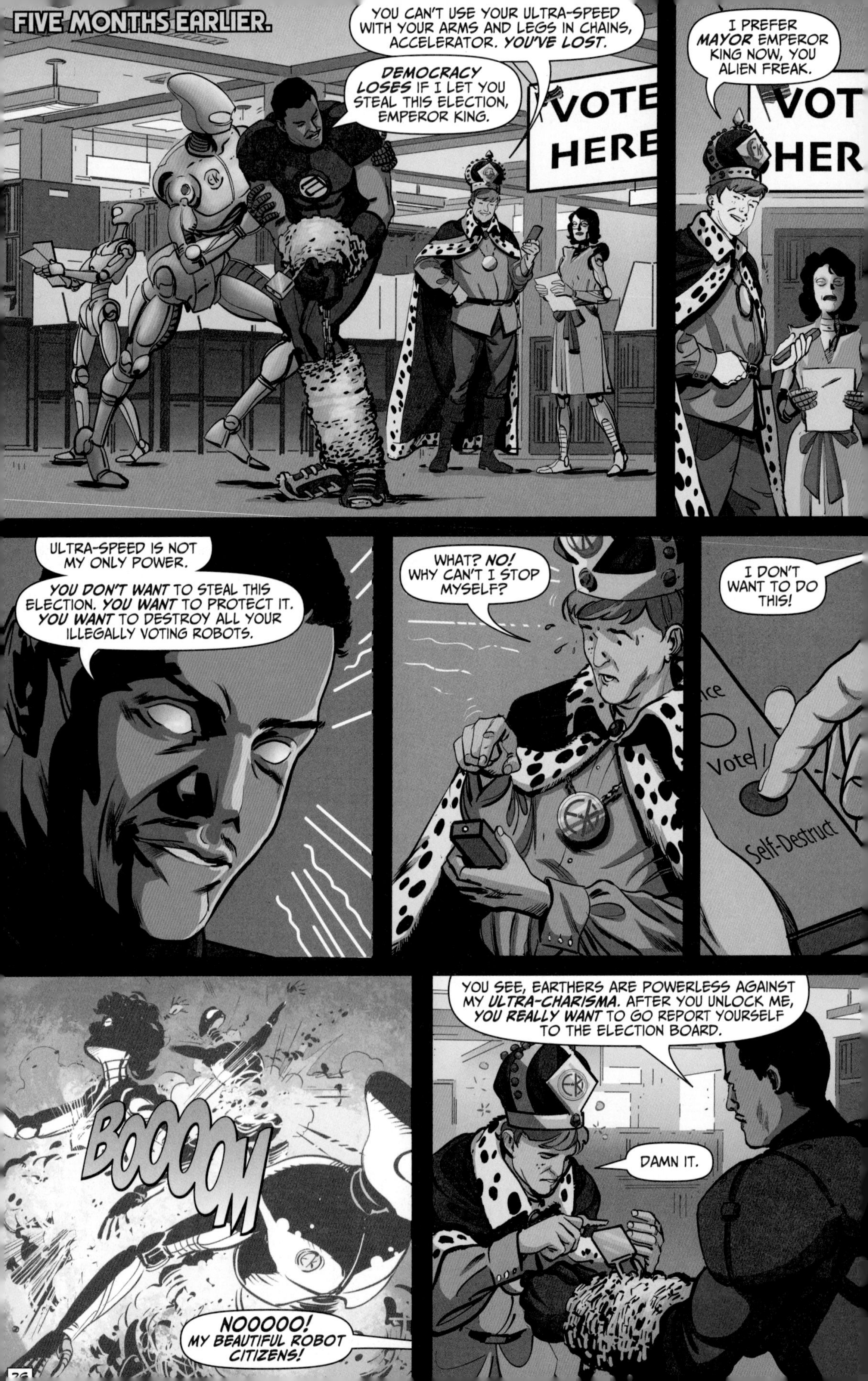
FIVE MONTHS EARLIER.
YOU CAN'T USE YOUR ULTRA-SPEED WITH YOUR ARMS AND LEGS IN CHAINS, ACCELERATOR. *YOU'VE LOST.*
DEMOCRACY LOSES IF I LET YOU STEAL THIS ELECTION, EMPEROR KING.
VOTE HERE
I PREFER *MAYOR* EMPEROR KING NOW, YOU ALIEN FREAK.
ULTRA-SPEED IS NOT MY ONLY POWER.
YOU DON'T WANT TO STEAL THIS ELECTION. *YOU WANT* TO PROTECT IT. *YOU WANT* TO DESTROY ALL YOUR ILLEGALLY VOTING ROBOTS.
WHAT? *NO!* WHY CAN'T I STOP MYSELF?
I DON'T WANT TO DO THIS!
Vote
Self-Destruct
BOOOOM
NOOOOO! MY BEAUTIFUL ROBOT CITIZENS!
YOU SEE, EARTHERS ARE POWERLESS AGAINST MY *ULTRA-CHARISMA.* AFTER YOU UNLOCK ME, *YOU REALLY WANT* TO GO REPORT YOURSELF TO THE ELECTION BOARD.
DAMN IT.

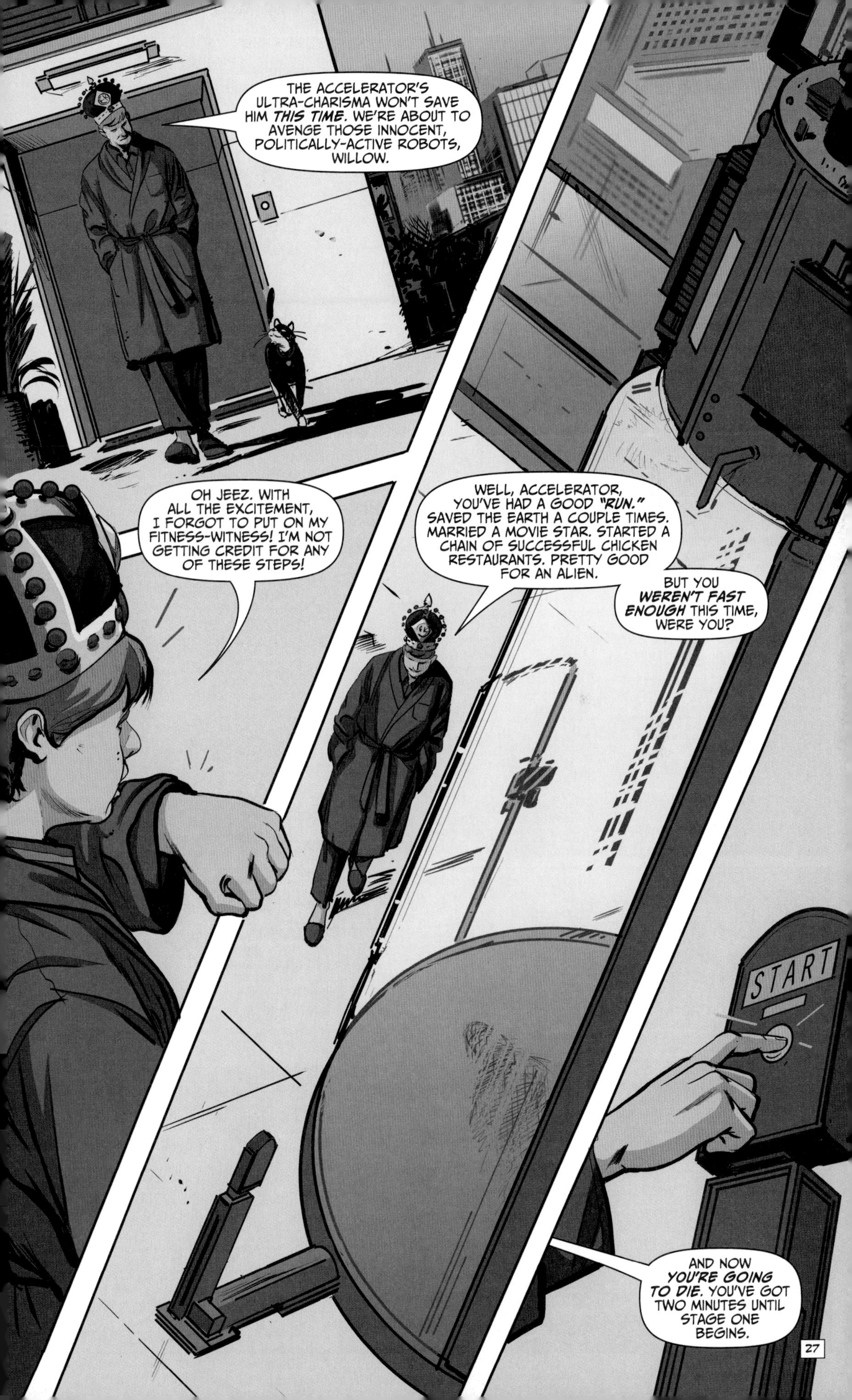
THE ACCELERATOR'S ULTRA-CHARISMA WON'T SAVE HIM THIS TIME. WE'RE ABOUT TO AVENGE THOSE INNOCENT, POLITICALLY-ACTIVE ROBOTS, WILLOW.
OH JEEZ. WITH ALL THE EXCITEMENT, I FORGOT TO PUT ON MY FITNESS-WITNESS! I'M NOT GETTING CREDIT FOR ANY OF THESE STEPS!
WELL, ACCELERATOR, YOU'VE HAD A GOOD "RUN." SAVED THE EARTH A COUPLE TIMES. MARRIED A MOVIE STAR. STARTED A CHAIN OF SUCCESSFUL CHICKEN RESTAURANTS. PRETTY GOOD FOR AN ALIEN.
BUT YOU WEREN'T FAST ENOUGH THIS TIME, WERE YOU?
START
AND NOW YOU'RE GOING TO DIE. YOU'VE GOT TWO MINUTES UNTIL STAGE ONE BEGINS.

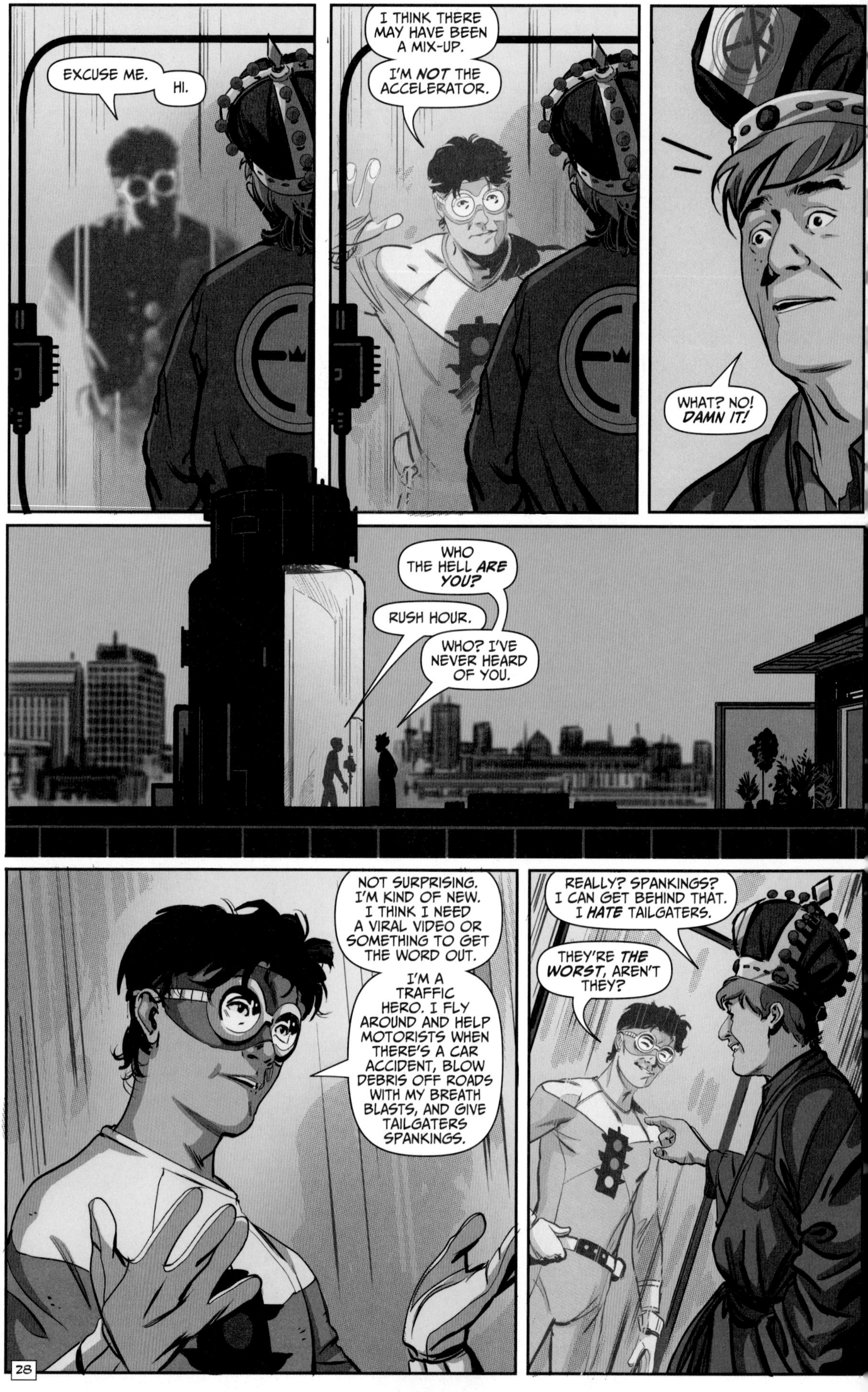
EXCUSE ME.
HI.
I THINK THERE MAY HAVE BEEN A MIX-UP.
I'M *NOT* THE ACCELERATOR.
WHAT? NO! *DAMN IT!*
WHO THE HELL *ARE YOU?*
RUSH HOUR.
WHO? I'VE NEVER HEARD OF YOU.
NOT SURPRISING. I'M KIND OF NEW. I THINK I NEED A VIRAL VIDEO OR SOMETHING TO GET THE WORD OUT.
I'M A TRAFFIC HERO. I FLY AROUND AND HELP MOTORISTS WHEN THERE'S A CAR ACCIDENT, BLOW DEBRIS OFF ROADS WITH MY BREATH BLASTS, AND GIVE TAILGATERS SPANKINGS.
REALLY? SPANKINGS? I CAN GET BEHIND THAT. I *HATE* TAILGATERS.
THEY'RE *THE WORST*, AREN'T THEY?

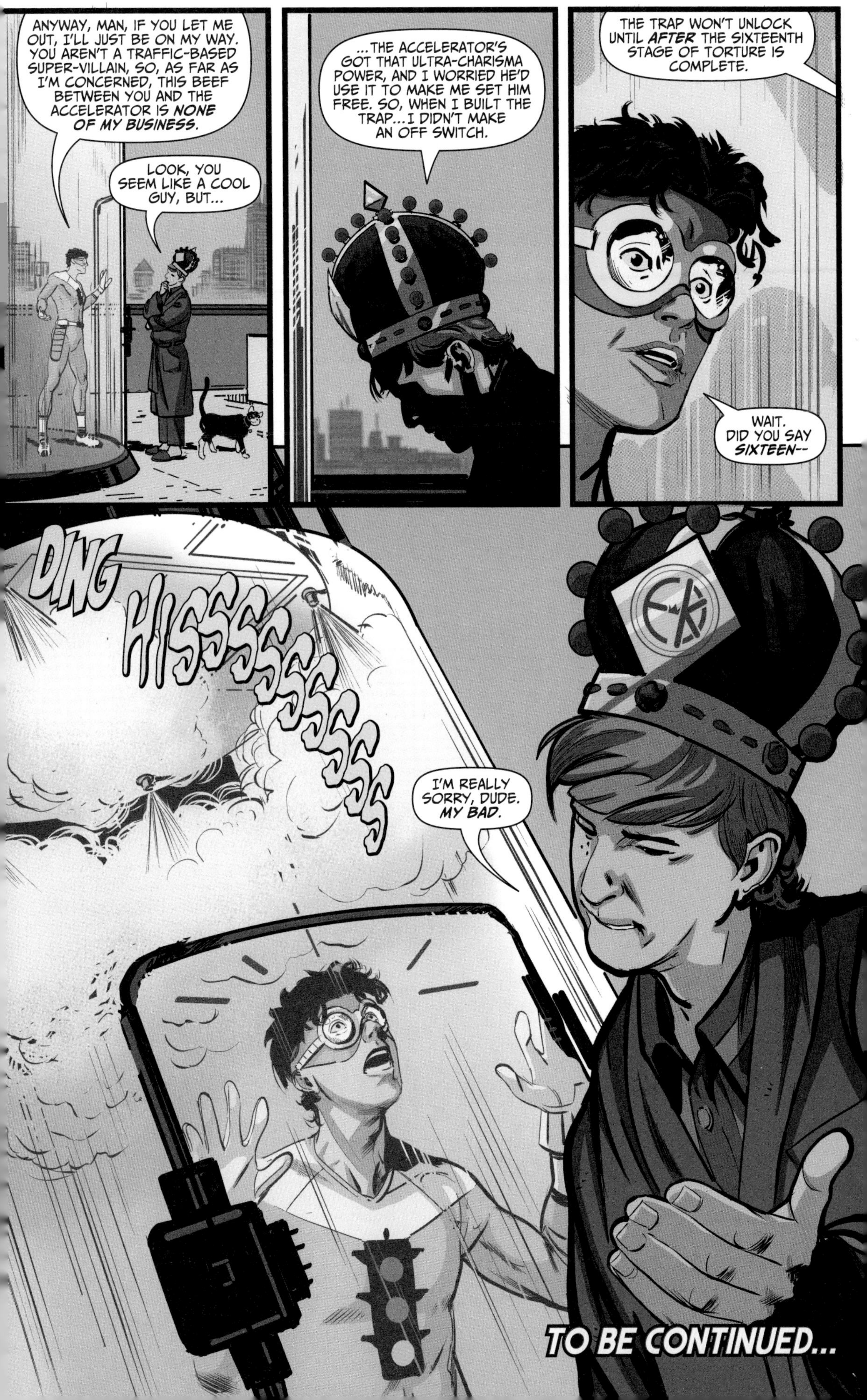
ANYWAY, MAN, IF YOU LET ME OUT, I'LL JUST BE ON MY WAY. YOU AREN'T A TRAFFIC-BASED SUPER-VILLAIN, SO, AS FAR AS I'M CONCERNED, THIS BEEF BETWEEN YOU AND THE ACCELERATOR IS *NONE OF MY BUSINESS.*
LOOK, YOU SEEM LIKE A COOL GUY, BUT...
...THE ACCELERATOR'S GOT THAT ULTRA-CHARISMA POWER, AND I WORRIED HE'D USE IT TO MAKE ME SET HIM FREE. SO, WHEN I BUILT THE TRAP...I DIDN'T MAKE AN OFF SWITCH.
THE TRAP WON'T UNLOCK UNTIL *AFTER* THE SIXTEENTH STAGE OF TORTURE IS COMPLETE.
WAIT. DID YOU SAY *SIXTEEN--*
DING
HISSSSSSSSSS
I'M REALLY SORRY, DUDE. *MY BAD.*
TO BE CONTINUED...

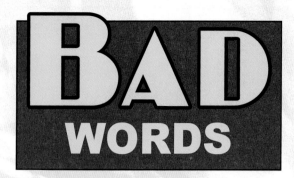

BAD WORDS

Bouncing Baby Bryce, one of MY BAD's writers, here. We sent out some advance digital copies of MY BAD #1 to get your reactions. Let's see what people had to say.

Mark and Bryce,
What is this? Who are you people? How do I unsubscribe?

> Terry
> Helena, Montana

Thanks for taking the time to reach out, Terry. I can tell MY BAD #1 left you with lots of questions. Don't worry! Everything will be explained in upcoming issues.

* * *

Bryce,
I'm your mother, and despite what's happened in the past, I'll always love you. But I'm a busy woman and I've told you more than once that I don't have time for this shit.

> Sharey
> North Bend, Oregon

Glad you enjoyed it, Mother. I love you too. If Father will let me visit, I'd love to swing by and say "hi." Give me a call if he says it's okay.

* * *

Bryce and Mark,
My laptop makes a terrible noise and shuts down every time I click on the file you sent. It's scaring the cat.

> Sally
> Orlando, Florida

To be honest, Sally, I'm a bit old-fashioned and still enjoy the look and feel of a physical comic book in my hands. But I have to admit that, like you, I think digital comics are pretty dang cool too! I'm glad you and your cat are enjoying the "book." While MY BAD is not intended to be read by cats, we're okay with it when it happens.

* * *

Mark and Bryce,
Two writers? What are you people trying to pull? This seems pretty sus. Before I take the risk and try reading this thing, can you explain how your writing process works?

> Monique
> Vancouver, B.C.

Thanks for reaching out, Monique. Yes, having two writers on one comic book is exciting. As far as how the process works, Mark handles the verbs and adverbs and I tackle the nouns, adjectives, and articles. We think this process yields some pretty impressive results, don't you?

* * *

Looks like we have room for one last correspondence...

Mr. Russell and Mr. Ingman,
You may think you're good people, but you're not. Good people don't do things like this. Stop immediately.

> Reggie
> Des Moines, Iowa

Thanks, Reggie. It's thoughtful words like yours that make all the sleepless nights and cocaine binges worth it.

TOM'S TOOLBOX!

Greetings, assembled AHOYniks! Timeless Tom here!

Didja know that AHOY has admirers in nearly every kingdom, republic, and principality around this big blue marble we call Earth? Well, bear with me, fond foreigners, 'cause this month I'm directing my remarks solely to our American readers! In fact, if you're not a dyed-in-the-wool Yankee Doodle Dandy, I ask that you fight the urge to peek at the rest of this column! After all, a nation's gotta have *some* secrets! Come back next month, AHOY-ardent outlanders! And don't cry—you'll get your turn! You'll *all* get your turn!

So! My fellow Americans! Didja ever stop and realize that this great country of ours is like one of AHOY's periodically published portions of picto-literature? Think about that next time you dig the details of our dazzling dramas! Note how harmonically the colors blend—how cyan and yellow become Manchild's emerald complexion, how magenta and cyan team up to tone Emperor King's silk shirt! Isn't that just like our magnificent, monarchy-smashing melting pot? We at AHOY are bursting with pride at the homeland's hearty history of amalgamating Americans of many colors and most faiths! And it doesn't just apply to how strange you look or weirdly you worship! Our masterfully manufactured consent unites most kinds of people—Republicans and Democrats,

Beethoven lovers and Beatlemaniacs, fellas and women—in brotherhood! And that's why every one of our cavortin' characters—even every *villain*—sheds a tear while saluting Old Glory's spectacular stars and sensational stripes! Now, if you'll excuse me, your emotionally overcome Chief needs a double shot of something strong!

Occupare omnes terras,

Tom

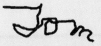

NEXT: Why did Rush Hour run into Emperor King's trap? Has Emperor King learned that the Chandelier is Jamington Winthrop? The answer to one of these questions awaits, along with a circus-peanut-flavored variant cover by Jonathan Case, ***December 8!***

—Bryce

COWER
UNSURE
DESPISE
ACID

COMING AHOY-TRACTIONS

EDGAR ALLAN POE'S SNIFTER OF DEATH #2 (Writers: Dean Motter and Holly Interlandi. Artists: Dean Motter and Greg Scott. Cover: Richard Williams.)—An automaton equipped to defeat an educated human in the game of chess? Preposterous! Poe himself undertakes to pierce the mechanical mystery in "Chess Player." Plus! An ostensibly helpful bit of software tries to dominate a writer's creative process in "Angle of the Odd." Our special "Dread of Devices" issue closes out with prose stories and a poem. In comics shops *November 10!*

SNELSON: COMEDY IS DYING #4 (Writer: Paul Constant. Artist: Fred Harper.)—Cue the laugh track! Comedian Melville Snelson doesn't know how many oxycontins he took. *(Laughter)* His shows are bombing. *(Laughter)* His website is attracting trolls who threaten violence. *(Laughter)* A comic he identifies with just committed suicide. *(Laughter, applause)* Time for a near-death experience with the possibility of a fatal encore. *(Crickets)* Plus: prose & pix, AHOY-style! *November 17!*

BLACK'S MYTH #5 (Writer: Eric Palicki. Artist; Wendell Cavalcanti. Cover: Liana Kangas.)—Final issue of the hit werewolf crime story! Will Strummer figure out who shot her? Is it the same person who stole the bullets? Will there be a "why" to go with the "who?" Will Ben and Aster ever get their beer? Find out in the thrilling conclusion *November 24!*

Write to MY BAD—or any AHOY mag—at letters@comicsahoy.com. Snail mail: PO Box 189, DeWitt, NY 13214. Mark "OK to print" if it is.

AND! Subscribe to the free, funny-as-anything AHOY Comics Newsletter at bit.ly/newsahoy.

PLUS! Use this case-sensitive link to access 35 pages of free—as in no cost to you—SNELSON: bit.ly/Snelson.

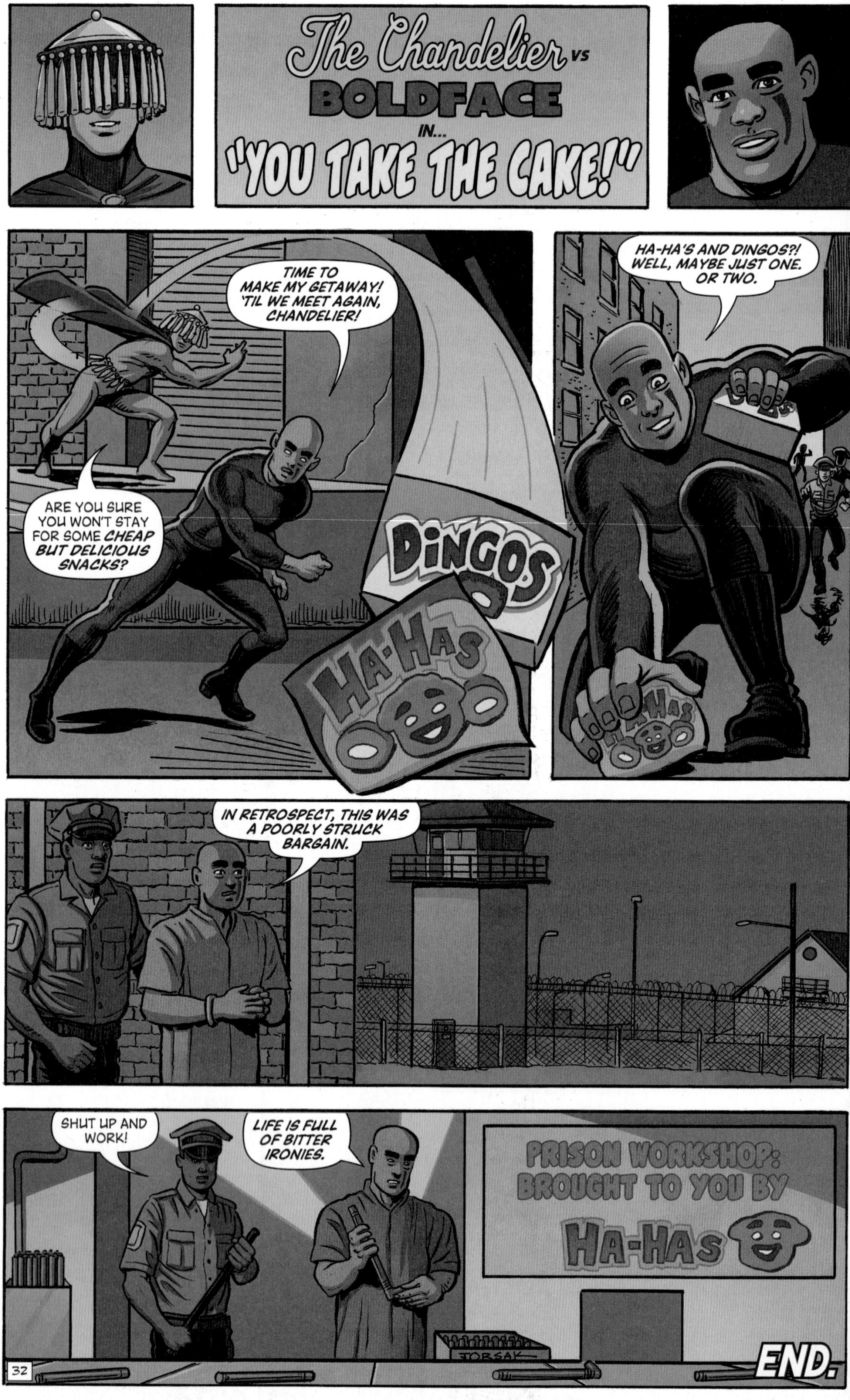
The Chandelier vs
BOLDFACE
in...
"YOU TAKE THE CAKE!"
TIME TO MAKE MY GETAWAY! 'TIL WE MEET AGAIN, CHANDELIER!
ARE YOU SURE YOU WON'T STAY FOR SOME CHEAP BUT DELICIOUS SNACKS?
DINGOS
HA-HAS
HA-HA'S AND DINGOS?! WELL, MAYBE JUST ONE. OR TWO.
IN RETROSPECT, THIS WAS A POORLY STRUCK BARGAIN.
SHUT UP AND WORK!
LIFE IS FULL OF BITTER IRONIES.
PRISON WORKSHOP: BROUGHT TO YOU BY
HA-HAS
JOBSAK
END.

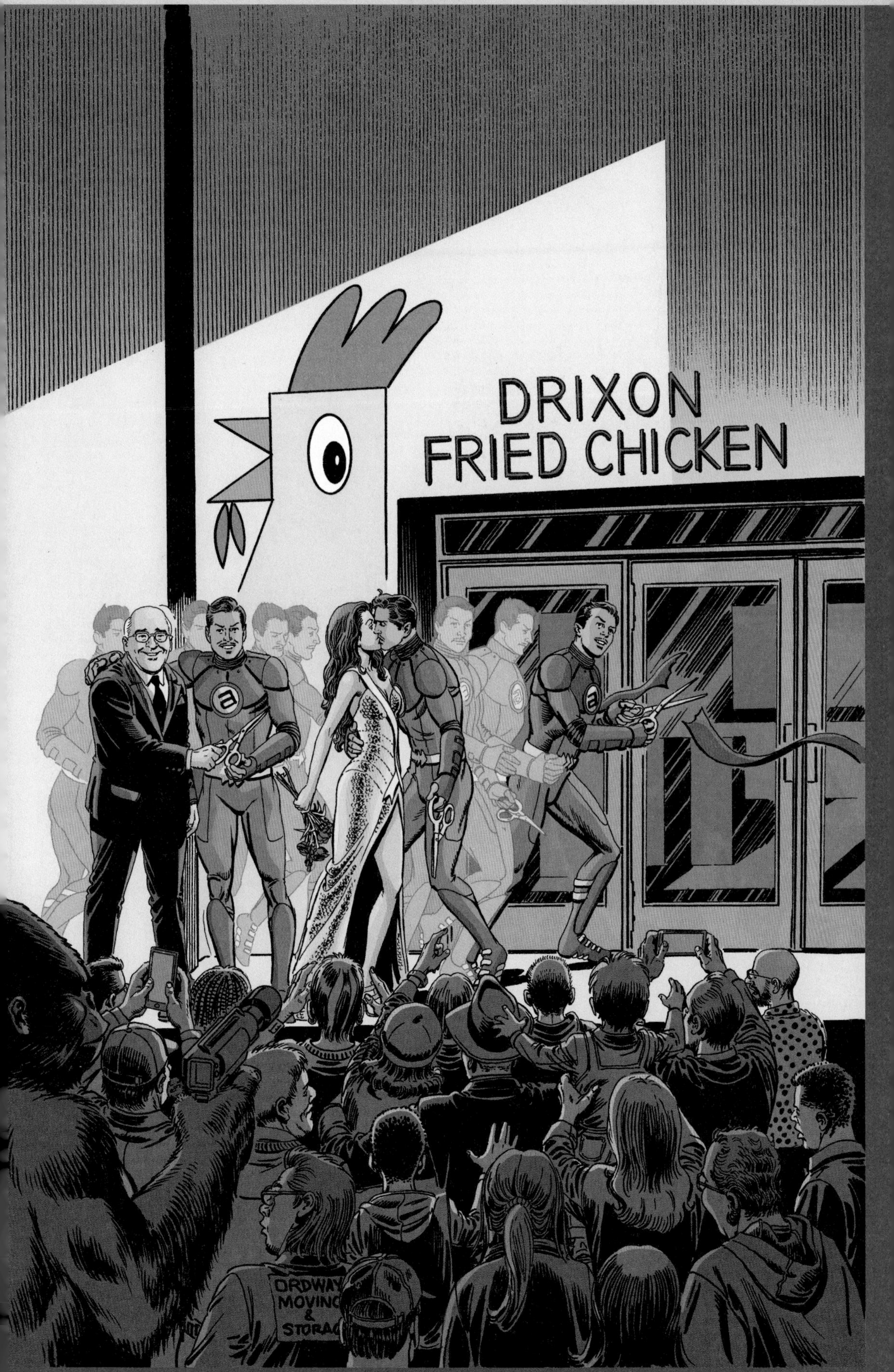
DRIXON
FRIED CHICKEN
ORDWAY
MOVING
&
STORAG

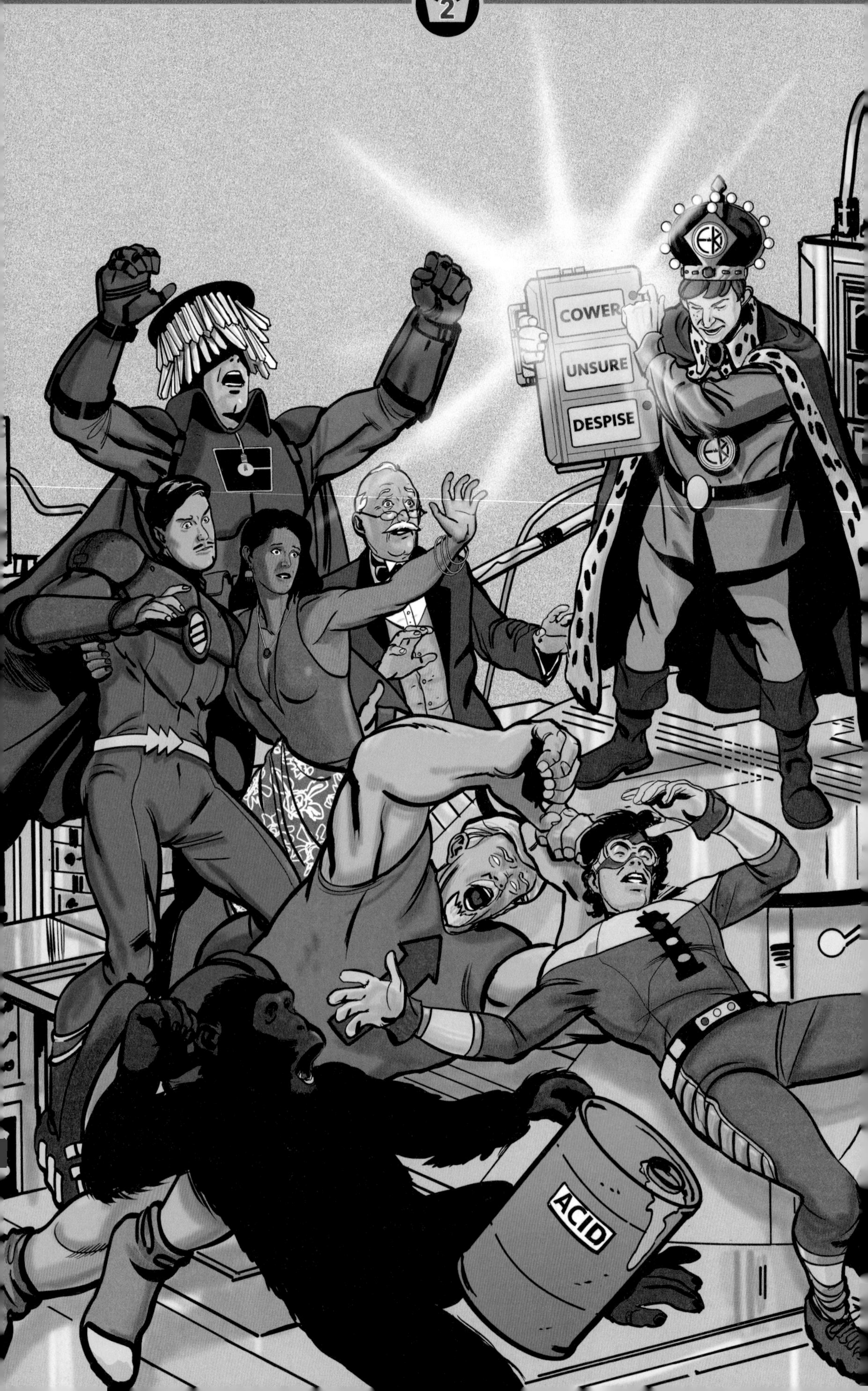
COWER
UNSURE
DESPISE
ACID

2

"I HAVE TRAVELED EXTENSIVELY IN CONCORD."

-HENRY DAVID THOREAU

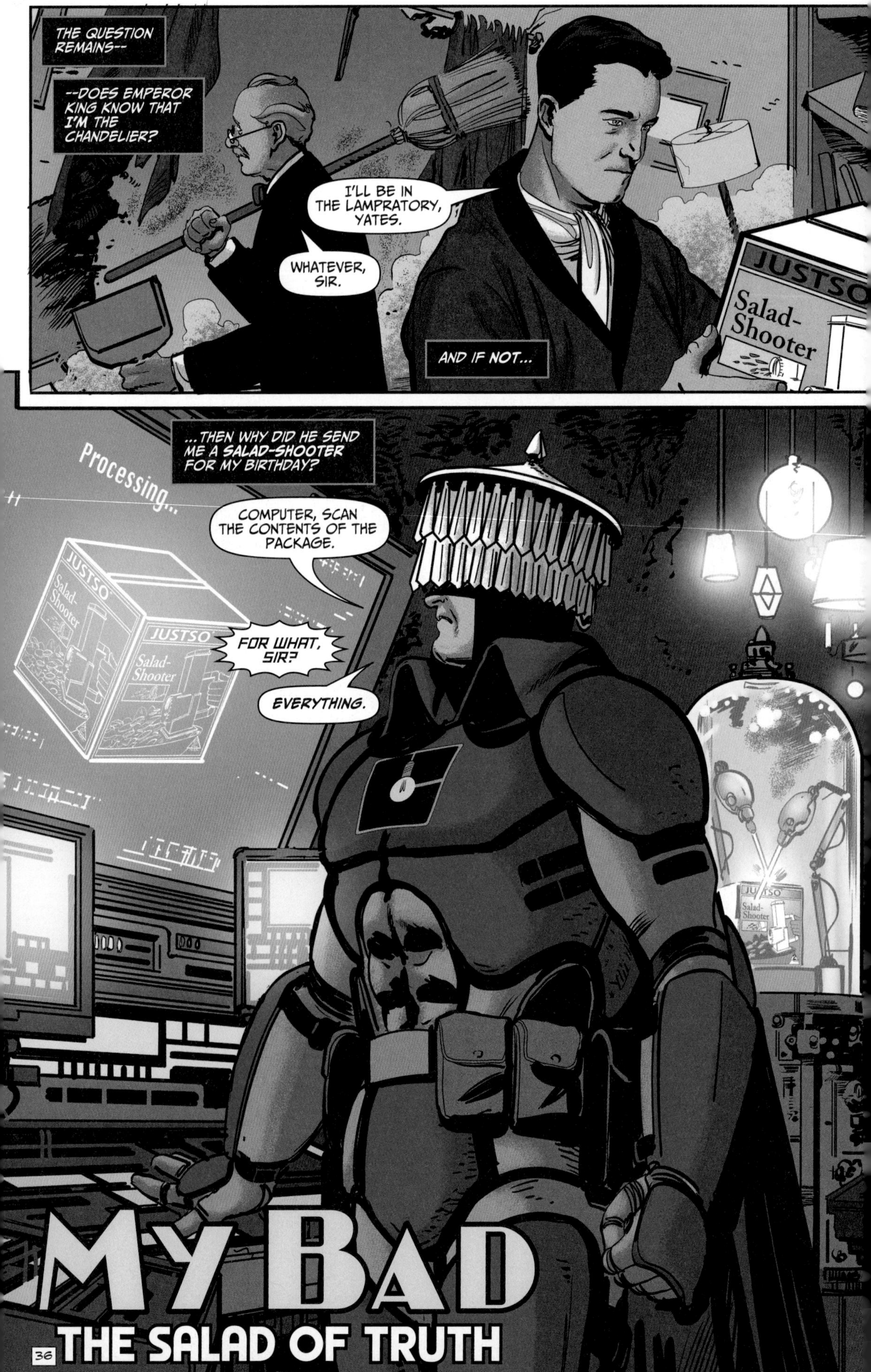
THE QUESTION REMAINS--
--DOES EMPEROR KING KNOW THAT **I'M** THE CHANDELIER?
I'LL BE IN THE LAMPRATORY, YATES.
WHATEVER, SIR.
JUSTSO Salad-Shooter
AND IF NOT...
...THEN WHY DID HE SEND ME A **SALAD-SHOOTER** FOR MY BIRTHDAY?
Processing...
COMPUTER, SCAN THE CONTENTS OF THE PACKAGE.
JUSTSO Salad-Shooter
FOR WHAT, SIR?
EVERYTHING.
MY BAD
THE SALAD OF TRUTH

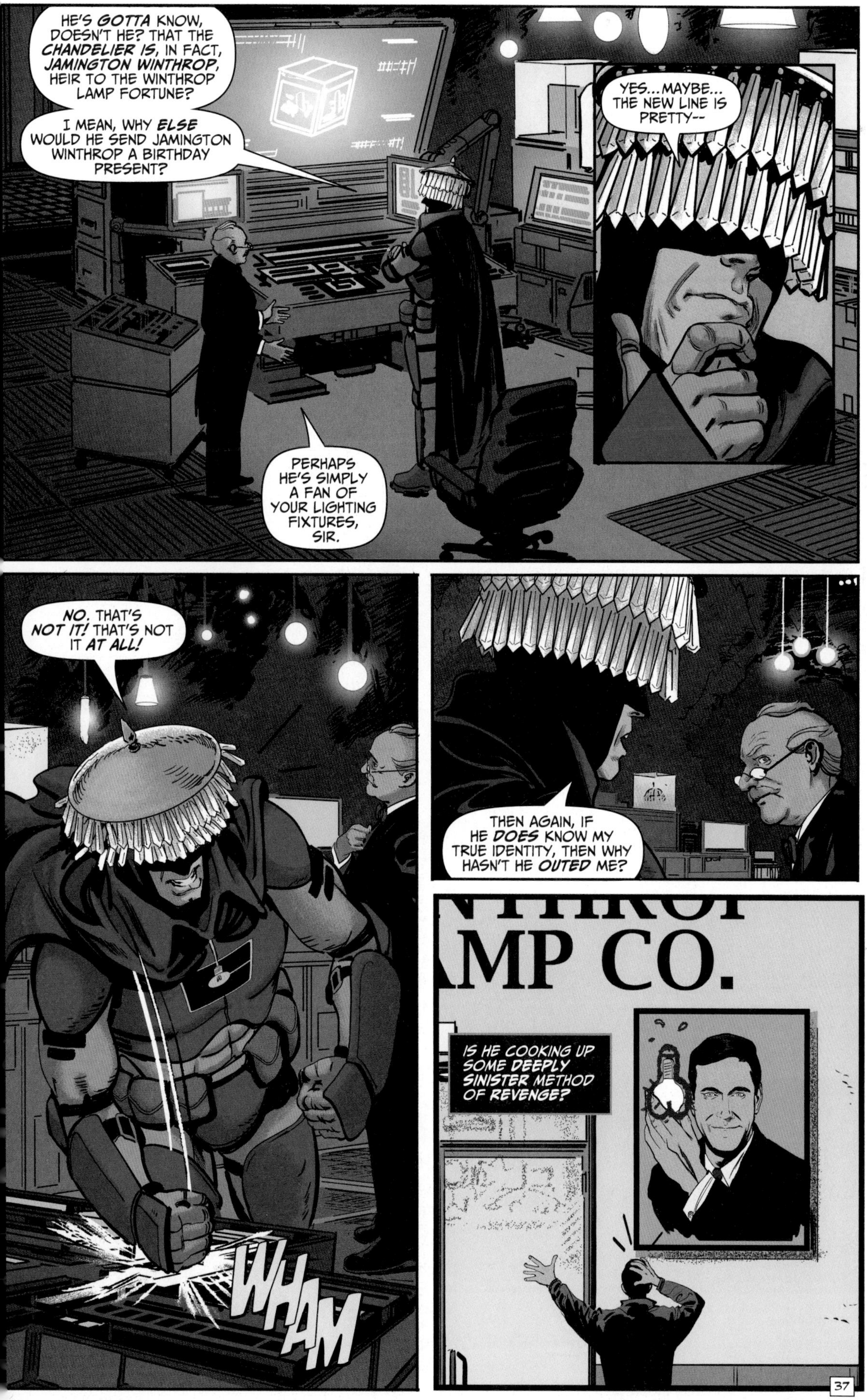
HE'S *GOTTA* KNOW, DOESN'T HE? THAT THE ***CHANDELIER IS,*** IN FACT, ***JAMINGTON WINTHROP,*** HEIR TO THE WINTHROP LAMP FORTUNE?
I MEAN, WHY ***ELSE*** WOULD HE SEND JAMINGTON WINTHROP A BIRTHDAY PRESENT?
PERHAPS HE'S SIMPLY A FAN OF YOUR LIGHTING FIXTURES, SIR.
YES...MAYBE... THE NEW LINE IS PRETTY--
NO. THAT'S ***NOT IT!*** THAT'S NOT IT ***AT ALL!***
WHAM
THEN AGAIN, IF HE ***DOES*** KNOW MY TRUE IDENTITY, THEN WHY HASN'T HE ***OUTED*** ME?
AMP CO.
*IS HE COOKING UP SOME **DEEPLY SINISTER** METHOD OF **REVENGE?***

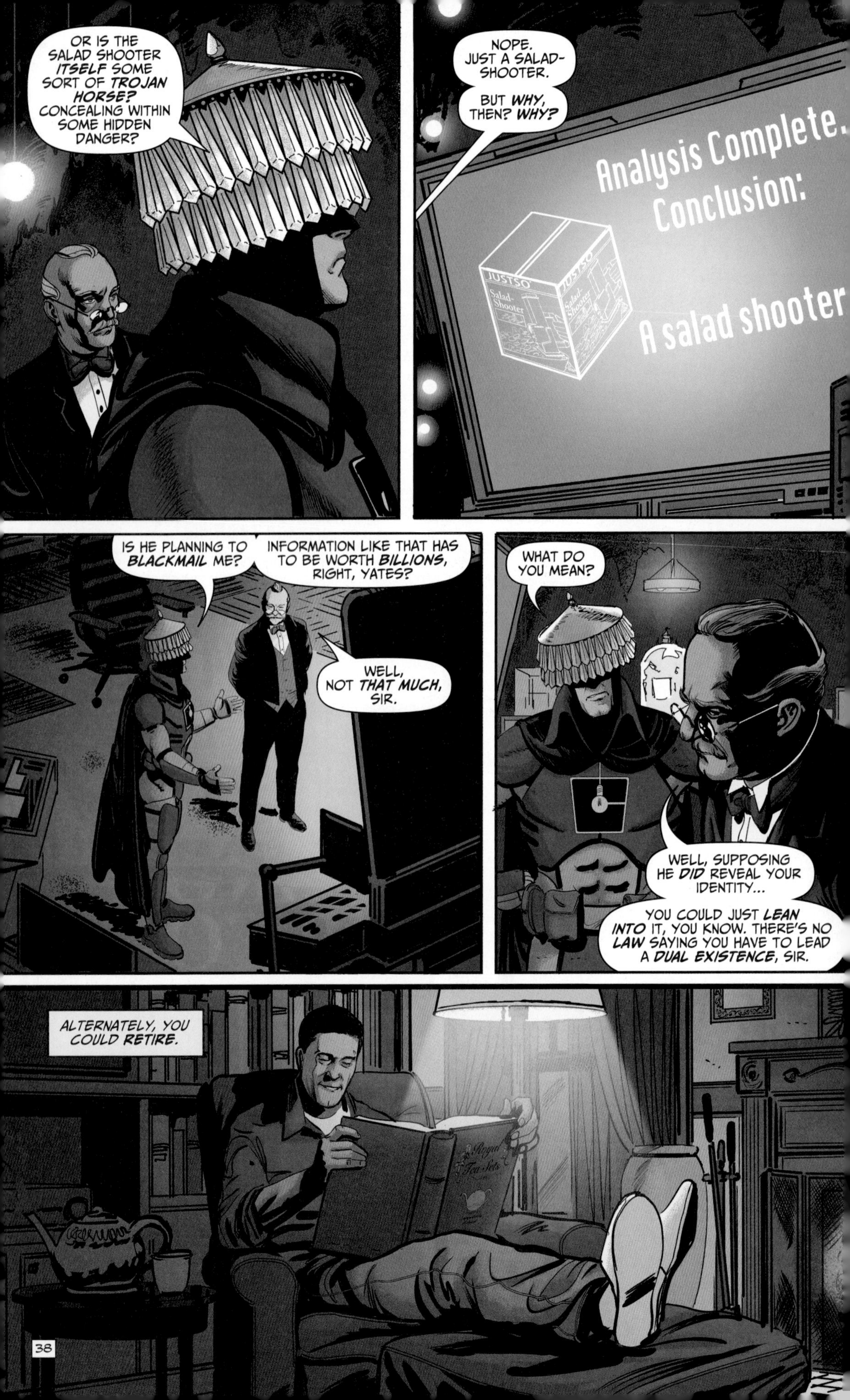

OR IS THE SALAD SHOOTER *ITSELF* SOME SORT OF *TROJAN HORSE?* CONCEALING WITHIN SOME HIDDEN DANGER?
NOPE. JUST A SALAD-SHOOTER.
BUT *WHY*, THEN? *WHY?*
Analysis Complete. Conclusion:
JUSTSO Salad-Shooter
A salad shooter
IS HE PLANNING TO *BLACKMAIL* ME?
INFORMATION LIKE THAT HAS TO BE WORTH *BILLIONS*, RIGHT, YATES?
WELL, NOT *THAT MUCH*, SIR.
WHAT DO YOU MEAN?
WELL, SUPPOSING HE *DID* REVEAL YOUR IDENTITY...
YOU COULD JUST *LEAN INTO* IT, YOU KNOW. THERE'S NO *LAW* SAYING YOU HAVE TO LEAD A *DUAL EXISTENCE*, SIR.
ALTERNATELY, YOU COULD *RETIRE*.
Royal Tea-Sets

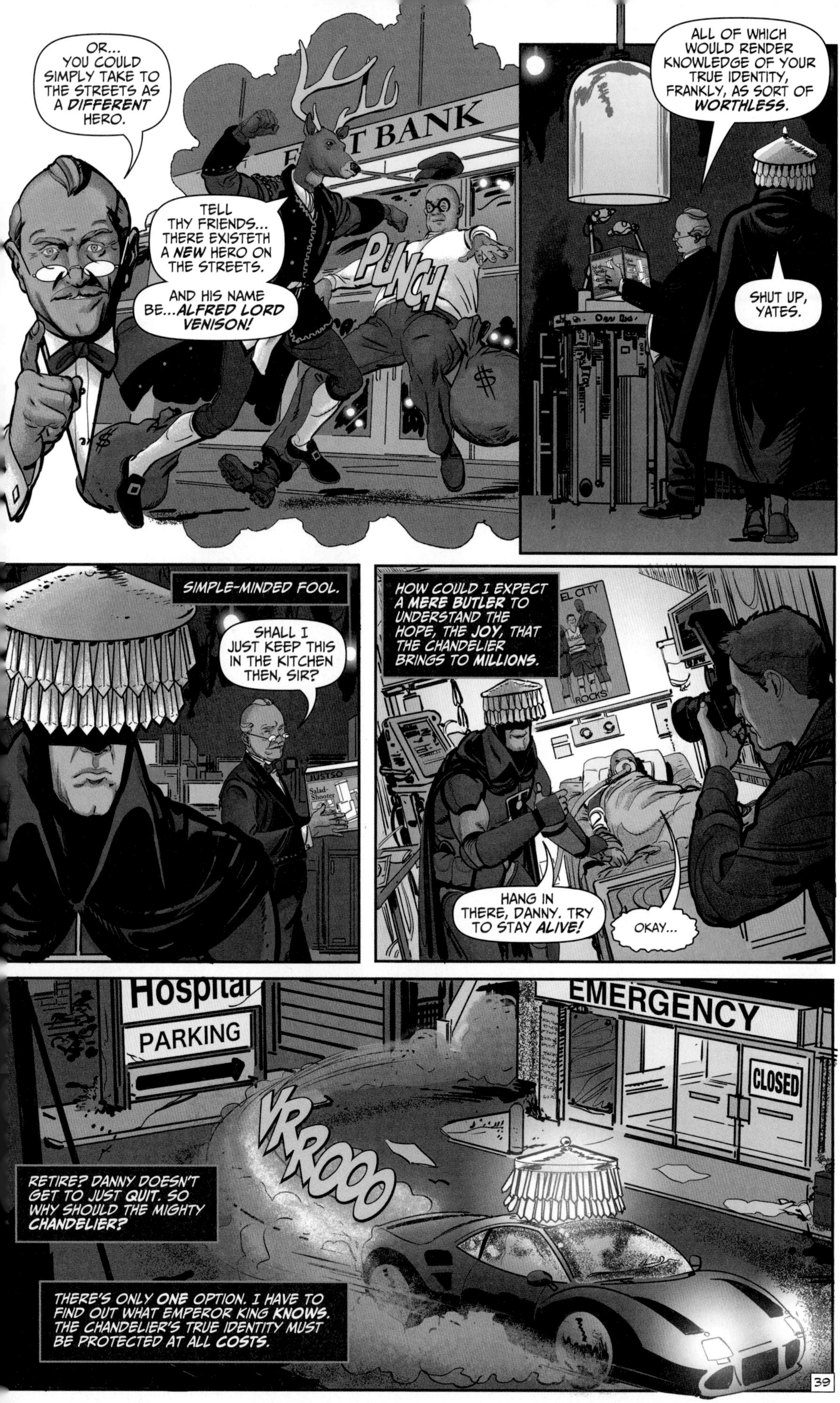
OR... YOU COULD SIMPLY TAKE TO THE STREETS AS A *DIFFERENT* HERO.
BANK
TELL THY FRIENDS... THERE EXISTETH A *NEW* HERO ON THE STREETS.
AND HIS NAME BE...*ALFRED LORD VENISON!*
PUNCH
ALL OF WHICH WOULD RENDER KNOWLEDGE OF YOUR TRUE IDENTITY, FRANKLY, AS SORT OF *WORTHLESS.*
SHUT UP, YATES.
SIMPLE-MINDED FOOL.
SHALL I JUST KEEP THIS IN THE KITCHEN THEN, SIR?
Salad-Shooter
*HOW COULD I EXPECT A **MERE BUTLER** TO UNDERSTAND THE HOPE, THE **JOY**, THAT THE CHANDELIER BRINGS TO **MILLIONS**.*
HANG IN THERE, DANNY. TRY TO STAY *ALIVE!*
OKAY...
Hospital
PARKING
EMERGENCY
CLOSED
VRROOO
*RETIRE? DANNY DOESN'T GET TO JUST **QUIT**. SO WHY SHOULD THE MIGHTY **CHANDELIER?***
*THERE'S ONLY **ONE** OPTION. I HAVE TO FIND OUT WHAT EMPEROR KING **KNOWS**. THE CHANDELIER'S TRUE IDENTITY MUST BE PROTECTED AT ALL **COSTS**.*

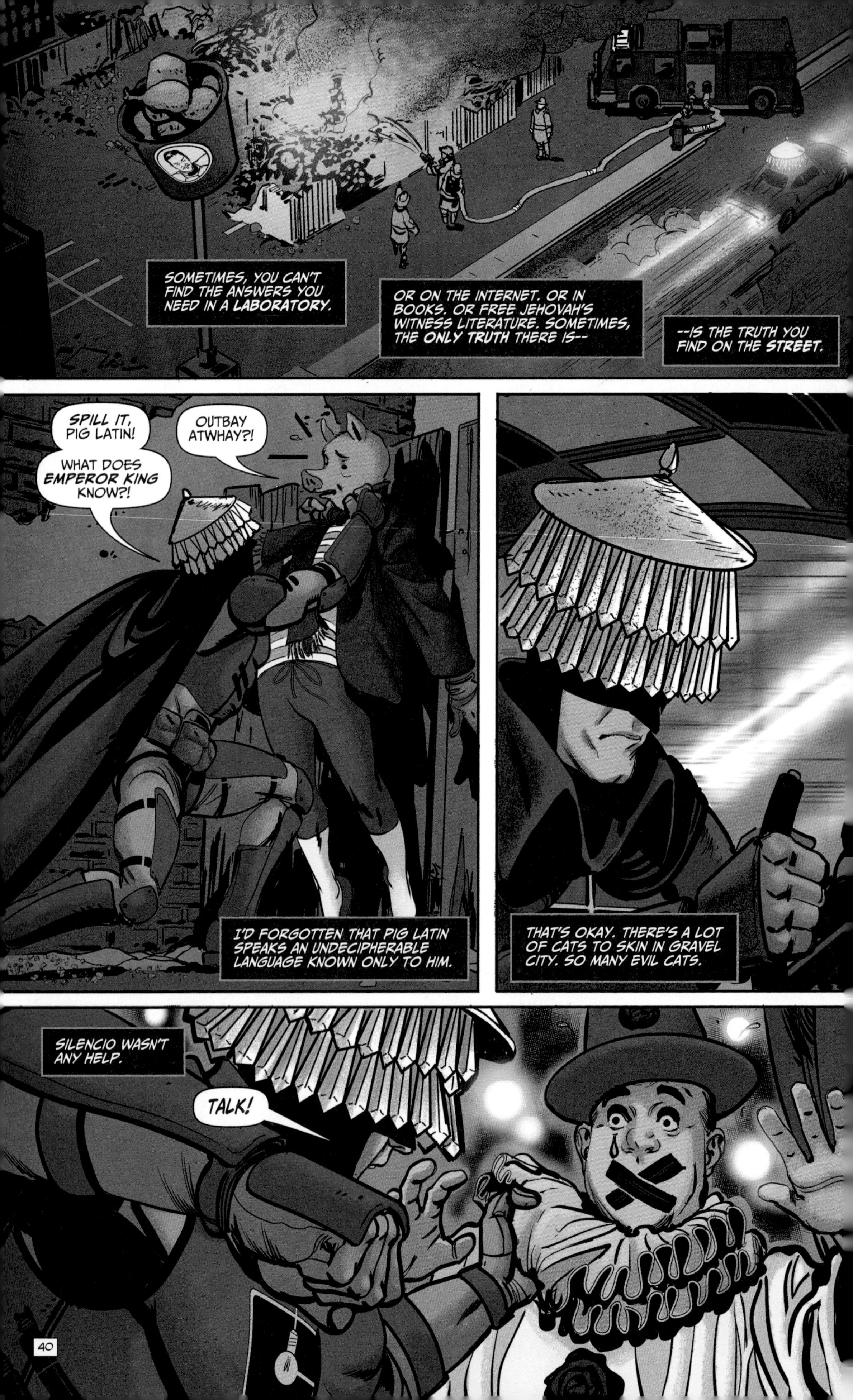
SOMETIMES, YOU CAN'T FIND THE ANSWERS YOU NEED IN A **LABORATORY.**
OR ON THE INTERNET. OR IN BOOKS. OR FREE JEHOVAH'S WITNESS LITERATURE. SOMETIMES, THE **ONLY TRUTH** THERE IS--
--IS THE TRUTH YOU FIND ON THE **STREET.**
SPILL IT, PIG LATIN!
WHAT DOES ***EMPEROR KING*** KNOW?!
OUTBAY ATWHAY?!
I'D FORGOTTEN THAT PIG LATIN SPEAKS AN UNDECIPHERABLE LANGUAGE KNOWN ONLY TO HIM.
THAT'S OKAY. THERE'S A LOT OF CATS TO SKIN IN GRAVEL CITY. SO MANY EVIL CATS.
SILENCIO WASN'T ANY HELP.
TALK!

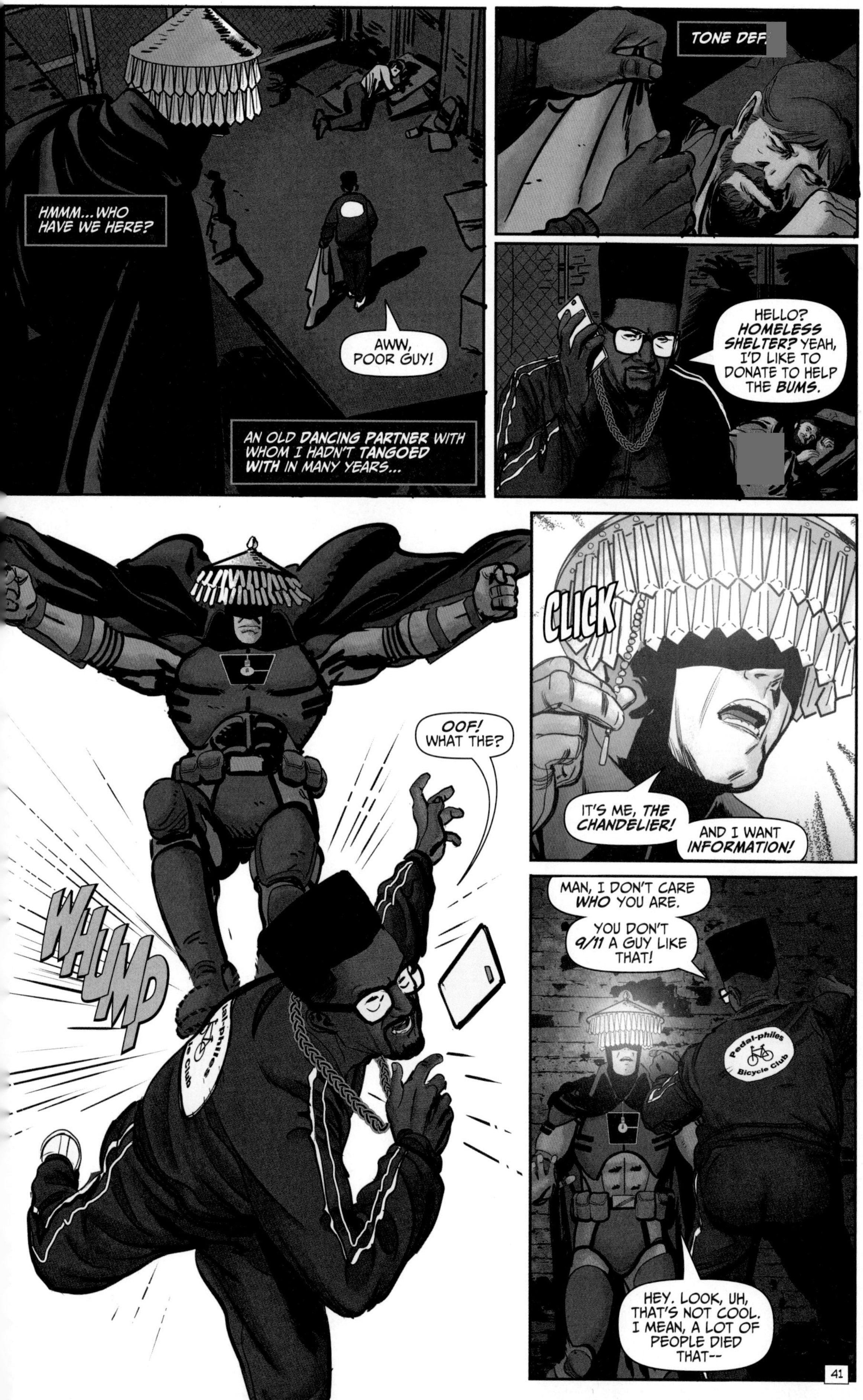
HMMM...WHO HAVE WE HERE?
AWW, POOR GUY!
AN OLD DANCING PARTNER WITH WHOM I HADN'T TANGOED WITH IN MANY YEARS...
TONE DEF
HELLO? HOMELESS SHELTER? YEAH, I'D LIKE TO DONATE TO HELP THE BUMS.
OOF! WHAT THE?
WHUMP
Pedal-philes Bicycle Club
CLICK
IT'S ME, THE CHANDELIER!
AND I WANT INFORMATION!
MAN, I DON'T CARE WHO YOU ARE.
YOU DON'T 9/11 A GUY LIKE THAT!
Pedal-philes Bicycle Club
HEY. LOOK, UH, THAT'S NOT COOL. I MEAN, A LOT OF PEOPLE DIED THAT--

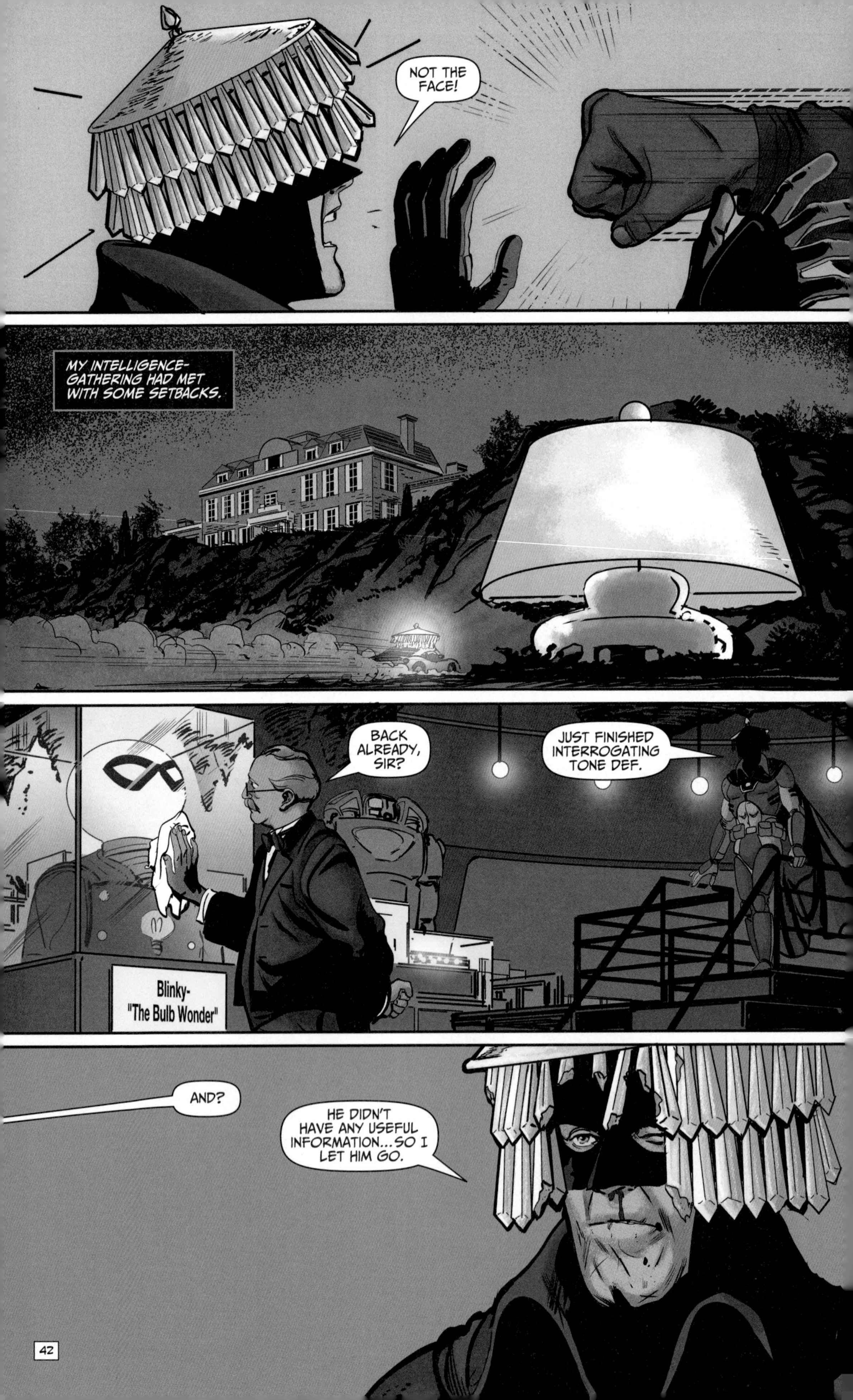
NOT THE FACE!
MY INTELLIGENCE-GATHERING HAD MET WITH SOME SETBACKS.
Blinky- "The Bulb Wonder"
BACK ALREADY, SIR?
JUST FINISHED INTERROGATING TONE DEF.
AND?
HE DIDN'T HAVE ANY USEFUL INFORMATION...SO I LET HIM GO.

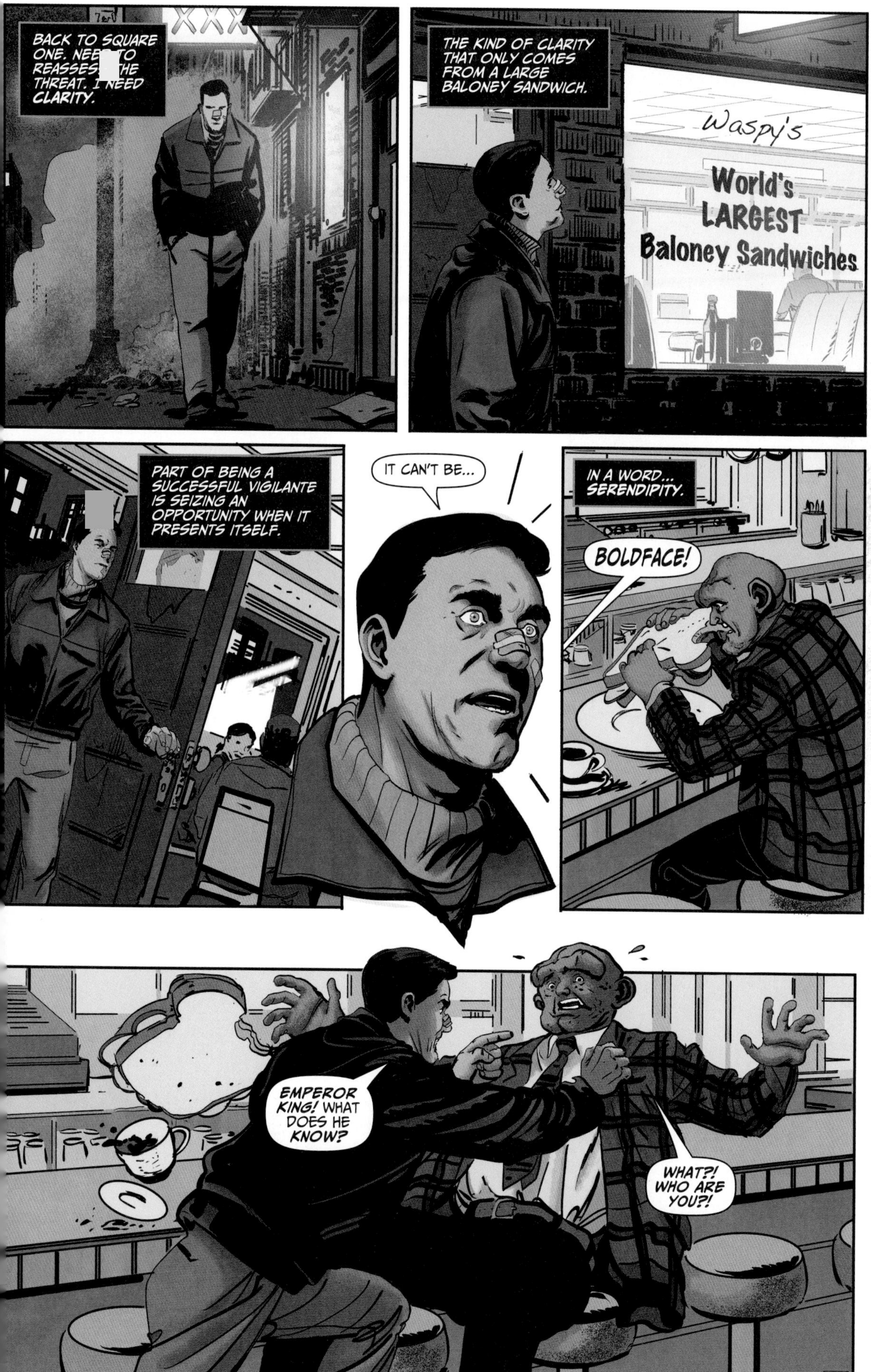
BACK TO SQUARE ONE. NEED TO REASSESS THE THREAT. I NEED CLARITY.
THE KIND OF CLARITY THAT ONLY COMES FROM A LARGE BALONEY SANDWICH.
Waspy's
World's LARGEST Baloney Sandwiches
PART OF BEING A SUCCESSFUL VIGILANTE IS SEIZING AN OPPORTUNITY WHEN IT PRESENTS ITSELF.
IT CAN'T BE...
IN A WORD... SERENDIPITY.
BOLDFACE!
EMPEROR KING! WHAT DOES HE KNOW?
WHAT?! WHO ARE YOU?!

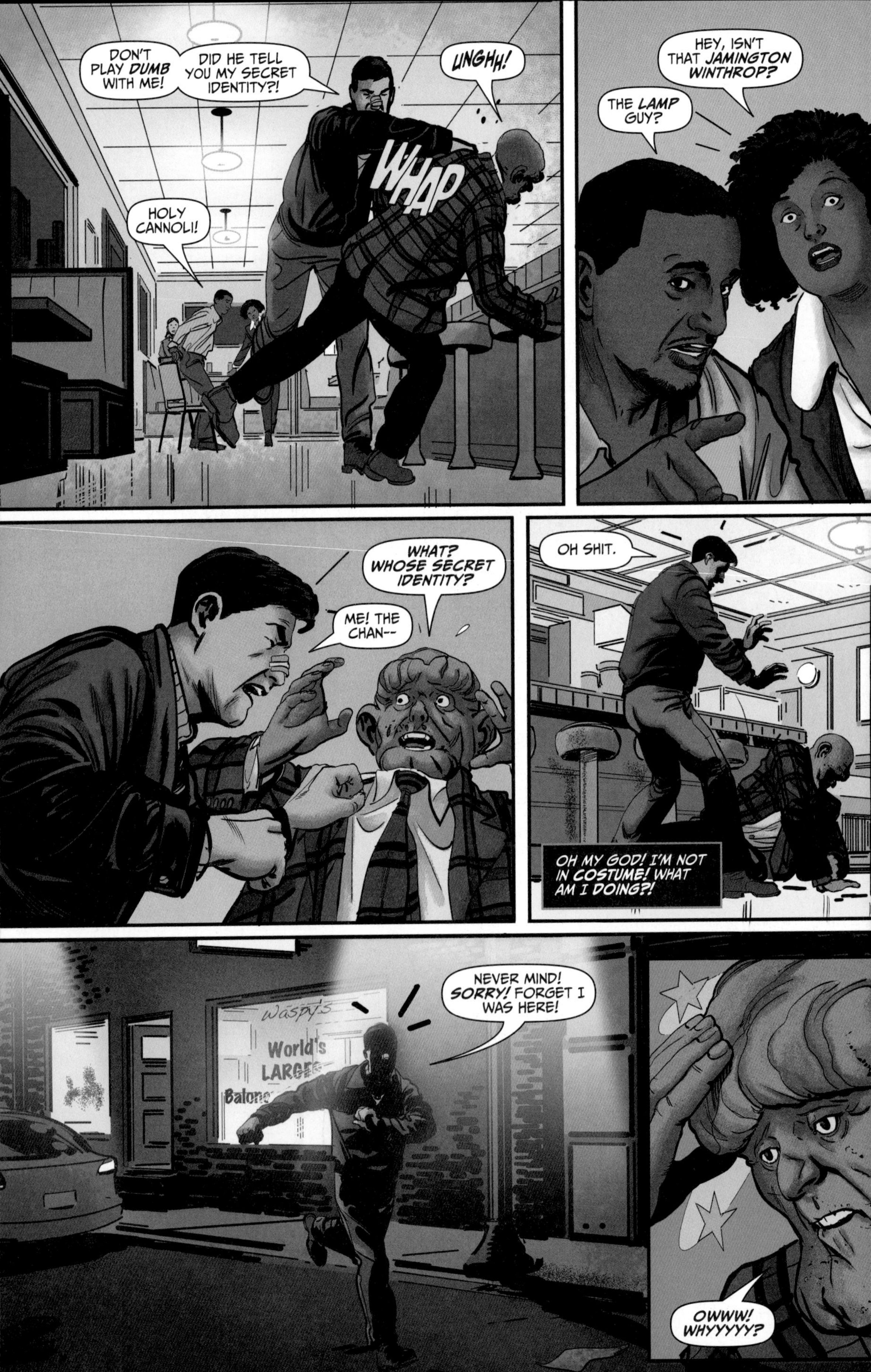

DON'T PLAY DUMB WITH ME!
DID HE TELL YOU MY SECRET IDENTITY?!
UNGHH!
WHAP
HOLY CANNOLI!
HEY, ISN'T THAT JAMINGTON WINTHROP?
THE LAMP GUY?
WHAT? WHOSE SECRET IDENTITY?
ME! THE CHAN--
OH SHIT.
OH MY GOD! I'M NOT IN COSTUME! WHAT AM I DOING?!
Waspy's
World's
NEVER MIND! SORRY! FORGET I WAS HERE!
OWWW! WHYYYYY?

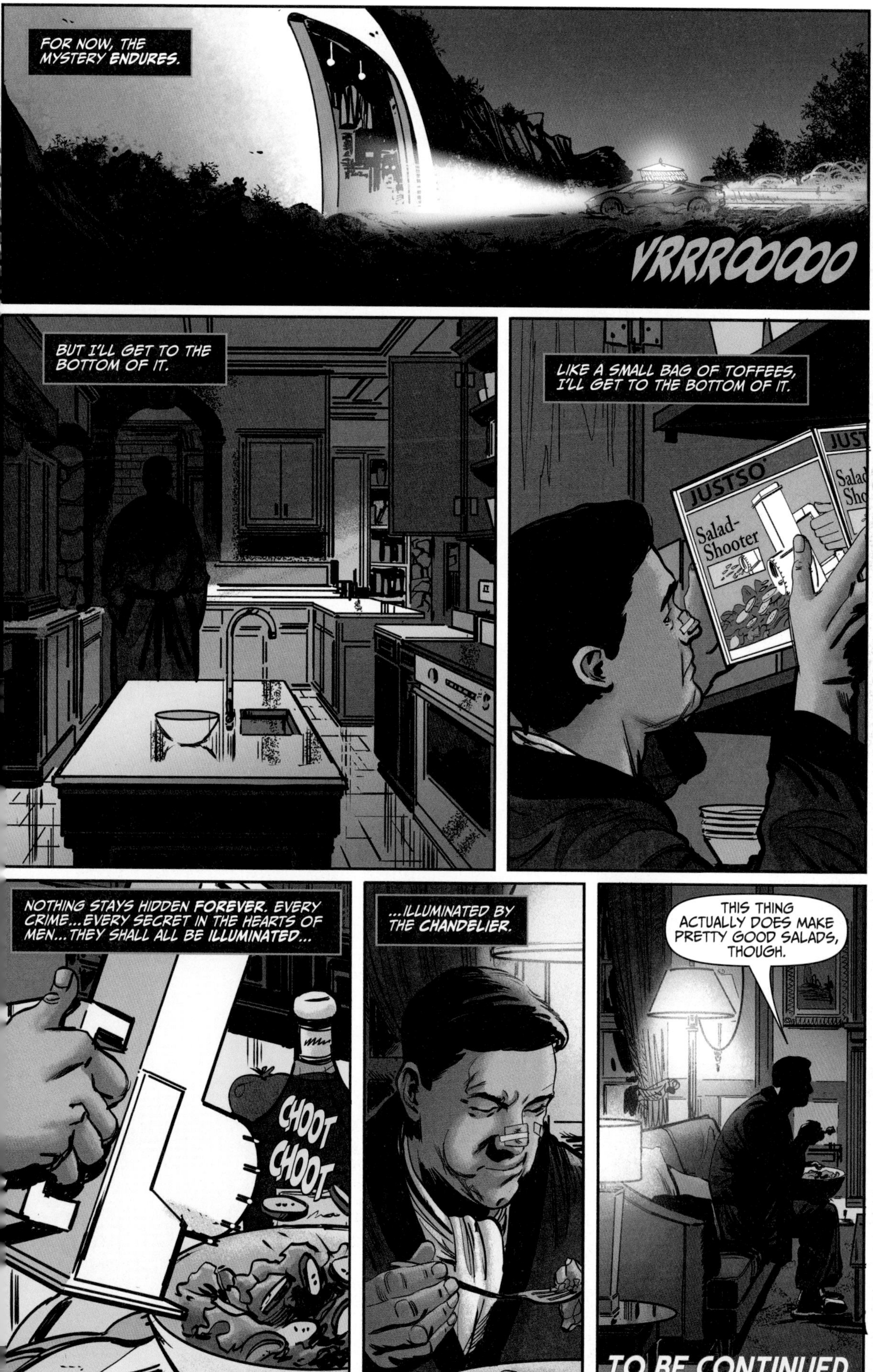
FOR NOW, THE MYSTERY ENDURES.
VRRROOOOO
BUT I'LL GET TO THE BOTTOM OF IT.
LIKE A SMALL BAG OF TOFFEES, I'LL GET TO THE BOTTOM OF IT.
JUSTSO
Salad-Shooter
NOTHING STAYS HIDDEN FOREVER. EVERY CRIME...EVERY SECRET IN THE HEARTS OF MEN...THEY SHALL ALL BE ILLUMINATED...
CHOOT CHOOT
...ILLUMINATED BY THE CHANDELIER.
THIS THING ACTUALLY DOES MAKE PRETTY GOOD SALADS, THOUGH.
TO BE CONTINUED.

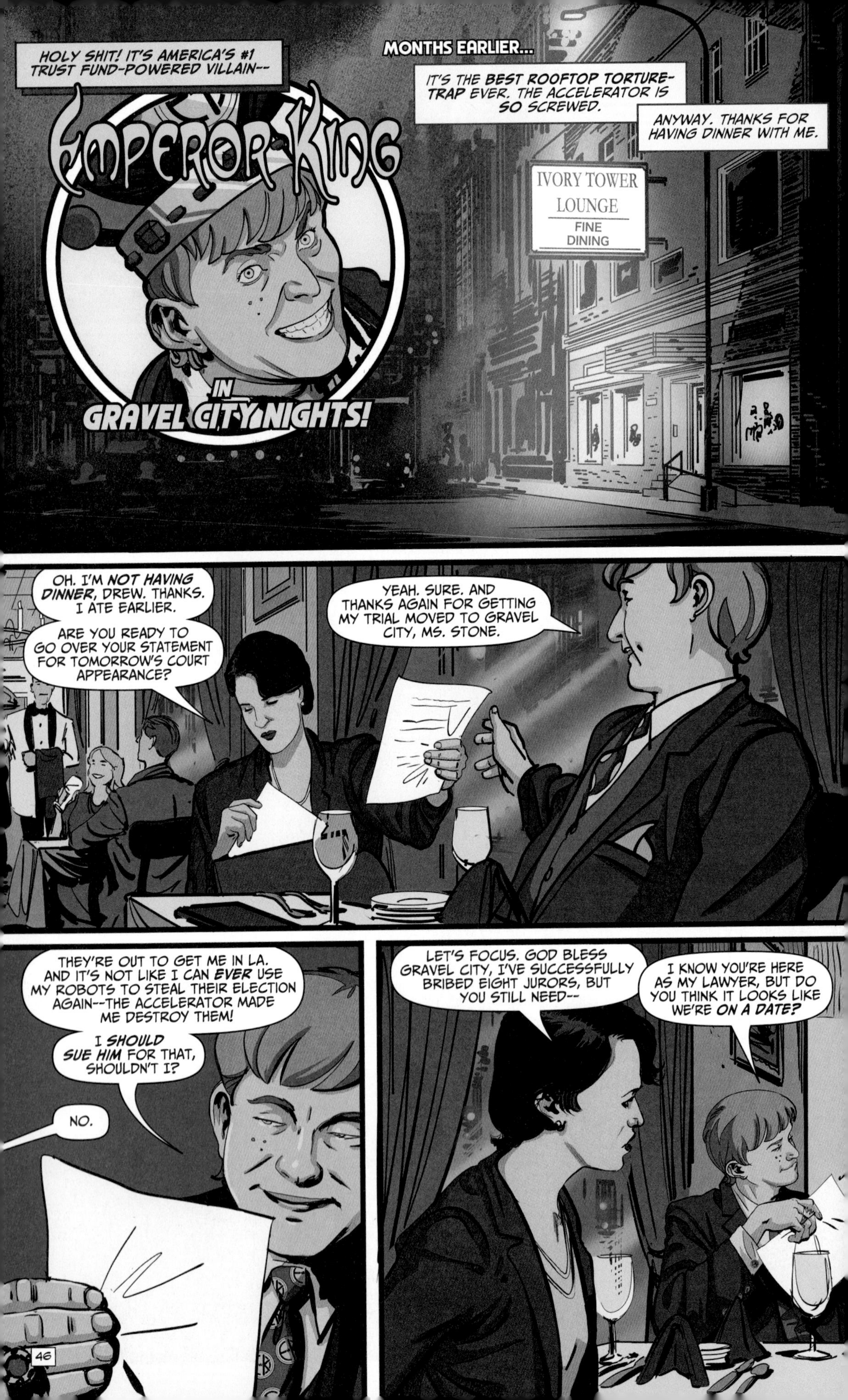
HOLY SHIT! IT'S AMERICA'S #1 TRUST FUND-POWERED VILLAIN--
EMPEROR KING
IN
GRAVEL CITY NIGHTS!
MONTHS EARLIER...
IT'S THE BEST ROOFTOP TORTURE-TRAP EVER. THE ACCELERATOR IS SO SCREWED.
ANYWAY. THANKS FOR HAVING DINNER WITH ME.
IVORY TOWER LOUNGE
FINE DINING
OH. I'M NOT HAVING DINNER, DREW. THANKS. I ATE EARLIER.
ARE YOU READY TO GO OVER YOUR STATEMENT FOR TOMORROW'S COURT APPEARANCE?
YEAH. SURE. AND THANKS AGAIN FOR GETTING MY TRIAL MOVED TO GRAVEL CITY, MS. STONE.
THEY'RE OUT TO GET ME IN LA. AND IT'S NOT LIKE I CAN EVER USE MY ROBOTS TO STEAL THEIR ELECTION AGAIN--THE ACCELERATOR MADE ME DESTROY THEM!
I SHOULD SUE HIM FOR THAT, SHOULDN'T I?
NO.
LET'S FOCUS. GOD BLESS GRAVEL CITY, I'VE SUCCESSFULLY BRIBED EIGHT JURORS, BUT YOU STILL NEED--
I KNOW YOU'RE HERE AS MY LAWYER, BUT DO YOU THINK IT LOOKS LIKE WE'RE ON A DATE?

I MEAN, *I KNOW WE'RE NOT.* BUT I BET THE OTHER DINERS THINK WE ARE. I BET THEY THINK I'M A REAL *LADIES' MAN.*

I DON'T KNOW... MAYBE.

ANYWAY. THIS IS IMPORTANT. YOUR TESTIMONY TOMORROW NEEDS TO--

OH, GREAT. NOT *HIM.*

WHO?

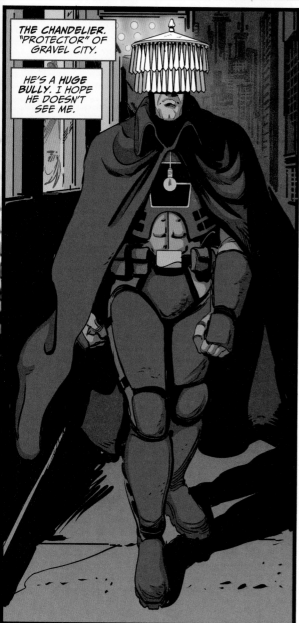

THE CHANDELIER. "PROTECTOR" OF GRAVEL CITY.

HE'S A *HUGE* BULLY. I HOPE HE DOESN'T SEE ME.

IS HE GONE? DID HE SEE ME?

DAMN IT. HE SAW ME, DIDN'T HE?

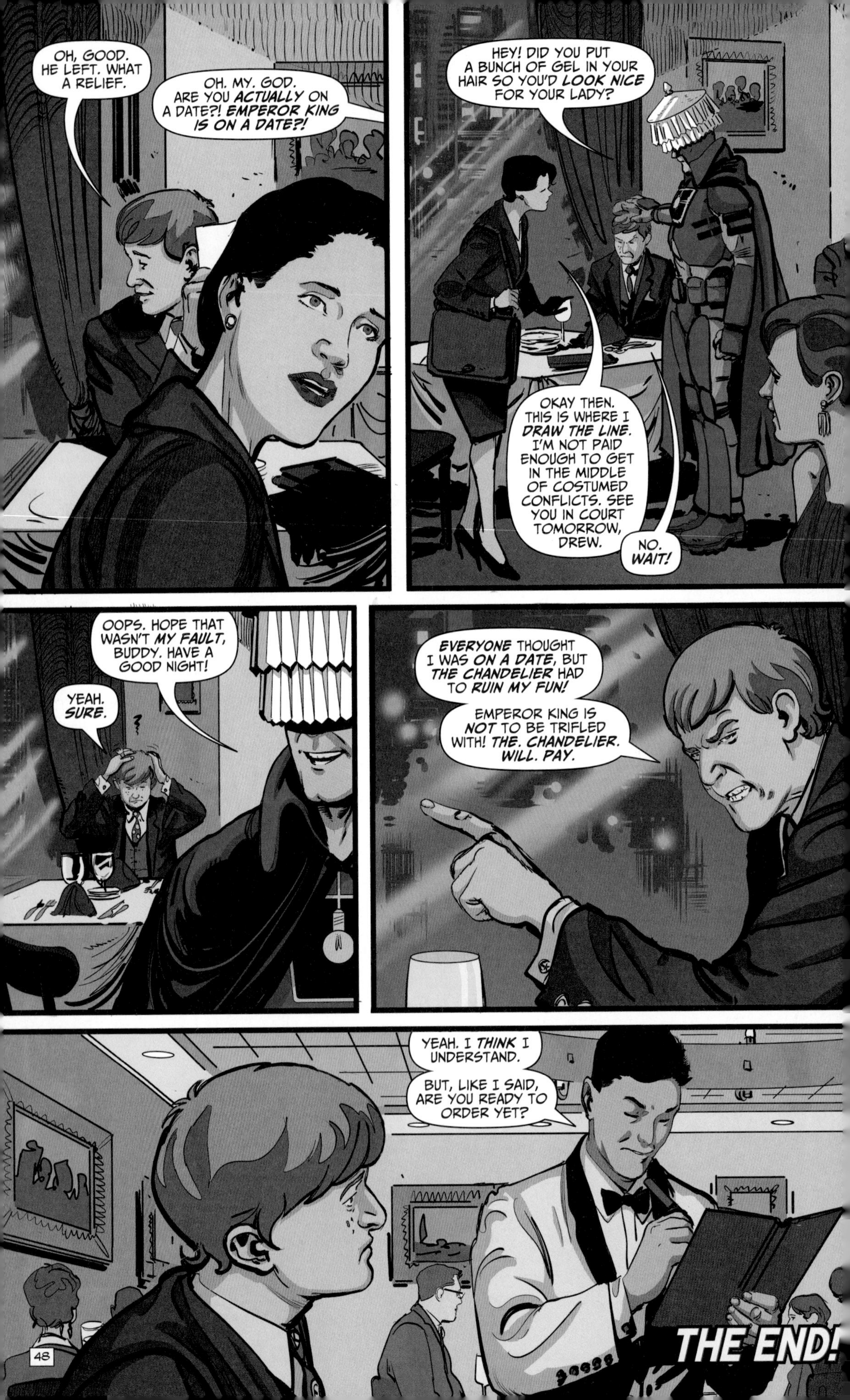
OH, GOOD. HE LEFT. WHAT A RELIEF.
OH. MY. GOD. ARE YOU ACTUALLY ON A DATE?! EMPEROR KING IS ON A DATE?!
HEY! DID YOU PUT A BUNCH OF GEL IN YOUR HAIR SO YOU'D LOOK NICE FOR YOUR LADY?
OKAY THEN. THIS IS WHERE I DRAW THE LINE. I'M NOT PAID ENOUGH TO GET IN THE MIDDLE OF COSTUMED CONFLICTS. SEE YOU IN COURT TOMORROW, DREW.
NO. WAIT!
OOPS. HOPE THAT WASN'T MY FAULT, BUDDY. HAVE A GOOD NIGHT!
YEAH. SURE.
?
EVERYONE THOUGHT I WAS ON A DATE, BUT THE CHANDELIER HAD TO RUIN MY FUN!
EMPEROR KING IS NOT TO BE TRIFLED WITH! THE. CHANDELIER. WILL. PAY.
YEAH. I THINK I UNDERSTAND.
BUT, LIKE I SAID, ARE YOU READY TO ORDER YET?
THE END!

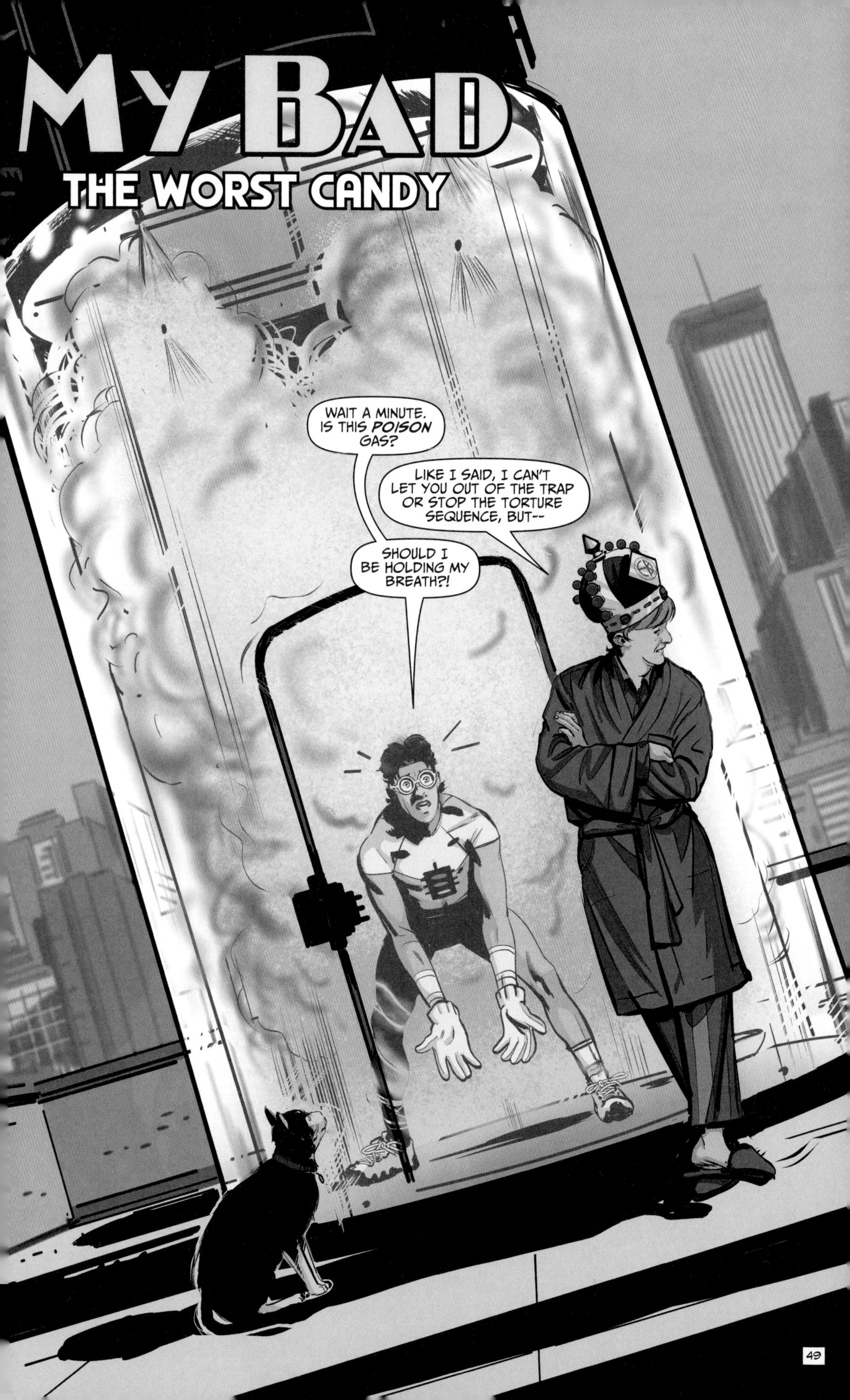
MY BAD
THE WORST CANDY
WAIT A MINUTE. IS THIS POISON GAS?
LIKE I SAID, I CAN'T LET YOU OUT OF THE TRAP OR STOP THE TORTURE SEQUENCE, BUT--
SHOULD I BE HOLDING MY BREATH?!

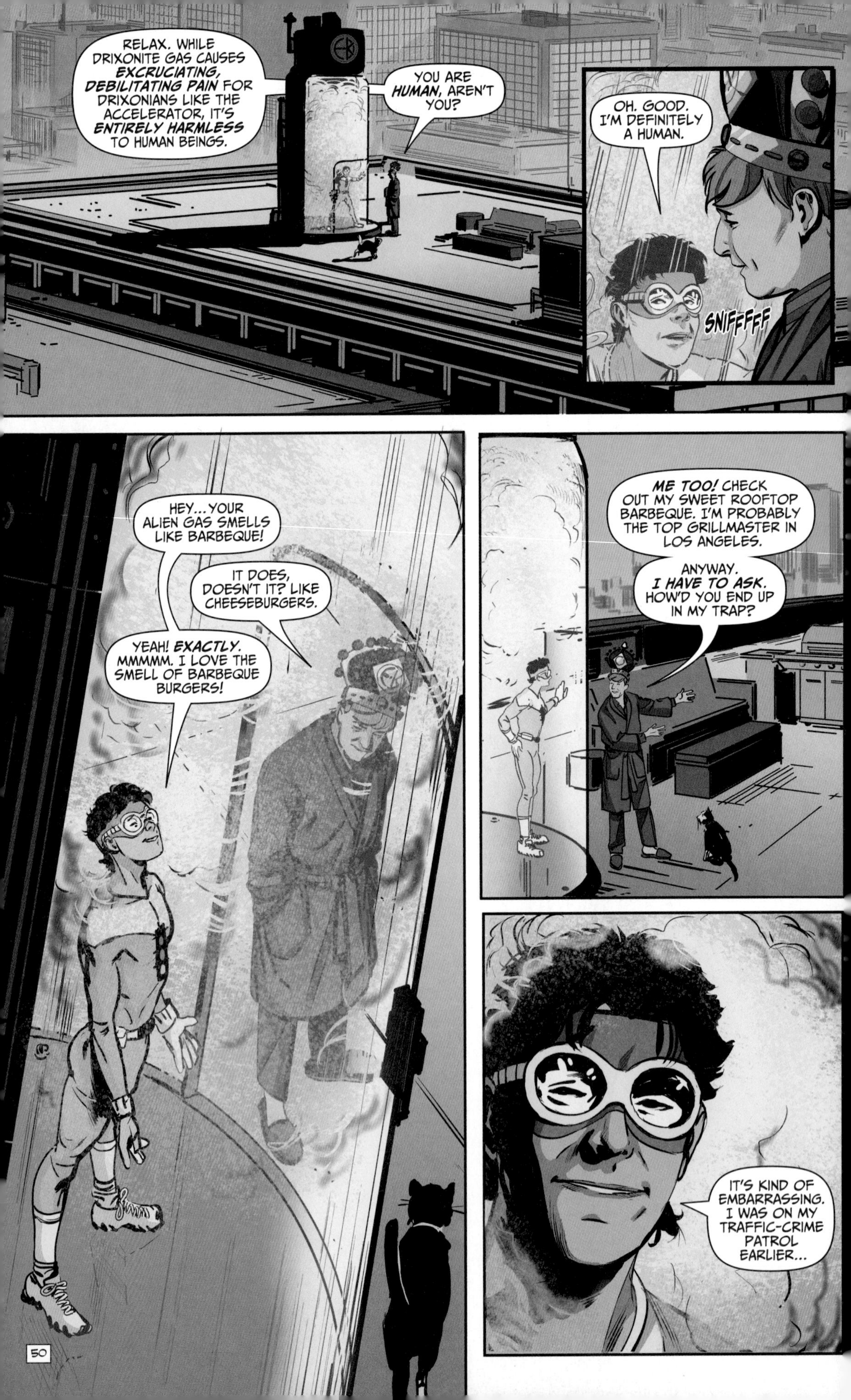

RELAX. WHILE DRIXONITE GAS CAUSES ***EXCRUCIATING, DEBILITATING PAIN*** FOR DRIXONIANS LIKE THE ACCELERATOR, IT'S ***ENTIRELY HARMLESS*** TO HUMAN BEINGS.
YOU ARE ***HUMAN,*** AREN'T YOU?
OH. GOOD. I'M DEFINITELY A HUMAN.
SNIFFFFFF
HEY... YOUR ALIEN GAS SMELLS LIKE BARBEQUE!
IT DOES, DOESN'T IT? LIKE CHEESEBURGERS.
YEAH! ***EXACTLY.*** MMMMM. I LOVE THE SMELL OF BARBEQUE BURGERS!
ME TOO! CHECK OUT MY SWEET ROOFTOP BARBEQUE. I'M PROBABLY THE TOP GRILLMASTER IN LOS ANGELES.
ANYWAY. ***I HAVE TO ASK.*** HOW'D YOU END UP IN MY TRAP?
IT'S KIND OF EMBARRASSING. I WAS ON MY TRAFFIC-CRIME PATROL EARLIER...

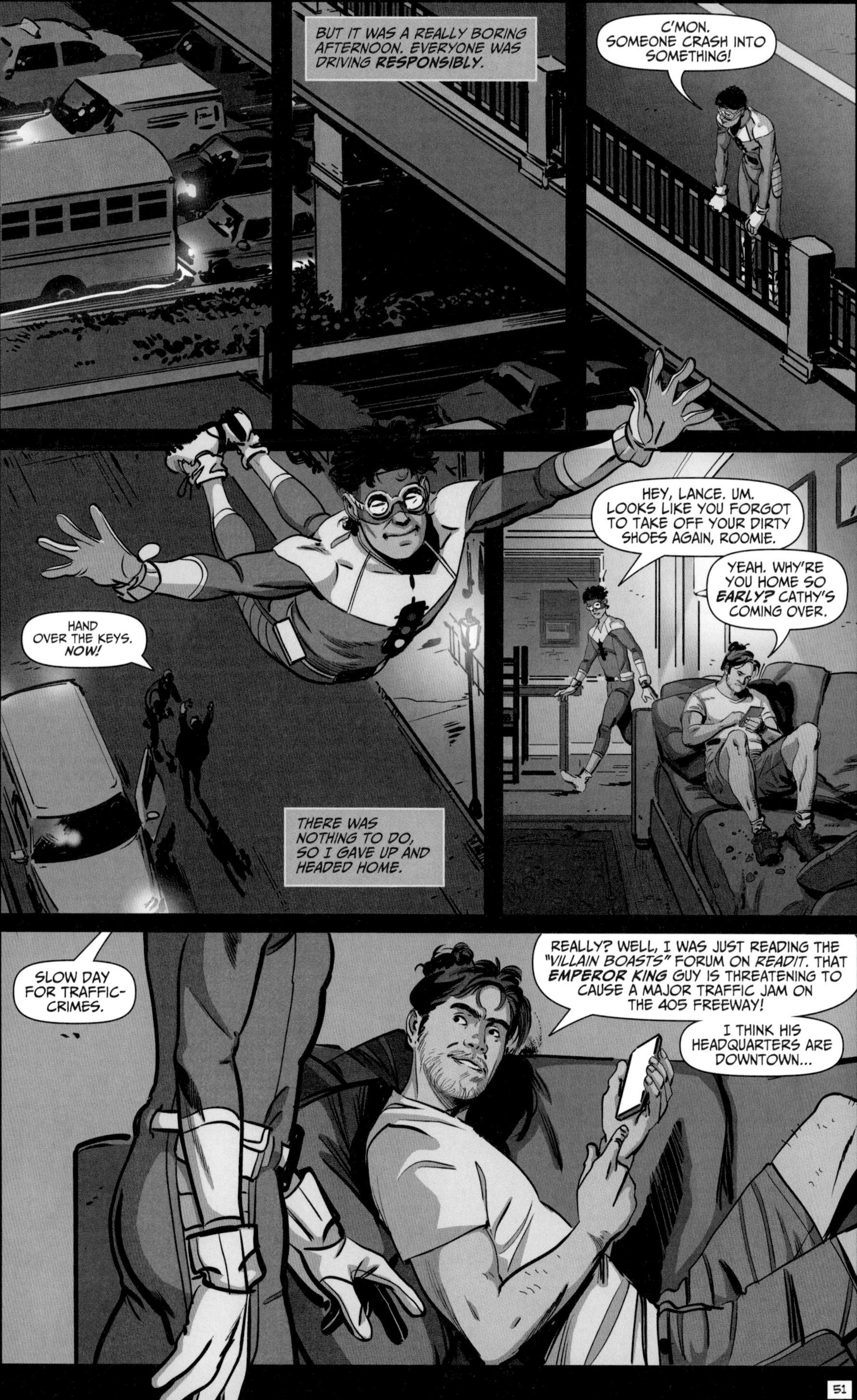
BUT IT WAS A REALLY BORING AFTERNOON. EVERYONE WAS DRIVING **RESPONSIBLY.**
C'MON. SOMEONE CRASH INTO SOMETHING!
HAND OVER THE KEYS. **NOW!**
THERE WAS NOTHING TO DO, SO I GAVE UP AND HEADED HOME.
HEY, LANCE. UM. LOOKS LIKE YOU FORGOT TO TAKE OFF YOUR DIRTY SHOES AGAIN, ROOMIE.
YEAH. WHY'RE YOU HOME SO ***EARLY?*** CATHY'S COMING OVER.
SLOW DAY FOR TRAFFIC-CRIMES.
REALLY? WELL, I WAS JUST READING THE *"VILLAIN BOASTS"* FORUM ON *READIT*. THAT ***EMPEROR KING*** GUY IS THREATENING TO CAUSE A MAJOR TRAFFIC JAM ON THE 405 FREEWAY!
I THINK HIS HEADQUARTERS ARE DOWNTOWN...

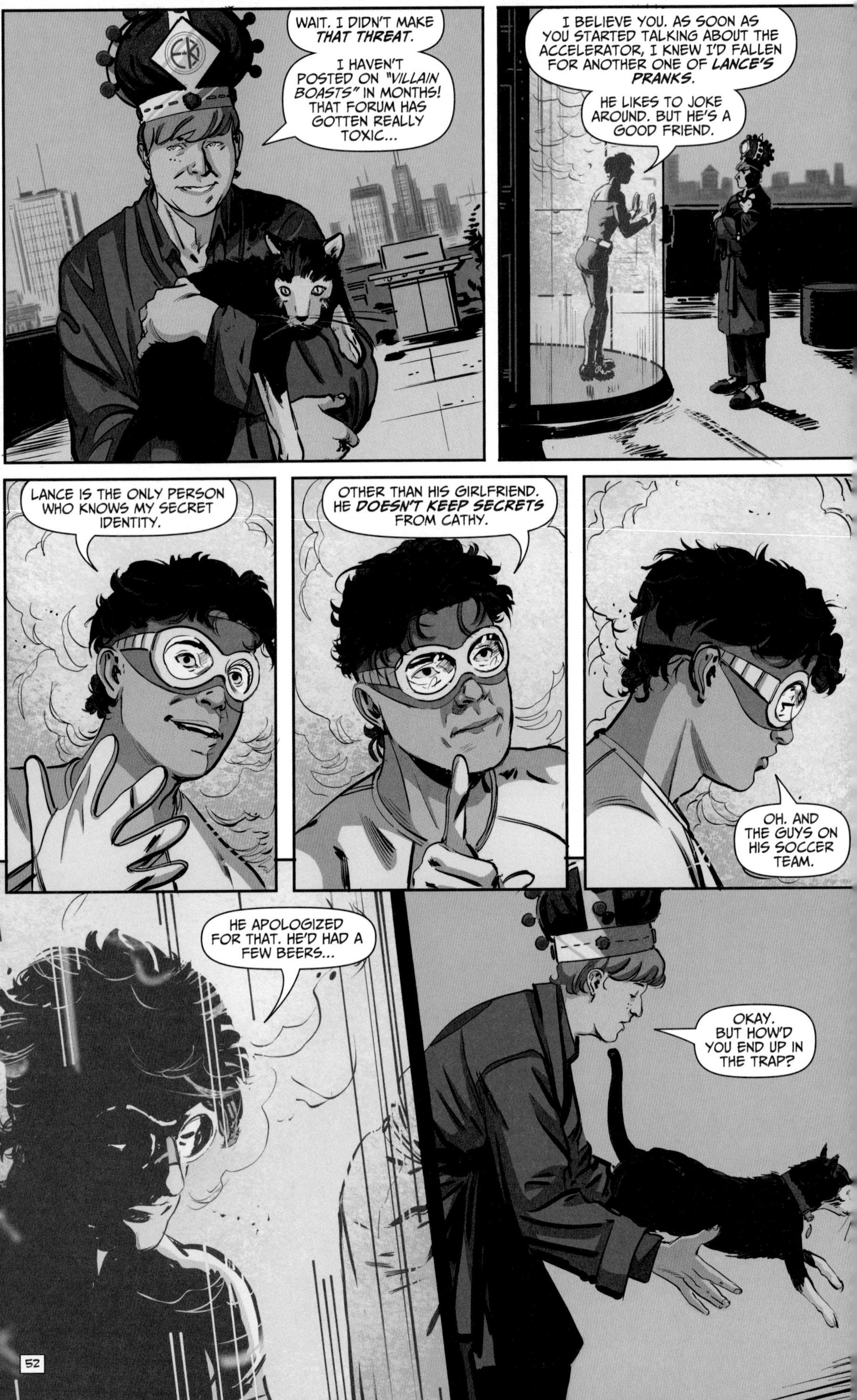
WAIT. I DIDN'T MAKE *THAT THREAT*.
I HAVEN'T POSTED ON *"VILLAIN BOASTS"* IN MONTHS! THAT FORUM HAS GOTTEN REALLY TOXIC...
I BELIEVE YOU. AS SOON AS YOU STARTED TALKING ABOUT THE ACCELERATOR, I KNEW I'D FALLEN FOR ANOTHER ONE OF ***LANCE'S PRANKS***.
HE LIKES TO JOKE AROUND. BUT HE'S A GOOD FRIEND.
LANCE IS THE ONLY PERSON WHO KNOWS MY SECRET IDENTITY.
OTHER THAN HIS GIRLFRIEND. HE ***DOESN'T KEEP SECRETS*** FROM CATHY.
OH. AND THE GUYS ON HIS SOCCER TEAM.
HE APOLOGIZED FOR THAT. HE'D HAD A FEW BEERS...
OKAY. BUT HOW'D YOU END UP IN THE TRAP?

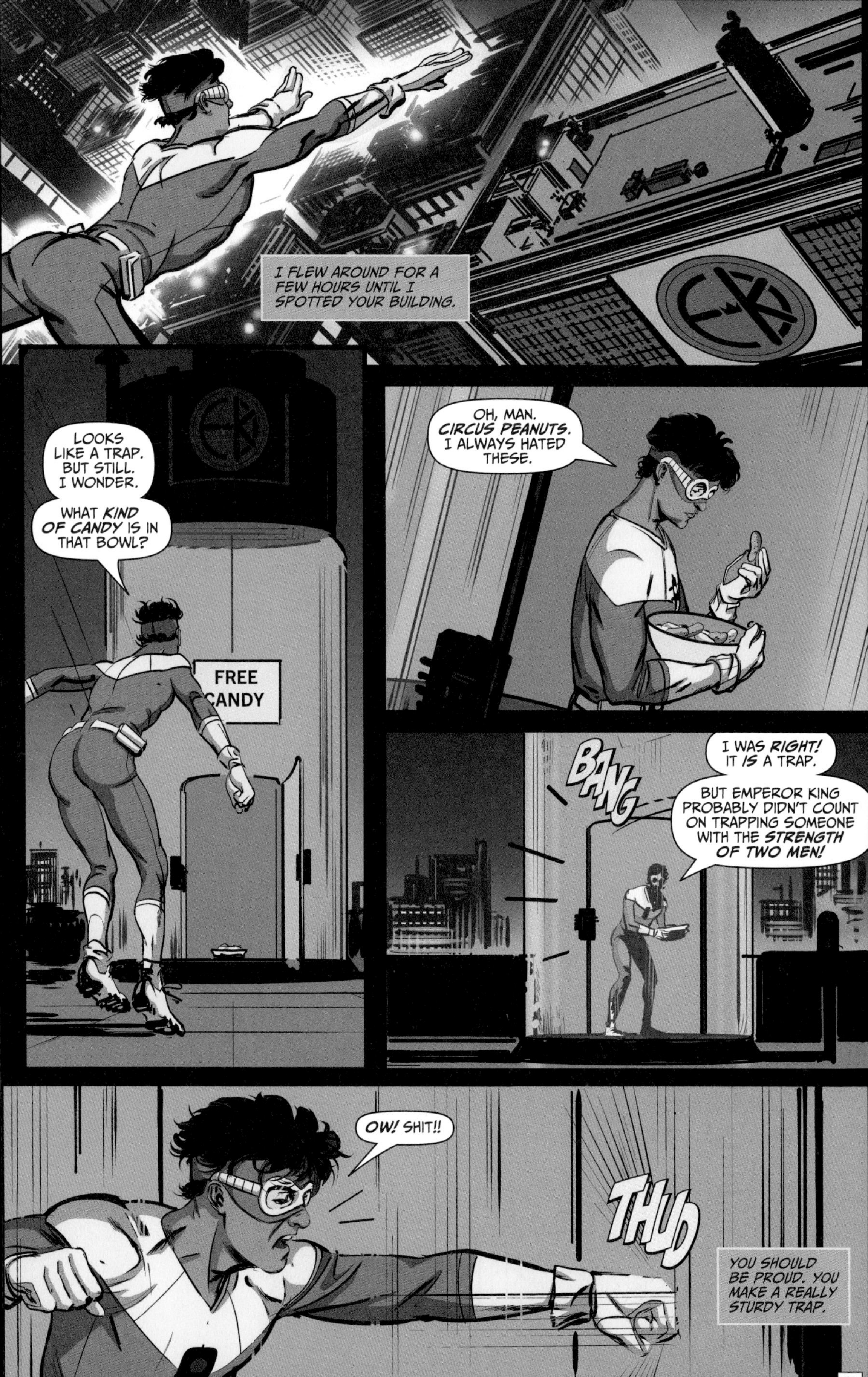
I FLEW AROUND FOR A FEW HOURS UNTIL I SPOTTED YOUR BUILDING.
LOOKS LIKE A TRAP. BUT STILL. I WONDER.
WHAT *KIND OF CANDY* IS IN THAT BOWL?
FREE CANDY
OH, MAN. ***CIRCUS PEANUTS.*** I ALWAYS HATED THESE.
BANG
I WAS *RIGHT!* IT *IS* A TRAP.
BUT EMPEROR KING PROBABLY DIDN'T COUNT ON TRAPPING SOMEONE WITH THE ***STRENGTH OF TWO MEN!***
OW! SHIT!!
THUD
YOU SHOULD BE PROUD. YOU MAKE A REALLY STURDY TRAP.

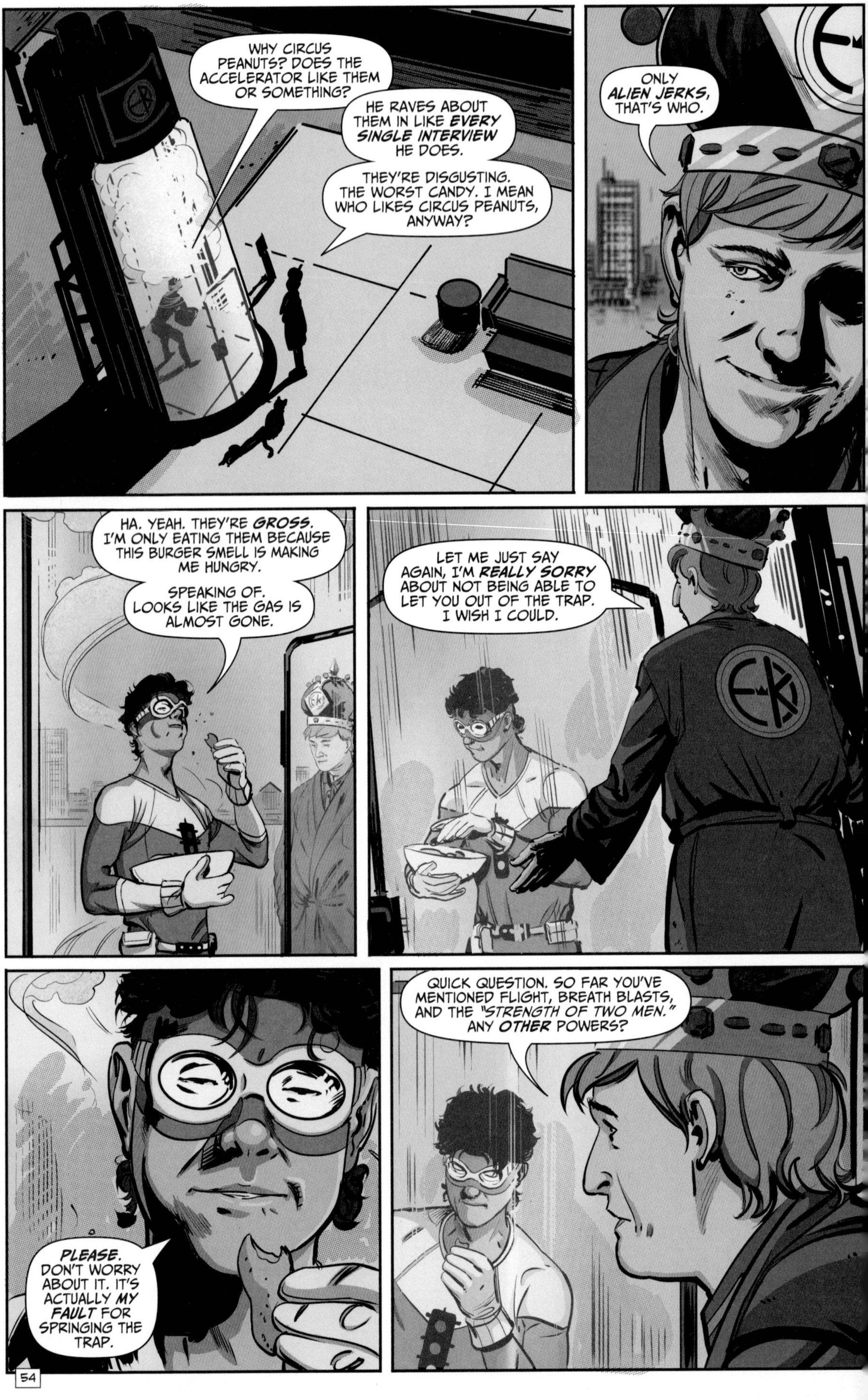
WHY CIRCUS PEANUTS? DOES THE ACCELERATOR LIKE THEM OR SOMETHING?
HE RAVES ABOUT THEM IN LIKE EVERY SINGLE INTERVIEW HE DOES.
THEY'RE DISGUSTING. THE WORST CANDY. I MEAN WHO LIKES CIRCUS PEANUTS, ANYWAY?
ONLY ALIEN JERKS, THAT'S WHO.
HA. YEAH. THEY'RE GROSS. I'M ONLY EATING THEM BECAUSE THIS BURGER SMELL IS MAKING ME HUNGRY.
SPEAKING OF. LOOKS LIKE THE GAS IS ALMOST GONE.
LET ME JUST SAY AGAIN, I'M REALLY SORRY ABOUT NOT BEING ABLE TO LET YOU OUT OF THE TRAP. I WISH I COULD.
PLEASE. DON'T WORRY ABOUT IT. IT'S ACTUALLY MY FAULT FOR SPRINGING THE TRAP.
QUICK QUESTION. SO FAR YOU'VE MENTIONED FLIGHT, BREATH BLASTS, AND THE "STRENGTH OF TWO MEN." ANY OTHER POWERS?

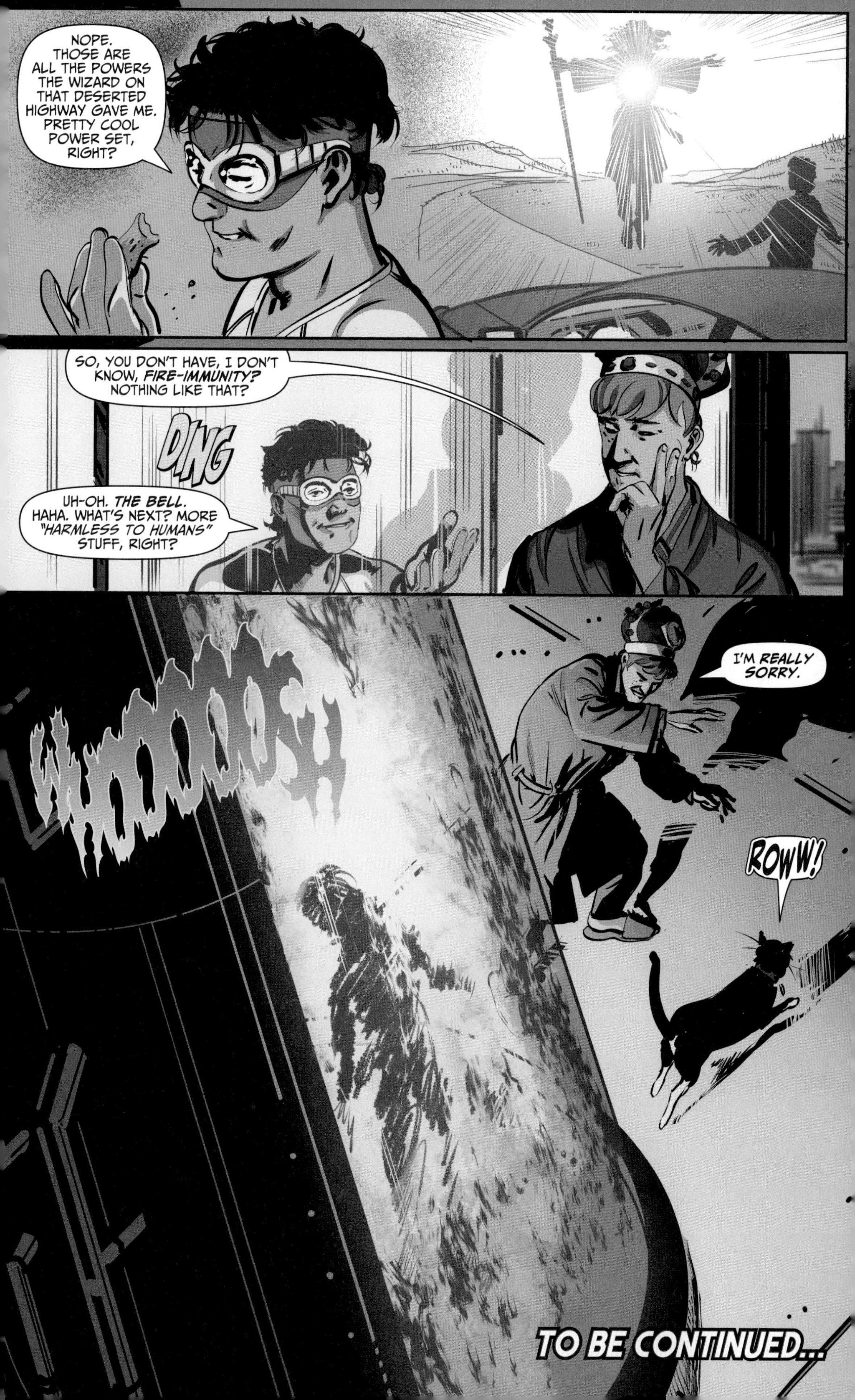
NOPE. THOSE ARE ALL THE POWERS THE WIZARD ON THAT DESERTED HIGHWAY GAVE ME. PRETTY COOL POWER SET, RIGHT?
SO, YOU DON'T HAVE, I DON'T KNOW, FIRE-IMMUNITY? NOTHING LIKE THAT?
DING
UH-OH. THE BELL. HAHA. WHAT'S NEXT? MORE "HARMLESS TO HUMANS" STUFF, RIGHT?
WHOOOSH
. . .
I'M REALLY SORRY.
ROWW!
TO BE CONTINUED...

BAD WORDS

Hey there, reader of mildly entertaining comic book letter columns, it's Bouncing Baby Bryce Ingman, your pal and MY BAD co-writer, back with another important installment of Bad Words! Right off the top let me say that the whole MY BAD team was blown away by the amazing response to issue one. We knew we were on to something with exciting new characters like the Chandelier, the Accelerator and Emperor King, but we had no idea the world would react **this** strongly. Being recommended by both Senate Minority Leader Mitch McConnell **and** retired football superstar O.J. Simpson on the same day is quite the honor. And when musical guest Da Baby dedicated a song to MY BAD on last week's Saturday Night Live, it was the icing on "da" cake. What an incredible ride.

Anyway, I suppose we should see what you normal, non-famous people have to say about MY BAD. (Although I can't imagine how any of your ramblings could be very exciting compared to the hilarious shout-out Jon Voight gave us on the Tonight Show last night. What a class act.)

Mark, Peter and Bryce,

I really enjoyed the first issue of MY BAD. Would you like to come over for dinner? I have a pizza oven.

Candice
Providence, RI

I was considering your offer until you started bragging about the pizza oven. Just because I have to cook my pizzas in a regular, non-pizza-specific oven and you have a cool, special pizza-only oven doesn't make you better than me, Candice. It makes you an elitist.

***

Humans,

I am an alien. I live in outer space.

Alien
Outer Space

I have to admit, that's pretty cool. I take back everything I said about our non-famous readers. You win "Letter of the Month" for this edition of Bad Words, Alien. Thanks for reading!

Bryce and Mark,

I have a complaint about MY BAD #1 and I think it's important for you guys to know my thoughts on the matter and consider the possibility that you've crossed a line. I only ask that you try to see the situation from my perspective and understand that I have been and always will be a fan. But I need to feel heard. And I don't think that's too much to ask.

The other day I accidentally sat on my copy of MY BAD #1 and when I stood up, it was stuck to my butt! I had to ask my neighbor to help me pull it off. It was really stuck! Could you please stop smearing glue on your covers?

Aside from that, I really, really enjoy the book. It's brilliant fun. Keep up the good work.

Max
Bend, OR

We get a lot of letters like this, so I guess it's time to address the issue. There is no glue smeared on our covers. In truth, our covers are embedded with magnets. Tiny magnets. And I'm guessing you're a war hero with a metal butt, aren't you, Max? So put your glue worries to bed, my friend. What you experienced were just regular, mildly radioactive, comic book magnets. Glad you're enjoying MY BAD, and thank you for your service.

***

Mark, Peter, and Bryce,

I'm a long haul trucker on the road 100 to 300 hours per week. Let me tell you, it can get pretty boring! That's why I had to thank you guys for the MY BAD audio book. It really helps me pass the time and keep my sanity! I love how the MY BAD audio book doesn't make any sound so you have to read it aloud to yourself as you drive. And Peter's art looks great! Definitely my favorite audio book ever.

I'm just going to rest my eyes for a few seconds. Don't let me fall asleep.

Antonio
America's Highways

Thanks, Antonio! I hope it's your truck that delivers MY BAD to all the comic book shops in America because I can tell you're the kind of conscientious fella who will make sure our precious comics get to their destination safe and on time!

***

Looks like we have room for one more letter...

Bryce,

Come home. I miss my husband and your son needs a father. He's starting to forget you! All I do is cry.

Deborah
Drain, OR

I'll be home soon, honey. Just a few more issues of MY BAD to write. Remember, as I explained to you in 2018, all AHOY comics must be written at AHOY Tower in Honolulu, Hawaii. It's in the company bylaws. Nothing I can do about it! Show Bryce Jr. my Instagram feed. I've been taking lots of beach selfies.

TOM'S TOOLBOX!

You know, they say there's no rest for the wicked—or the unabashedly intrepid!

Your Chief must fit into one of those wild categories, because when I'm not managing this mass of magnificent magazines, I'm probably off at one of the 290-or-so speaking gigs I do each and every year! I usually perform for three or four exhausting hours—promoting our properties, entertaining your enquiries, and pitching the AHOY lifestyle to assorted advisory boards, think tanks, yacht clubs, and other altruistic assemblies!

But prattling from podiums—plus conjuring comics—is not the totality of my tasks! Our pernicious publisher also requires me to race to the globe's most luxurious leisure spots, rub elbows with the moneyed and the mighty, and convert them to AHOYism! How do I do it? (Just between us: Since you're an AHOYnik, I know I can trust you to keep these secret steps under your sailor hat!)

- First, I make their acquaintance!
- Then, I flatter them!
- When absolutely necessary, I'll flourish the AHOY credit card for a huge round of highballs!
- And, building up to the dramatic dénouement, I will delicately imply that a sure-thing investment opportunity exists for their further enrichment!
- Suddenly, I'll get very quiet, appearing to regret a cat I let out of the bag!
- Before I know it, *they're* begging *me* to accept their filthy, fishy funds!

Yes, it looks like a workload that would kill an army—but, to Your Chief, it's not labor at all! I bring it blithely, because I believe in AHOY!

But what exactly *do* I believe? What *is* the AHOY Philosophy? We get so many postal cards and telegrams asking those questions that it's really starting to tick me off! What are

we busting our tails on these mags for? Aren't we making their themes and morals clear enough? Are we using too many big words? How stupid *are* you people?

Sorry. I never should have said that. It's been a long week of late nights, and Your Chief is feeling as fragile as Rush Hour after a dreadful day in Emperor King's dizzy death trap!

Tell you what, Fab Followers: Give us a smile and I'll answer your probing pleas right here in this space next issue!

Occupare omnes terras,

COMING AHOY-TRACTIONS

EDGAR ALLAN POE'S SNIFTER OF DEATH #3 (Writers: Tom Peyer and Bryce Abood. Artists: Greg Scott and Rick Geary. Cover: Richard Williams.)— It's MONSTER MONTH in the world's weirdest horror/humor anthology! Who is killing the classic creatures? Find out in "Edgar Allan Poe's Gore of Frankenstein"! How stupid were 19th century doctors? Learn the giant, bloodsucking answer in "Annabel's Leech"! In comics shops ***December 15!***

SNELSON: COMEDY IS DYING #5 (Writer: Paul Constant. Artist: Fred Harper.)— Last issue, a.k.a. the punchline! Comedian Melville Snelson's career-restoring flirtation with the online alt-right descends into crisis when he learns that his newest, loudest, and most loyal fans can also be described as "angry" and "gun-toting." ***December 22!***

NEXT: Disaster strikes The Chandelier when he compares his social media feed to those of more popular crimefighters! AND! A look back at the glory days when Rush Hour enforced safety compliance on America's thrilling freeways! See you next year—specifically, ***January 12!***

—Bryce

Write to MY BAD—or any AHOY Rockin' Pop Litform—at letters@comicsahoy.com. Snail mail: PO Box 189, DeWitt, NY 13214. Mark "OK to print" if it is. AND! Subscribe to the free, funny-as-anything AHOY Newsletter at bit.ly/newsahoy. PLUS! Use this case-sensitive link to access 35 pages of free—as in no cost to you—SNELSON: bit.ly/Snelson.

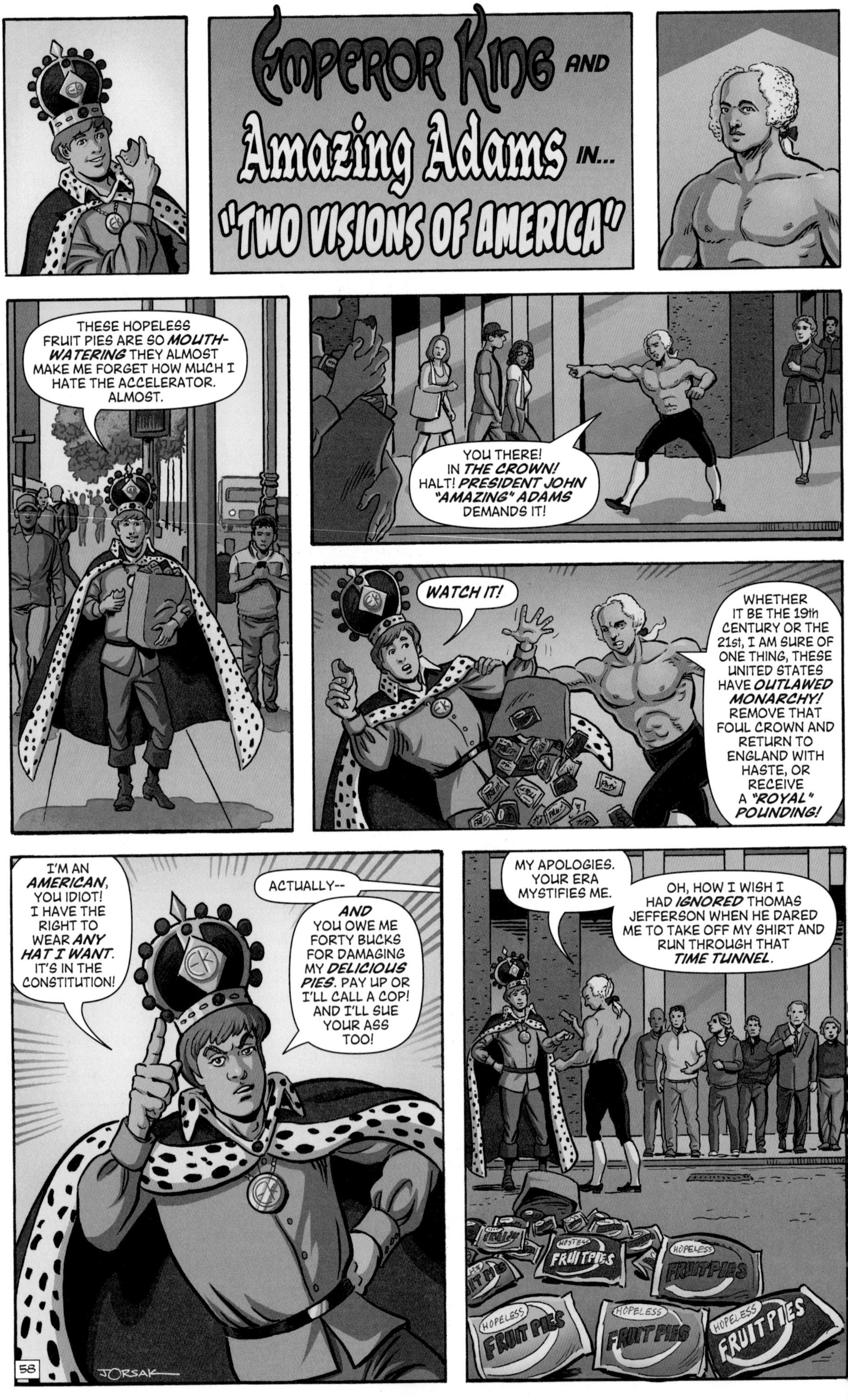
EMPEROR KING AND
Amazing Adams IN...
"TWO VISIONS OF AMERICA"
THESE HOPELESS FRUIT PIES ARE SO MOUTH-WATERING THEY ALMOST MAKE ME FORGET HOW MUCH I HATE THE ACCELERATOR. ALMOST.
YOU THERE! IN THE CROWN! HALT! PRESIDENT JOHN "AMAZING" ADAMS DEMANDS IT!
WATCH IT!
WHETHER IT BE THE 19th CENTURY OR THE 21st, I AM SURE OF ONE THING, THESE UNITED STATES HAVE OUTLAWED MONARCHY! REMOVE THAT FOUL CROWN AND RETURN TO ENGLAND WITH HASTE, OR RECEIVE A "ROYAL" POUNDING!
I'M AN AMERICAN, YOU IDIOT! I HAVE THE RIGHT TO WEAR ANY HAT I WANT. IT'S IN THE CONSTITUTION!
ACTUALLY--
AND YOU OWE ME FORTY BUCKS FOR DAMAGING MY DELICIOUS PIES. PAY UP OR I'LL CALL A COP! AND I'LL SUE YOUR ASS TOO!
JORSAK
MY APOLOGIES. YOUR ERA MYSTIFIES ME.
OH, HOW I WISH I HAD IGNORED THOMAS JEFFERSON WHEN HE DARED ME TO TAKE OFF MY SHIRT AND RUN THROUGH THAT TIME TUNNEL.
HOSTESS FRUIT PIES
HOPELESS FRUIT PIES
HOPELESS FRUIT PIES
HOPELESS FRUIT PIES
HOPELESS FRUIT PIES

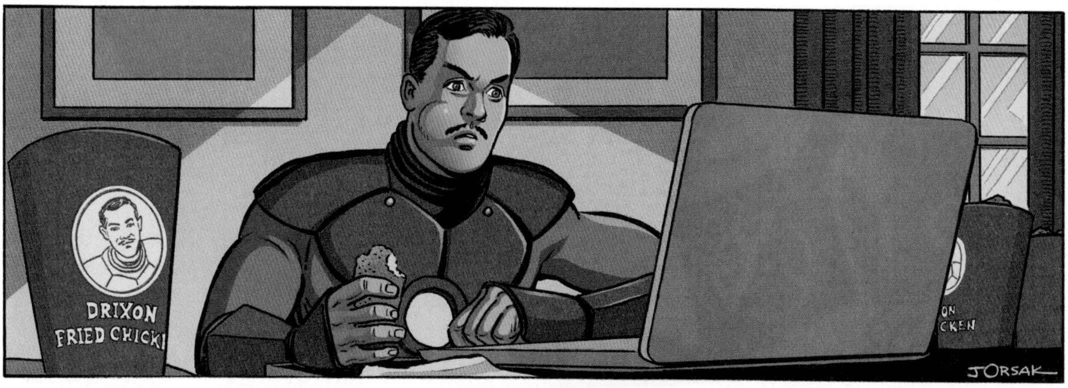
DRIXON
FRIED CHICKI
JORSAK

ASK THE ACCELERATOR

I am The Accelerator, an intergalactic hero and adventurer. I've pledged my life to protecting Earth, my adopted planet. I also own a chain of Drixon Fried Chicken restaurants located throughout the U.S. and Canada. Try our delicious new Spicy Chicken Milkshakes - available for a limited time! I love my human fans and have agreed to answer some questions that were submitted through your primitive internet system.

Loveandunderstanding675
Which is better? Earth or your home planet?

I will always love Drixon; I visit regularly. But your Earth is by far the best planet. Drixon's planetary government is oppressive. Too many rules, my Earther friends! For instance, they're so obsessed with making sure that every Drixonian has affordable, quality health care that they've outlawed private health insurance! I make a lot of money with my fried chicken restaurants, and I appreciate how, on Earth, I can use that money to enroll in premium health plans and hire better doctors than a poor person can. Fair is fair, right?

Bigpandagal900
Thanks for answering our questions, Mr. Accelerator. You're amazing. Just how fast can you run?

You're welcome, bigpandagal900. Honestly, I'm not sure what my top speed is. You see, I try not to run faster than the speed of light. If I move at a higher speed than that, my stomach gets queasy. Of course, the best remedy for an upset stomach is Drixon Fried Chicken. Check out our new location in Florida City, Florida!

Fireinmyhole53
Would you ever star in a movie? If so, what genre?

Well, as I'm sure you know, I speak all Earth languages (they're easy) and I've already "starred" in a series of Chinese animated films as Saipao-zhe, the rabbit sidekick to their awesome president, Xi Jinping. It was a lot of fun recording the voice. And the paycheck was excellent. Unfortunately, your American networks and streaming services have labeled the movies "blatant Chinese government propaganda." Which is ridiculous. INFALLIBLE LEADER AND RABBIT isn't propaganda. It's good, clean fun!

Delectabledrew14
Do you ever regret injuring the "villains" you encounter? To mention one completely random example, aren't you too hard on Emperor King? He doesn't even have super powers and you're constantly assaulting him!

I have a feeling this is Emperor King, so I'm going to ignore the second question and focus on what happened last week when I apprehended Dr. Fist-Punch. He was attacking the competitors at the Drixon Fried Chicken Eating Championship with that weird, giant fist of his. Kobayashi was vomiting. Joey Chestnut was crying. It was heartbreaking. Now. Did I overreact when I let purposefully let go of Dr. Fist-Punch while carrying him at 100mph? Perhaps. Will Dr. Fist-Punch recover? Also, perhaps. So, to answer your question, do I have any regrets? No. Because I will protect the rights of Earthers to eat grotesque amounts of food for the entertainment of others until the day I die!

Thecandymancan8
You're famously a huge fan of Circus Peanuts candy. Which color is your favorite?

Everyone knows that yellow Circus Peanuts are a perfect foodstuff. Why aren't more candies banana flavored? Shout-out to 97-year-old Circus Peanuts' creator Nathaniel Hepner. That man knows what makes a good snack! And remember, at Drixon Fried Chicken, Circus Peanuts are included with every value meal!

Eighblimon90
How do you respond to those of us who aren't sure we can trust the Accelerator due to your constant advertising for Drixon Fried Chicken and your other business interests? Do you, like some people say, "care more about Earth money than Earth people?"

This question breaks my heart. Let me remind you of what I said in a recent shoe commercial which features some of my original poetry, "**The humans of Earth have been so kind. Truer friends you'll never find. They've healed this Drixonian's wounded psyche. Check out the new Accelerator shoes from Nike.**" When I open my heart like that so publicly, it's hard to believe anyone could question my loyalties!

Well, that's all the questions we have room for this month. Say "hi" if you see me run by!

—The Accelerator

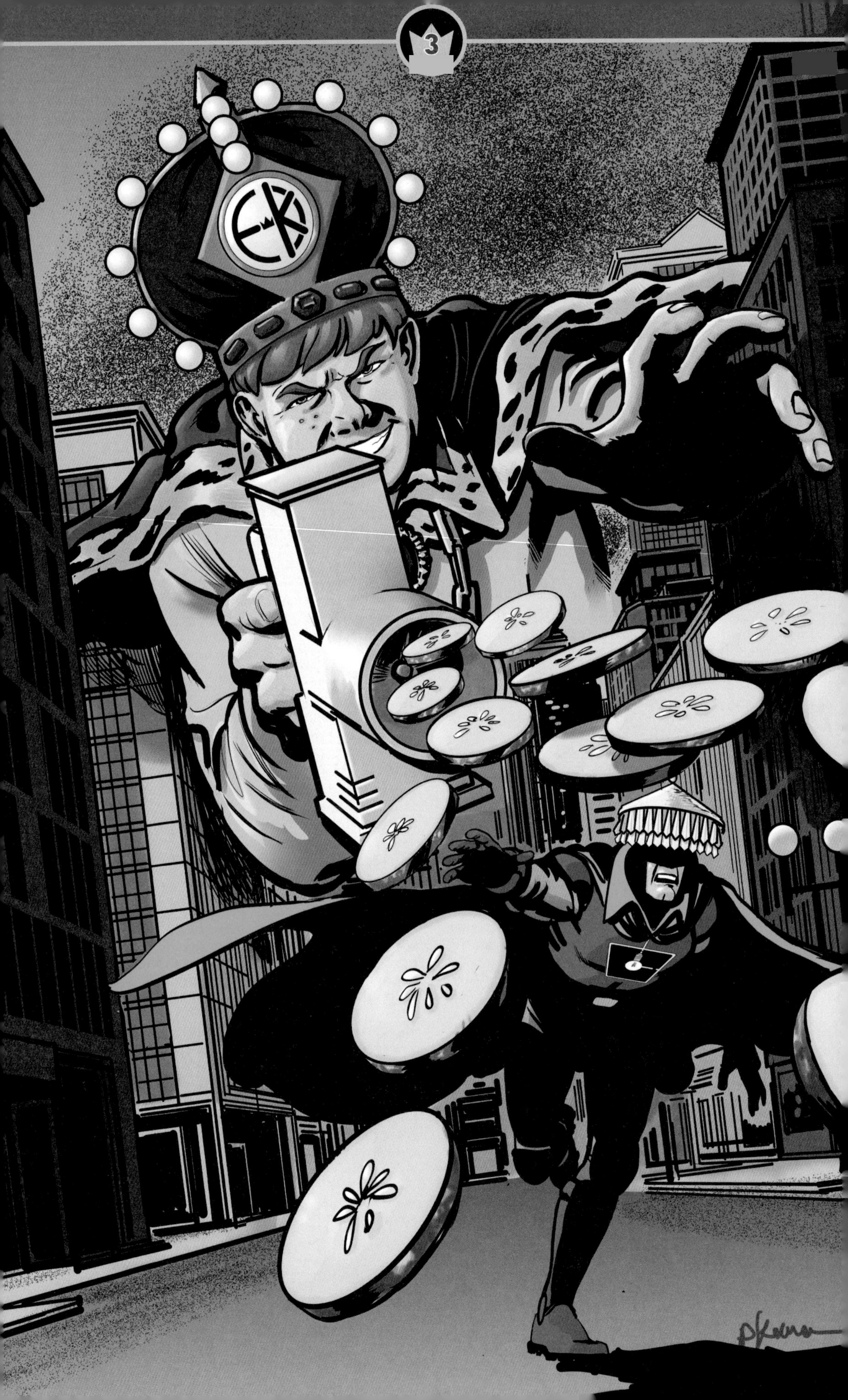
3

"LABOR CONQUERS ALL THINGS."

-OKLAHOMA STATE MOTTO

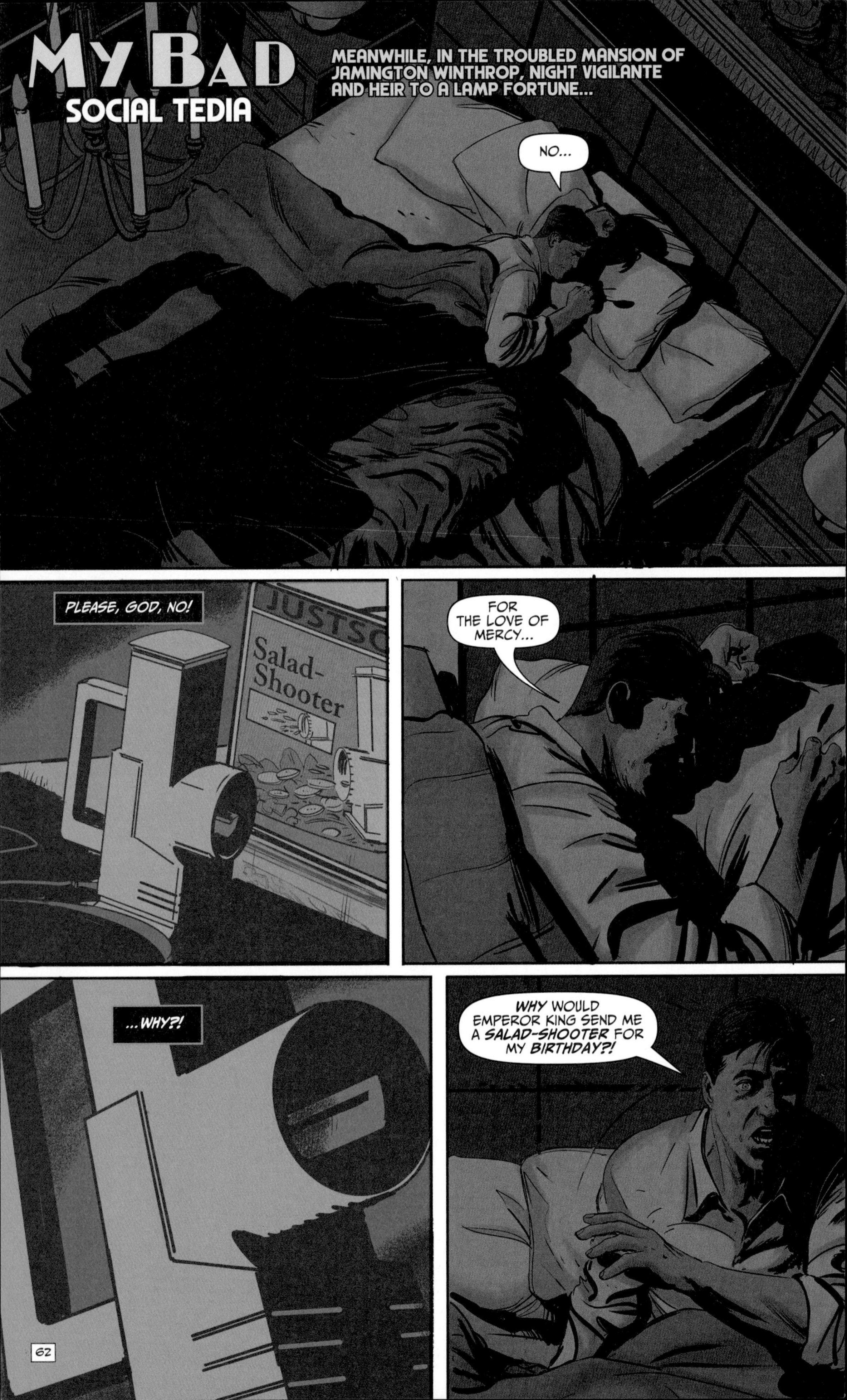
MY BAD
SOCIAL TEDIA
MEANWHILE, IN THE TROUBLED MANSION OF JAMINGTON WINTHROP, NIGHT VIGILANTE AND HEIR TO A LAMP FORTUNE...
NO...
PLEASE, GOD, NO!
JUSTSO
Salad-Shooter
FOR THE LOVE OF MERCY...
...WHY?!
WHY WOULD EMPEROR KING SEND ME A SALAD-SHOOTER FOR MY BIRTHDAY?!

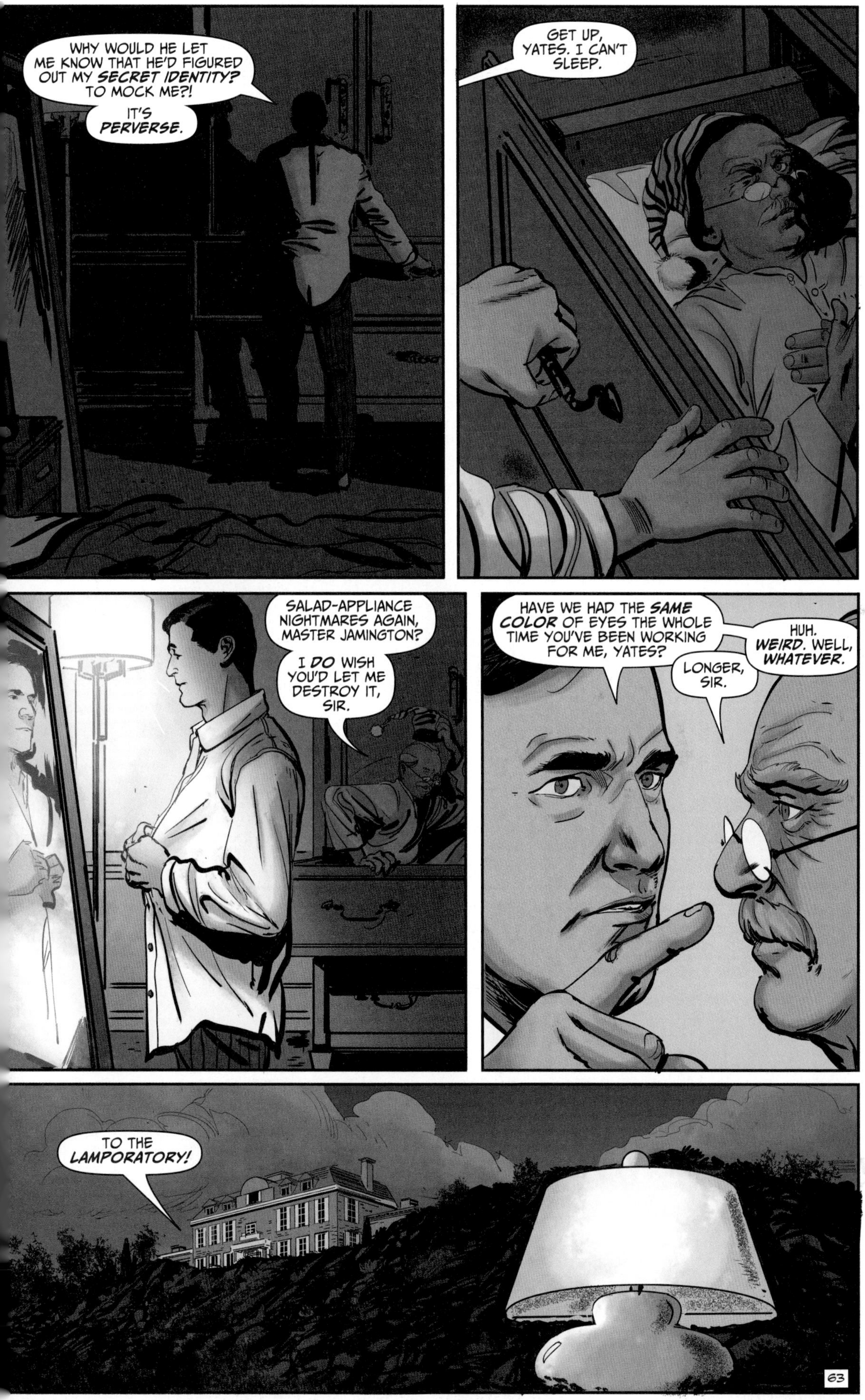
WHY WOULD HE LET ME KNOW THAT HE'D FIGURED OUT MY SECRET IDENTITY? TO MOCK ME?!
IT'S PERVERSE.
GET UP, YATES. I CAN'T SLEEP.
SALAD-APPLIANCE NIGHTMARES AGAIN, MASTER JAMINGTON?
I DO WISH YOU'D LET ME DESTROY IT, SIR.
HAVE WE HAD THE SAME COLOR OF EYES THE WHOLE TIME YOU'VE BEEN WORKING FOR ME, YATES?
LONGER, SIR.
HUH. WEIRD. WELL, WHATEVER.
TO THE LAMPORATORY!

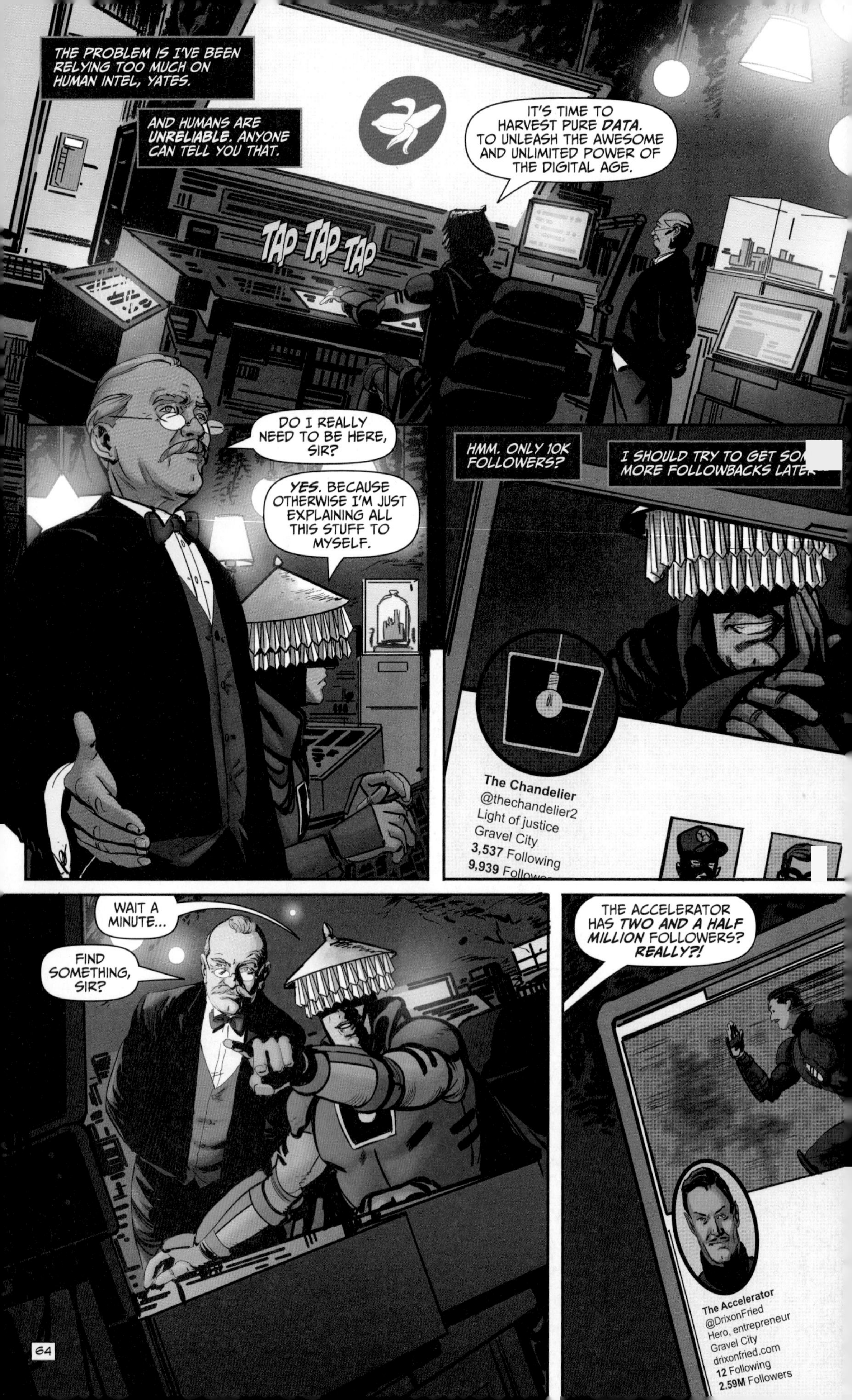
THE PROBLEM IS I'VE BEEN RELYING TOO MUCH ON HUMAN INTEL, YATES.
AND HUMANS ARE UNRELIABLE. ANYONE CAN TELL YOU THAT.
IT'S TIME TO HARVEST PURE DATA. TO UNLEASH THE AWESOME AND UNLIMITED POWER OF THE DIGITAL AGE.
TAP TAP TAP
DO I REALLY NEED TO BE HERE, SIR?
YES. BECAUSE OTHERWISE I'M JUST EXPLAINING ALL THIS STUFF TO MYSELF.
HMM. ONLY 10K FOLLOWERS?
I SHOULD TRY TO GET SOM
MORE FOLLOWBACKS LATE
The Chandelier
@thechandelier2
Light of justice
Gravel City
3,537 Following
9,939 Follow
WAIT A MINUTE...
FIND SOMETHING, SIR?
THE ACCELERATOR HAS TWO AND A HALF MILLION FOLLOWERS? REALLY?!
The Accelerator
@DrixonFried
Hero, entrepreneur
Gravel City
drixonfried.com
12 Following
2.59M Followers

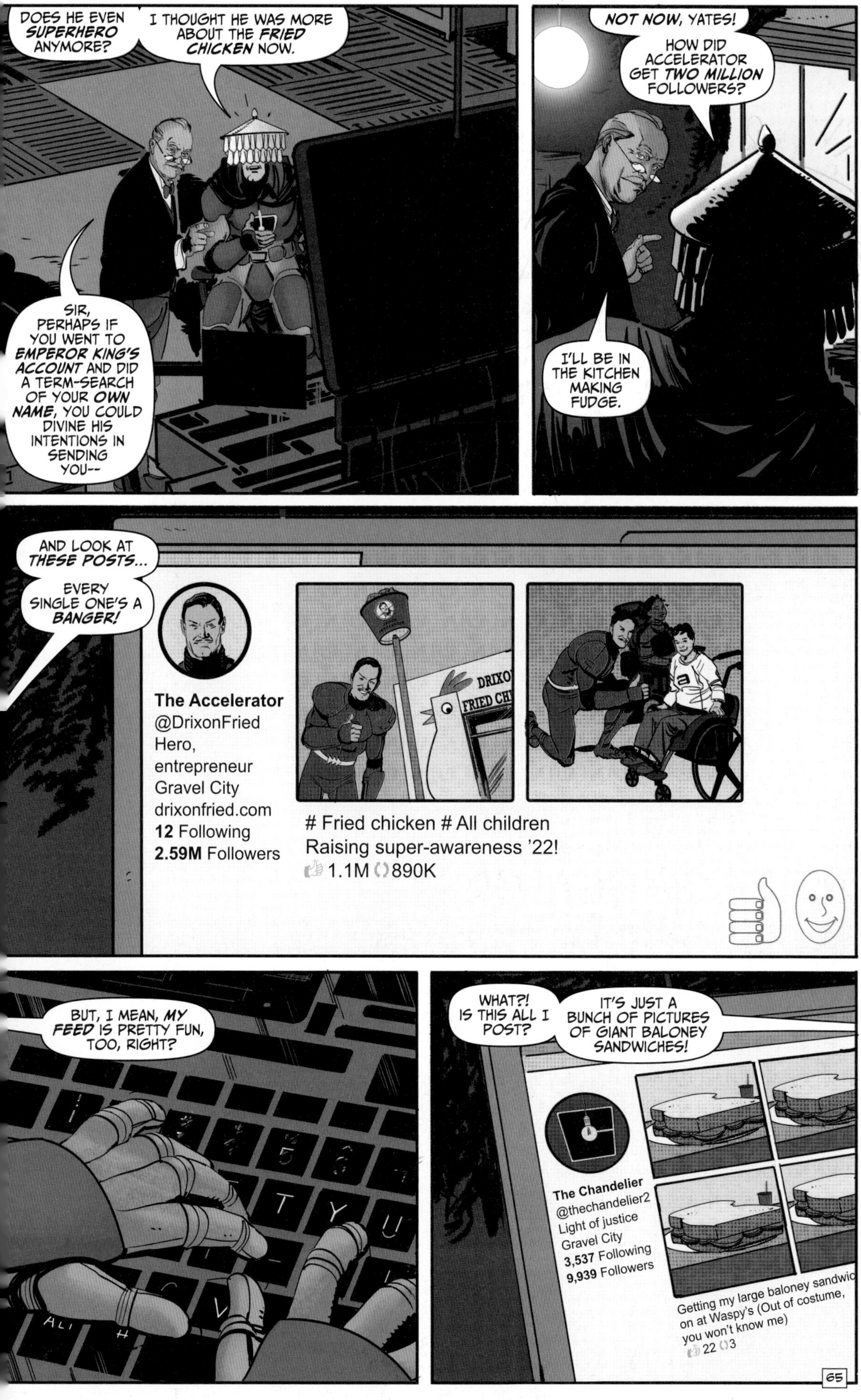
DOES HE EVEN SUPERHERO ANYMORE?
I THOUGHT HE WAS MORE ABOUT THE FRIED CHICKEN NOW.
SIR, PERHAPS IF YOU WENT TO EMPEROR KING'S ACCOUNT AND DID A TERM-SEARCH OF YOUR OWN NAME, YOU COULD DIVINE HIS INTENTIONS IN SENDING YOU--
NOT NOW, YATES!
HOW DID ACCELERATOR GET TWO MILLION FOLLOWERS?
I'LL BE IN THE KITCHEN MAKING FUDGE.
AND LOOK AT THESE POSTS...
EVERY SINGLE ONE'S A BANGER!
The Accelerator
@DrixonFried
Hero, entrepreneur
Gravel City
drixonfried.com
12 Following
2.59M Followers
DRIXON FRIED CHI
Fried chicken # All children
Raising super-awareness '22!
1.1M 890K
BUT, I MEAN, MY FEED IS PRETTY FUN, TOO, RIGHT?
WHAT?! IS THIS ALL I POST?
IT'S JUST A BUNCH OF PICTURES OF GIANT BALONEY SANDWICHES!
The Chandelier
@thechandelier2
Light of justice
Gravel City
3,537 Following
9,939 Followers
Getting my large baloney sandwic on at Waspy's (Out of costume, you won't know me)
22 3

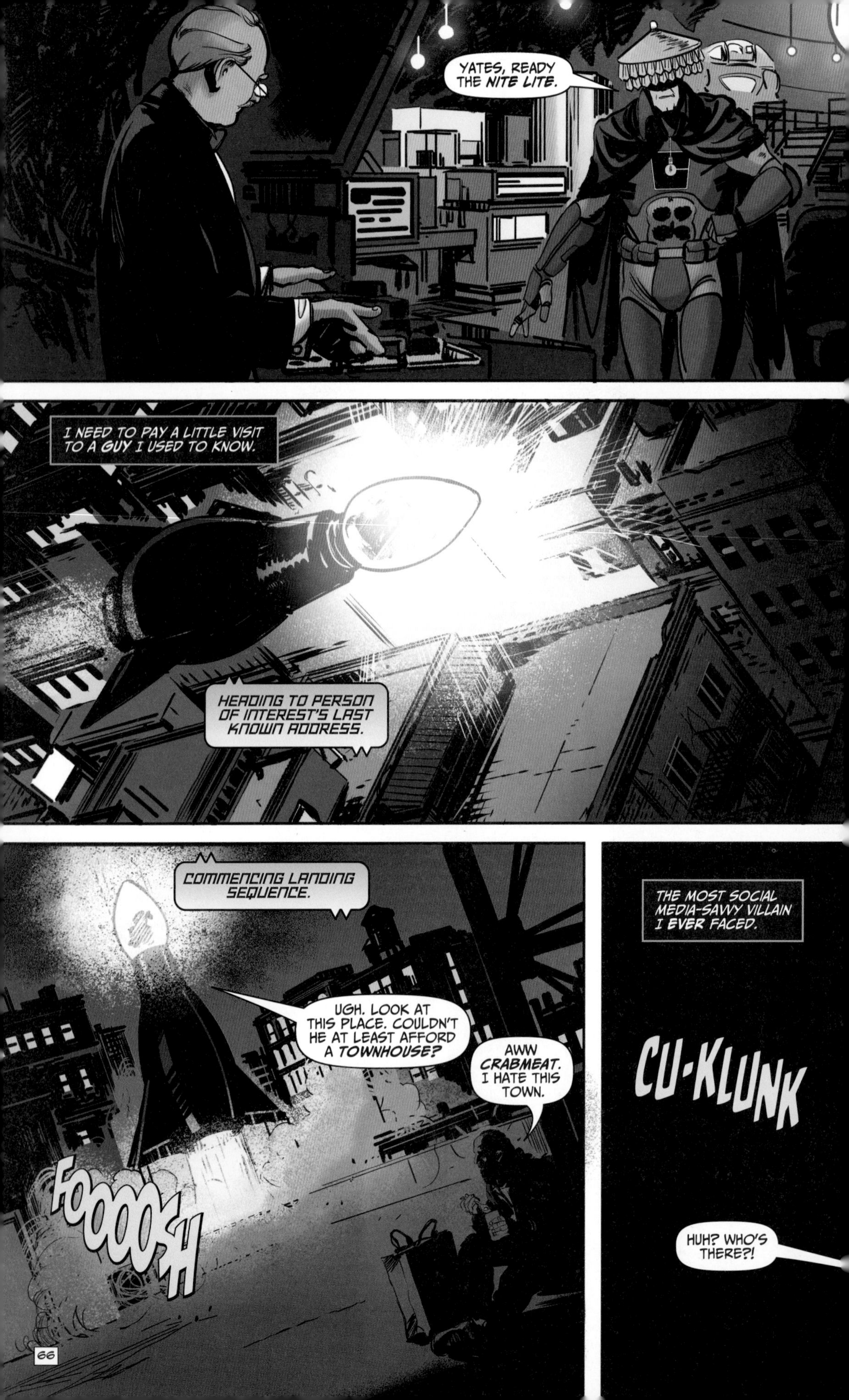
YATES, READY THE NITE LITE.
I NEED TO PAY A LITTLE VISIT TO A GUY I USED TO KNOW.
HEADING TO PERSON OF INTEREST'S LAST KNOWN ADDRESS.
COMMENCING LANDING SEQUENCE.
UGH. LOOK AT THIS PLACE. COULDN'T HE AT LEAST AFFORD A TOWNHOUSE?
AWW CRABMEAT. I HATE THIS TOWN.
FOOOOSH
THE MOST SOCIAL MEDIA-SAVVY VILLAIN I EVER FACED.
CU-KLUNK
HUH? WHO'S THERE?!

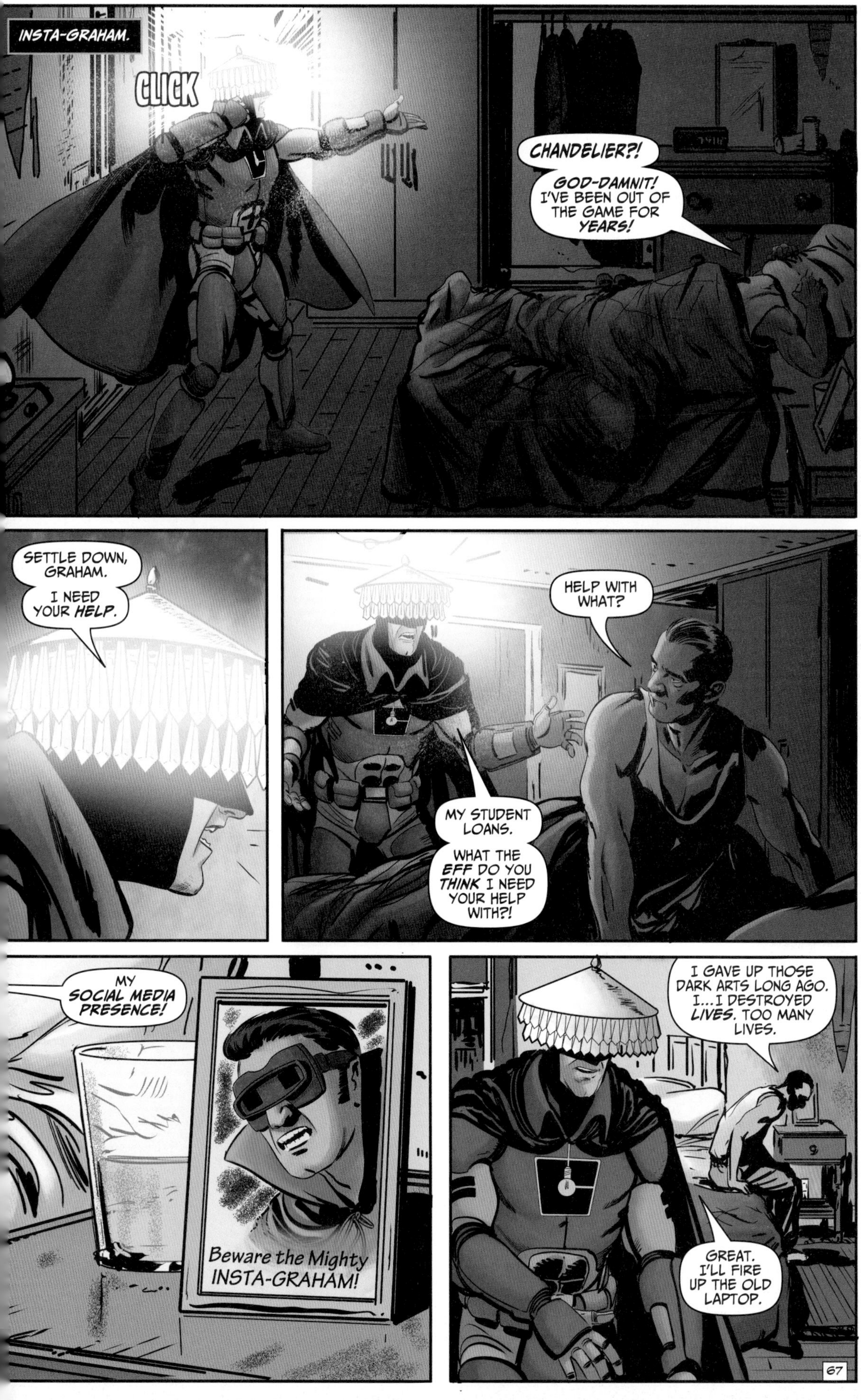
INSTA-GRAHAM.
CLICK
CHANDELIER?!
GOD-DAMNIT! I'VE BEEN OUT OF THE GAME FOR YEARS!
SETTLE DOWN, GRAHAM.
I NEED YOUR HELP.
HELP WITH WHAT?
MY STUDENT LOANS.
WHAT THE EFF DO YOU THINK I NEED YOUR HELP WITH?!
MY SOCIAL MEDIA PRESENCE!
Beware the Mighty INSTA-GRAHAM!
I GAVE UP THOSE DARK ARTS LONG AGO. I...I DESTROYED LIVES. TOO MANY LIVES.
GREAT. I'LL FIRE UP THE OLD LAPTOP.

I MEAN, HOW CAN THE ACCELERATOR *POSSIBLY* HAVE THAT MANY MORE FOLLOWERS THAN ME! HE'S ONLY BEEN ON THIS PLANET FOR FIVE YEARS!

EVEN *ACID CHIMP* HAS 20K FOLLOWERS.

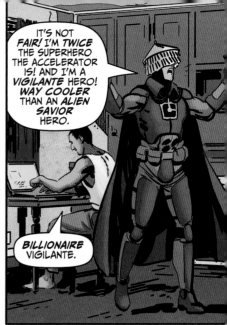

IT'S NOT *FAIR!* I'M *TWICE* THE SUPERHERO THE ACCELERATOR IS! AND I'M A *VIGILANTE* HERO! *WAY COOLER* THAN AN *ALIEN SAVIOR* HERO.

BILLIONAIRE VIGILANTE.

BILLIONAIRES ARE COOL.

HMM. I THINK I SEE THE *PROBLEM* WITH YOUR SOCIAL MEDIA PROFILE.

IT'S ALL ABOUT *YOU.*

YOU SEEM TO LABOR UNDER THE ILLUSION THAT YOU ARE *INHERENTLY FASCINATING.*

The Chandelier
@thechandelier2
Light of justice
Gravel City
3,537 Following
9,939 Followers

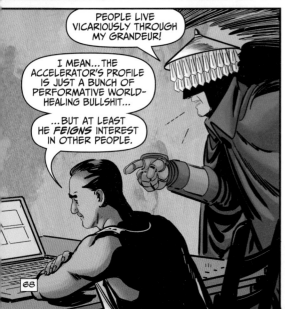

PEOPLE LIVE VICARIOUSLY THROUGH MY GRANDEUR!

I MEAN...THE ACCELERATOR'S PROFILE IS JUST A BUNCH OF PERFORMATIVE WORLD-HEALING BULLSHIT...

...BUT AT LEAST HE *FEIGNS* INTEREST IN OTHER PEOPLE.

IS THERE NO *FIXING* IT?

WHAT? THE FACT THAT YOU'RE A *SOCIOPATH?*

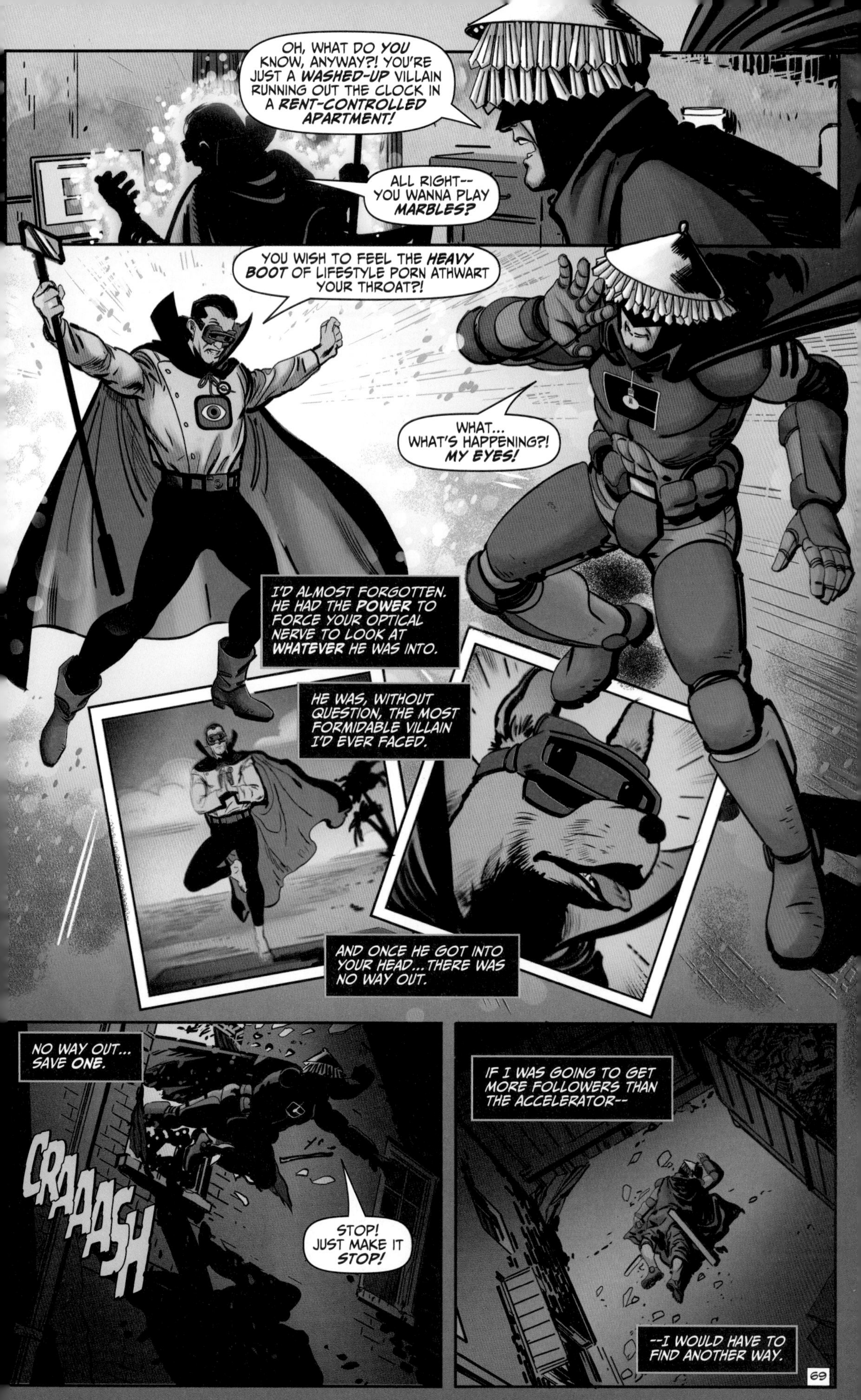
OH, WHAT DO YOU KNOW, ANYWAY?! YOU'RE JUST A WASHED-UP VILLAIN RUNNING OUT THE CLOCK IN A RENT-CONTROLLED APARTMENT!
ALL RIGHT-- YOU WANNA PLAY MARBLES?
YOU WISH TO FEEL THE HEAVY BOOT OF LIFESTYLE PORN ATHWART YOUR THROAT?!
WHAT... WHAT'S HAPPENING?! MY EYES!
I'D ALMOST FORGOTTEN. HE HAD THE POWER TO FORCE YOUR OPTICAL NERVE TO LOOK AT WHATEVER HE WAS INTO.
HE WAS, WITHOUT QUESTION, THE MOST FORMIDABLE VILLAIN I'D EVER FACED.
AND ONCE HE GOT INTO YOUR HEAD...THERE WAS NO WAY OUT.
NO WAY OUT... SAVE ONE.
CRAAASH
STOP! JUST MAKE IT STOP!
IF I WAS GOING TO GET MORE FOLLOWERS THAN THE ACCELERATOR--
--I WOULD HAVE TO FIND ANOTHER WAY.

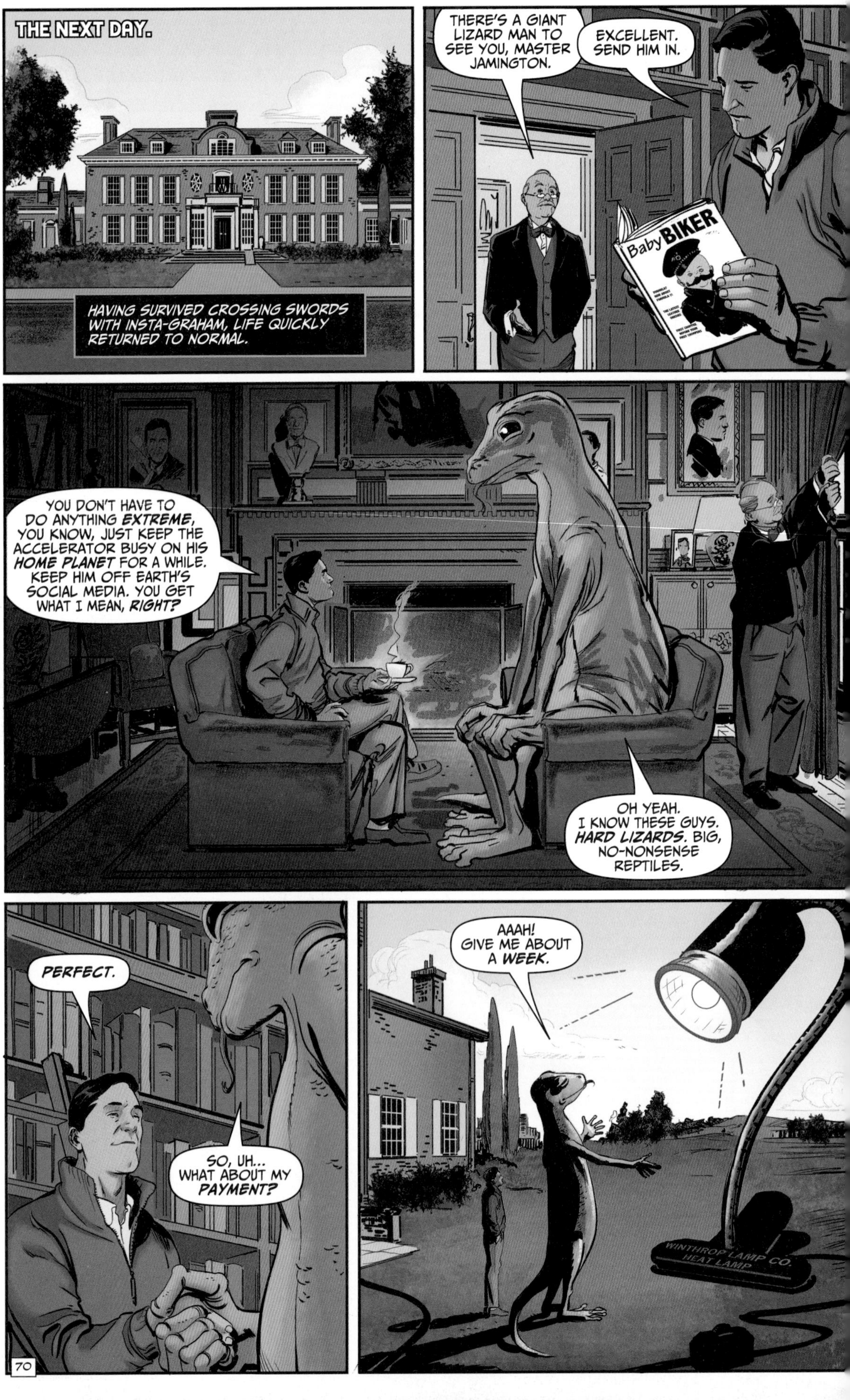
THE NEXT DAY.
HAVING SURVIVED CROSSING SWORDS WITH INSTA-GRAHAM, LIFE QUICKLY RETURNED TO NORMAL.
THERE'S A GIANT LIZARD MAN TO SEE YOU, MASTER JAMINGTON.
EXCELLENT. SEND HIM IN.
Baby BIKER
YOU DON'T HAVE TO DO ANYTHING *EXTREME*, YOU KNOW, JUST KEEP THE ACCELERATOR BUSY ON HIS *HOME PLANET* FOR A WHILE. KEEP HIM OFF EARTH'S SOCIAL MEDIA. YOU GET WHAT I MEAN, *RIGHT?*
OH YEAH. I KNOW THESE GUYS. *HARD LIZARDS*. BIG, NO-NONSENSE REPTILES.
PERFECT.
SO, UH... WHAT ABOUT MY *PAYMENT?*
AAAH! GIVE ME ABOUT A *WEEK*.
WINTHROP LAMP CO.
HEAT LAMP

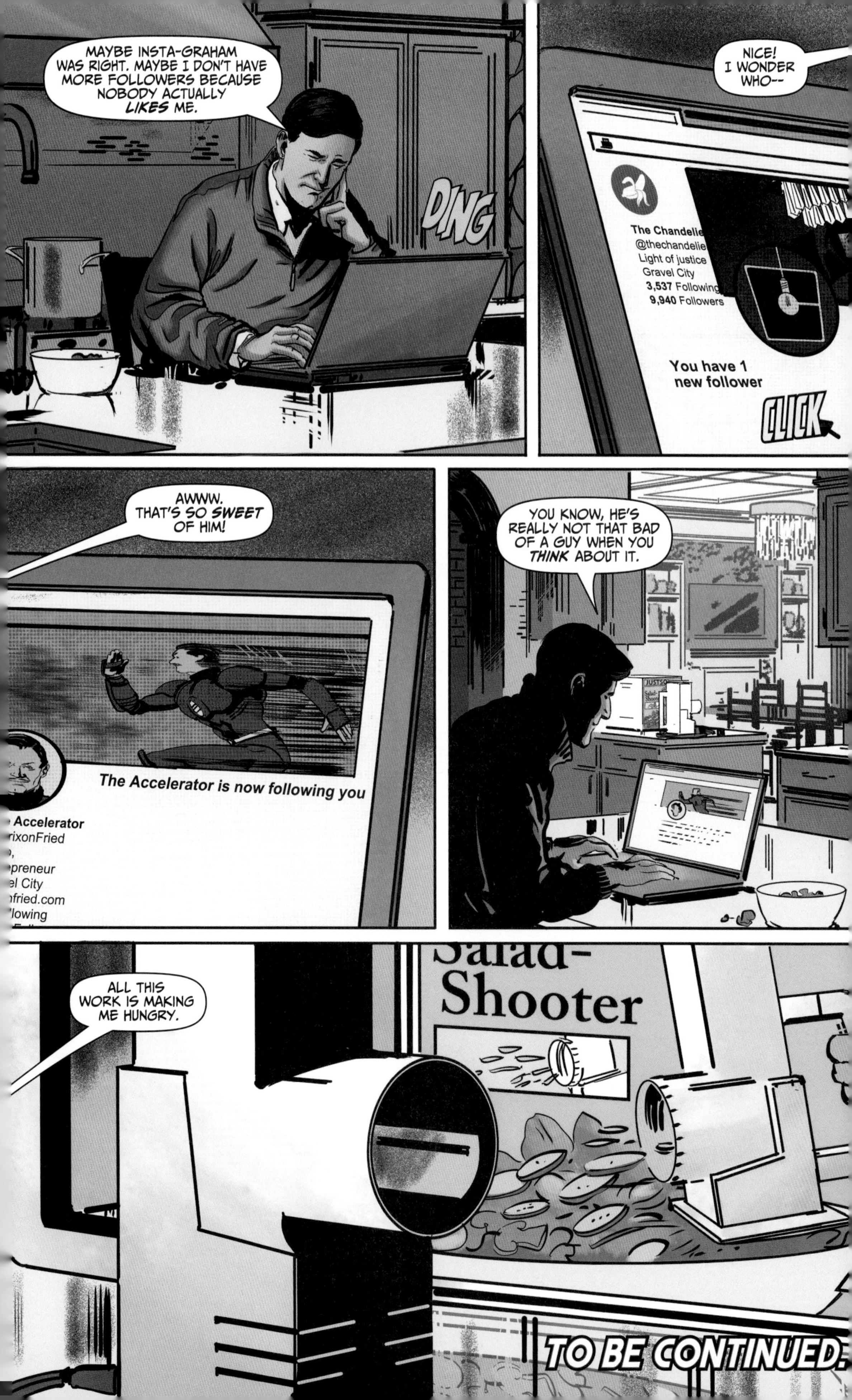
MAYBE INSTA-GRAHAM WAS RIGHT. MAYBE I DON'T HAVE MORE FOLLOWERS BECAUSE NOBODY ACTUALLY ***LIKES*** ME.
DING
NICE! I WONDER WHO--
The Chandelie
@thechandelie
Light of justice
Gravel City
3,537 Following
9,940 Followers
You have 1 new follower
CLICK
AWWW. THAT'S SO ***SWEET*** OF HIM!
The Accelerator is now following you
Accelerator
rixonFried
preneur
el City
nfried.com
lowing
YOU KNOW, HE'S REALLY NOT THAT BAD OF A GUY WHEN YOU ***THINK*** ABOUT IT.
ALL THIS WORK IS MAKING ME HUNGRY.
Shooter
TO BE CONTINUED.

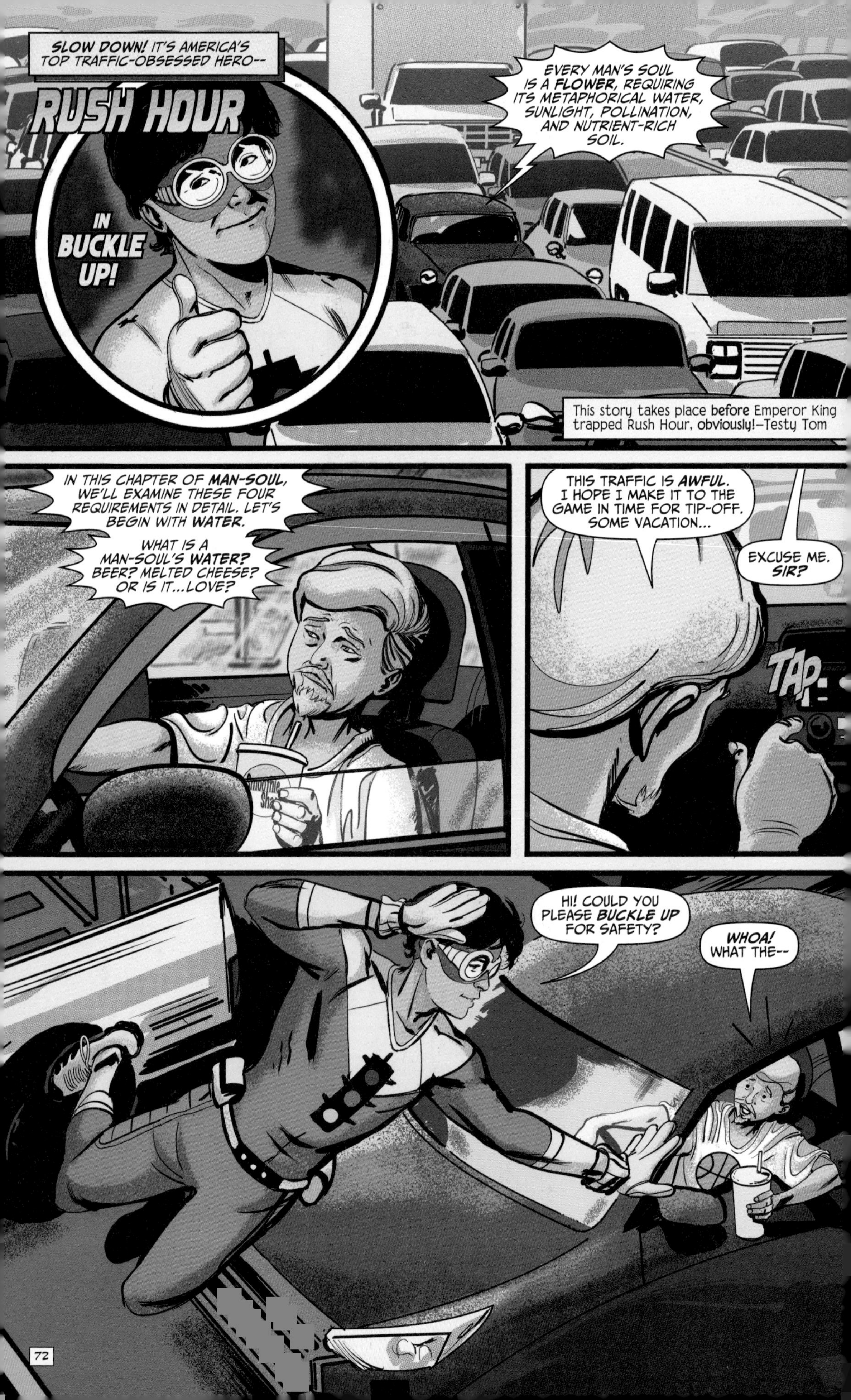
SLOW DOWN! IT'S AMERICA'S TOP TRAFFIC-OBSESSED HERO--
RUSH HOUR
IN BUCKLE UP!
EVERY MAN'S SOUL IS A FLOWER, REQUIRING ITS METAPHORICAL WATER, SUNLIGHT, POLLINATION, AND NUTRIENT-RICH SOIL.
This story takes place before Emperor King trapped Rush Hour, obviously!—Testy Tom
IN THIS CHAPTER OF MAN-SOUL, WE'LL EXAMINE THESE FOUR REQUIREMENTS IN DETAIL. LET'S BEGIN WITH WATER.
WHAT IS A MAN-SOUL'S WATER? BEER? MELTED CHEESE? OR IS IT...LOVE?
THIS TRAFFIC IS AWFUL. I HOPE I MAKE IT TO THE GAME IN TIME FOR TIP-OFF. SOME VACATION...
EXCUSE ME. SIR?
TAP
HI! COULD YOU PLEASE BUCKLE UP FOR SAFETY?
WHOA! WHAT THE--

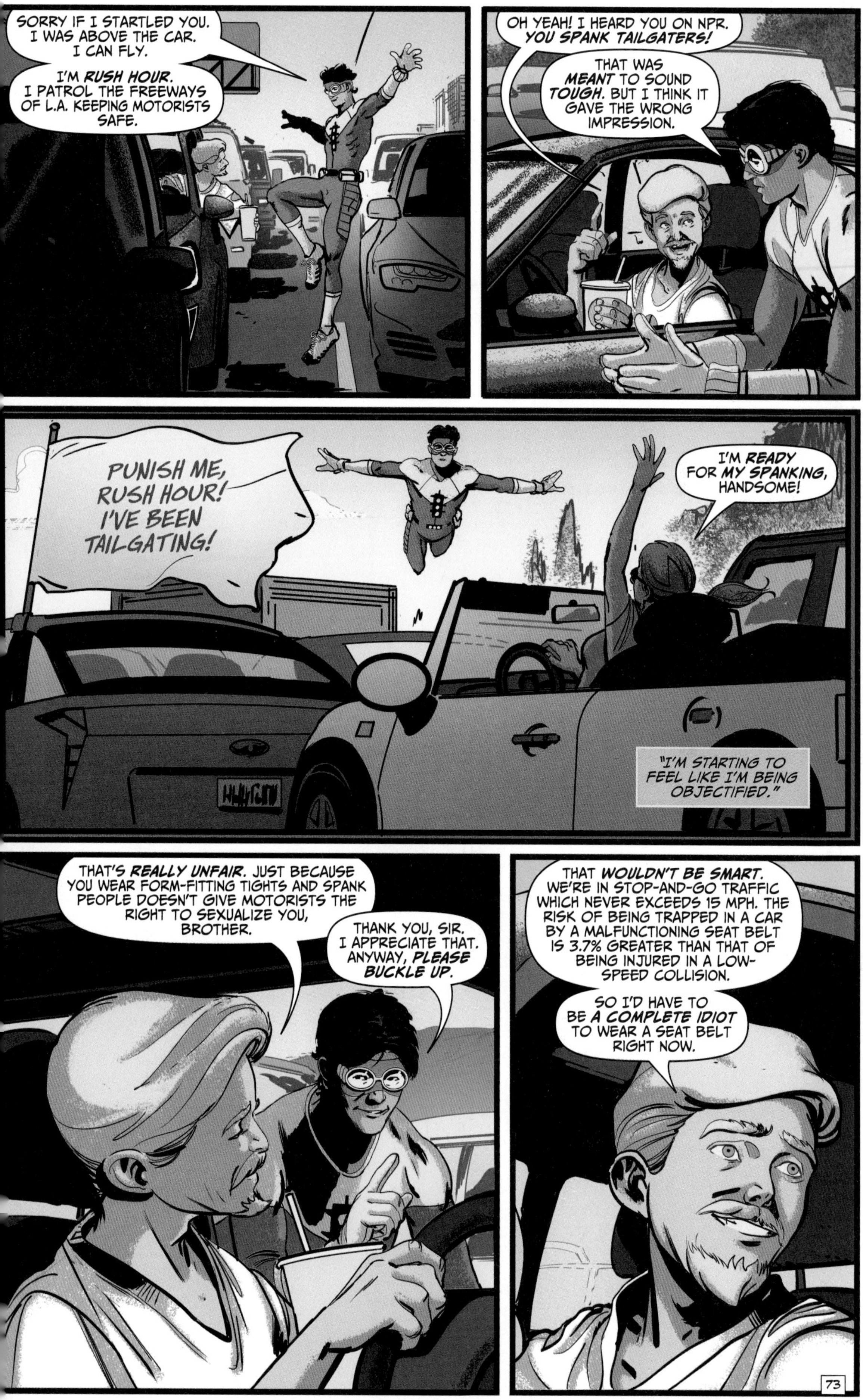
SORRY IF I STARTLED YOU. I WAS ABOVE THE CAR. I CAN FLY.
I'M **RUSH HOUR**. I PATROL THE FREEWAYS OF L.A. KEEPING MOTORISTS SAFE.
OH YEAH! I HEARD YOU ON NPR. ***YOU SPANK TAILGATERS!***
THAT WAS ***MEANT*** TO SOUND ***TOUGH***. BUT I THINK IT GAVE THE WRONG IMPRESSION.
PUNISH ME, RUSH HOUR! I'VE BEEN TAILGATING!
I'M ***READY*** FOR ***MY SPANKING***, HANDSOME!
"I'M STARTING TO FEEL LIKE I'M BEING OBJECTIFIED."
THAT'S ***REALLY UNFAIR***. JUST BECAUSE YOU WEAR FORM-FITTING TIGHTS AND SPANK PEOPLE DOESN'T GIVE MOTORISTS THE RIGHT TO SEXUALIZE YOU, BROTHER.
THANK YOU, SIR. I APPRECIATE THAT. ANYWAY, ***PLEASE BUCKLE UP***.
THAT ***WOULDN'T BE SMART***. WE'RE IN STOP-AND-GO TRAFFIC WHICH NEVER EXCEEDS 15 MPH. THE RISK OF BEING TRAPPED IN A CAR BY A MALFUNCTIONING SEAT BELT IS 3.7% GREATER THAN THAT OF BEING INJURED IN A LOW-SPEED COLLISION.
SO I'D HAVE TO BE ***A COMPLETE IDIOT*** TO WEAR A SEAT BELT RIGHT NOW.

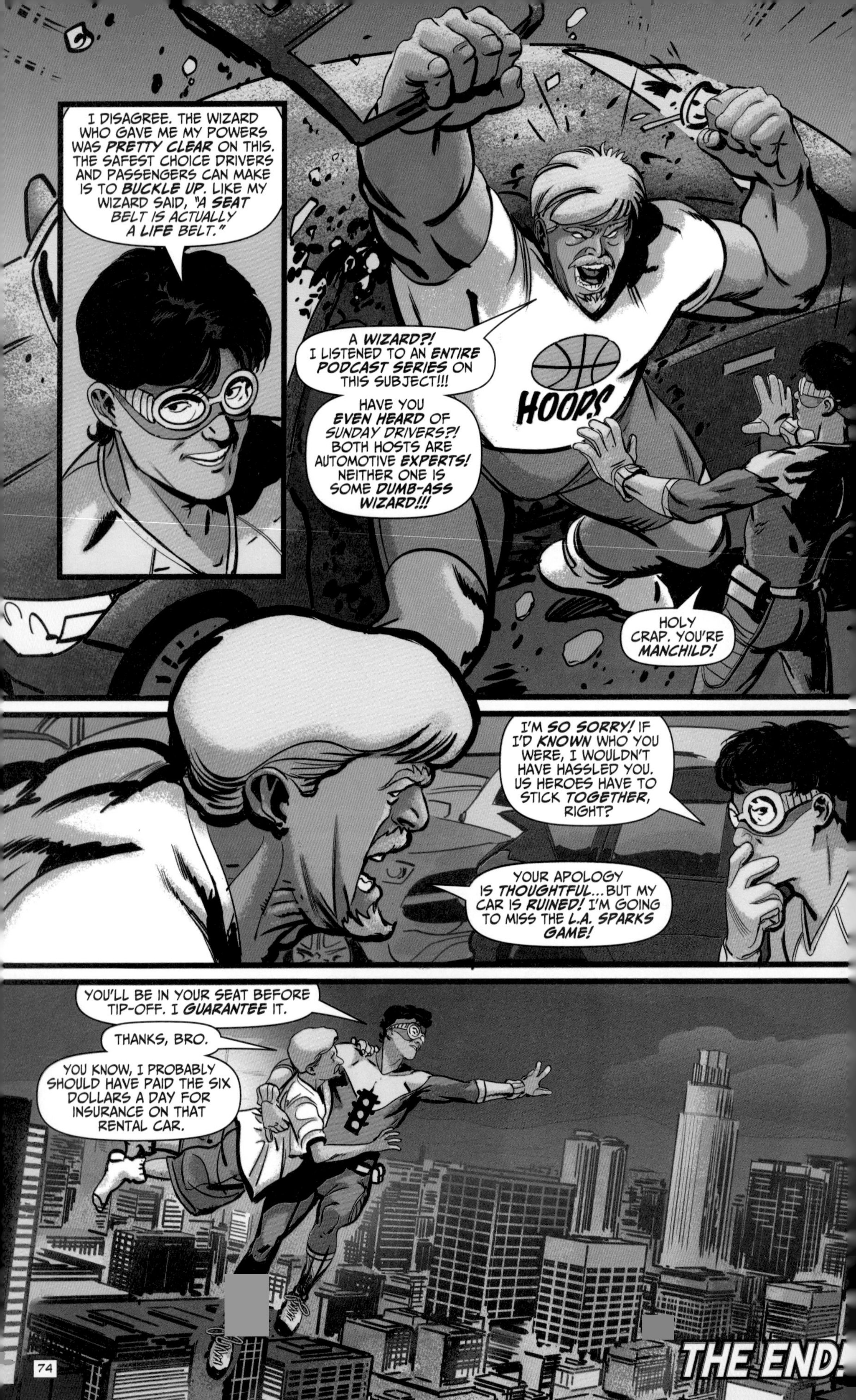
I DISAGREE. THE WIZARD WHO GAVE ME MY POWERS WAS PRETTY CLEAR ON THIS. THE SAFEST CHOICE DRIVERS AND PASSENGERS CAN MAKE IS TO BUCKLE UP. LIKE MY WIZARD SAID, "A SEAT BELT IS ACTUALLY A LIFE BELT."
A WIZARD?! I LISTENED TO AN ENTIRE PODCAST SERIES ON THIS SUBJECT!!!
HAVE YOU EVEN HEARD OF SUNDAY DRIVERS?! BOTH HOSTS ARE AUTOMOTIVE EXPERTS! NEITHER ONE IS SOME DUMB-ASS WIZARD!!!
HOOPS
HOLY CRAP. YOU'RE MANCHILD!
I'M SO SORRY! IF I'D KNOWN WHO YOU WERE, I WOULDN'T HAVE HASSLED YOU. US HEROES HAVE TO STICK TOGETHER, RIGHT?
YOUR APOLOGY IS THOUGHTFUL... BUT MY CAR IS RUINED! I'M GOING TO MISS THE L.A. SPARKS GAME!
YOU'LL BE IN YOUR SEAT BEFORE TIP-OFF. I GUARANTEE IT.
THANKS, BRO.
YOU KNOW, I PROBABLY SHOULD HAVE PAID THE SIX DOLLARS A DAY FOR INSURANCE ON THAT RENTAL CAR.
THE END!

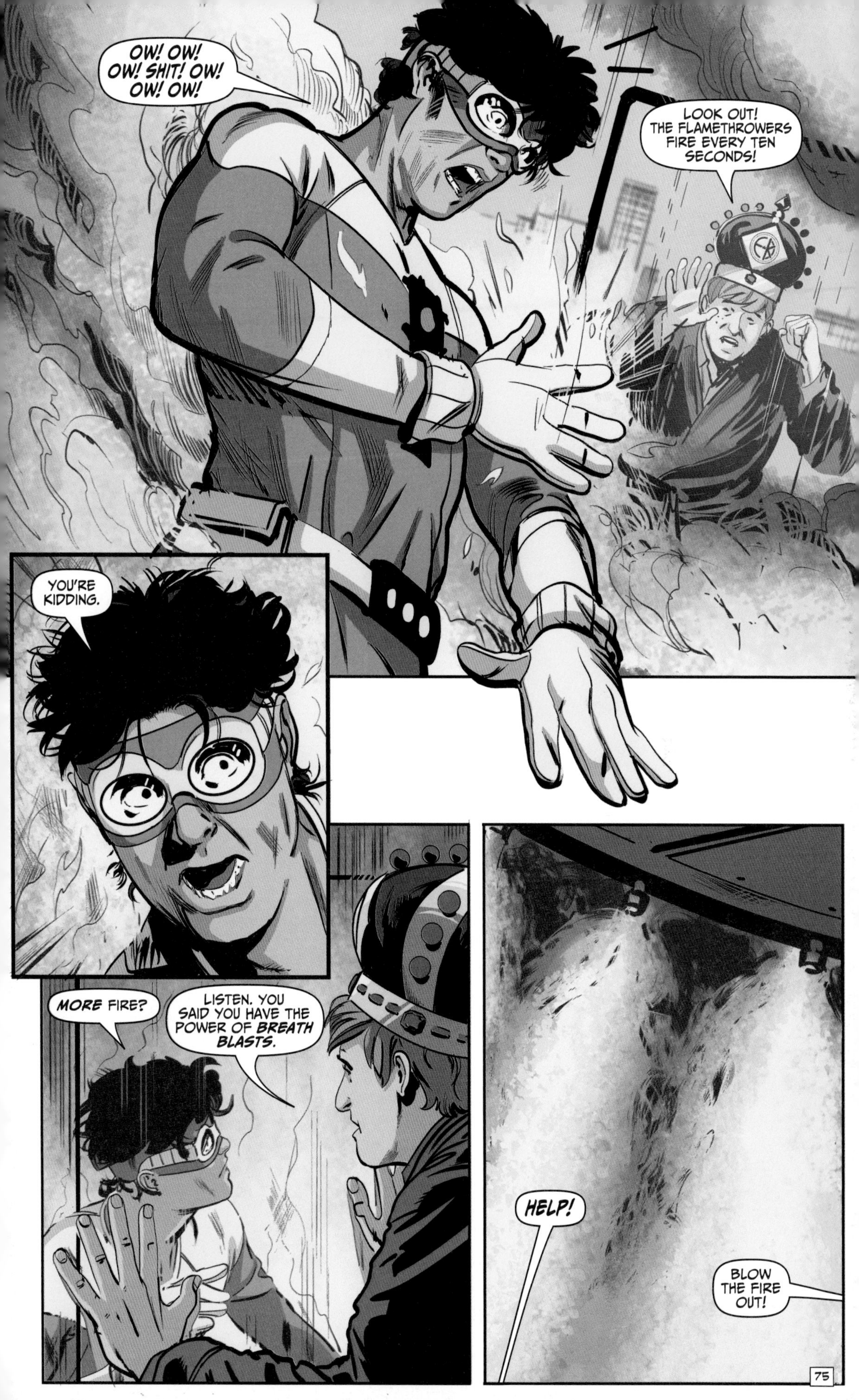
OW! OW! OW! SHIT! OW! OW! OW!
LOOK OUT! THE FLAMETHROWERS FIRE EVERY TEN SECONDS!
YOU'RE KIDDING.
MORE FIRE?
LISTEN. YOU SAID YOU HAVE THE POWER OF BREATH BLASTS.
HELP!
BLOW THE FIRE OUT!

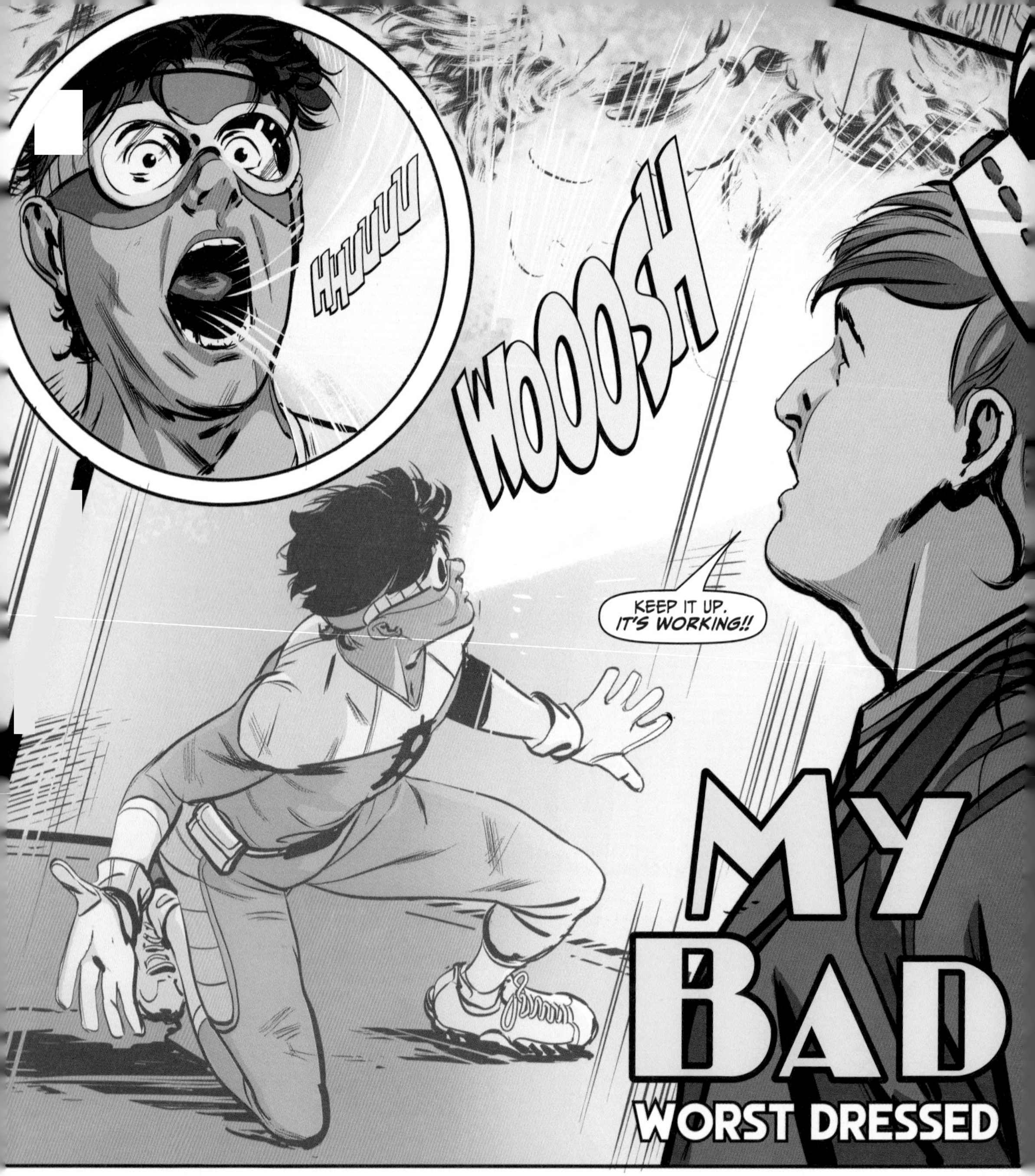
HHUUUU
WOOOSH
KEEP IT UP. IT'S WORKING!!
MY BAD
WORST DRESSED

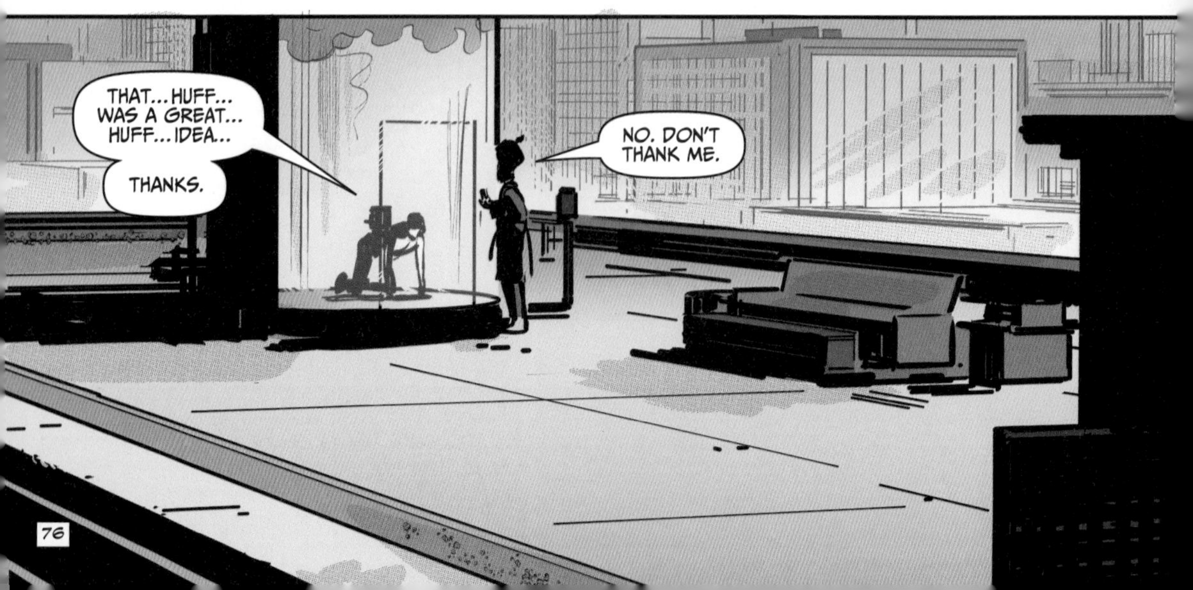
THAT...HUFF... WAS A GREAT... HUFF...IDEA...
THANKS.
NO. DON'T THANK ME.

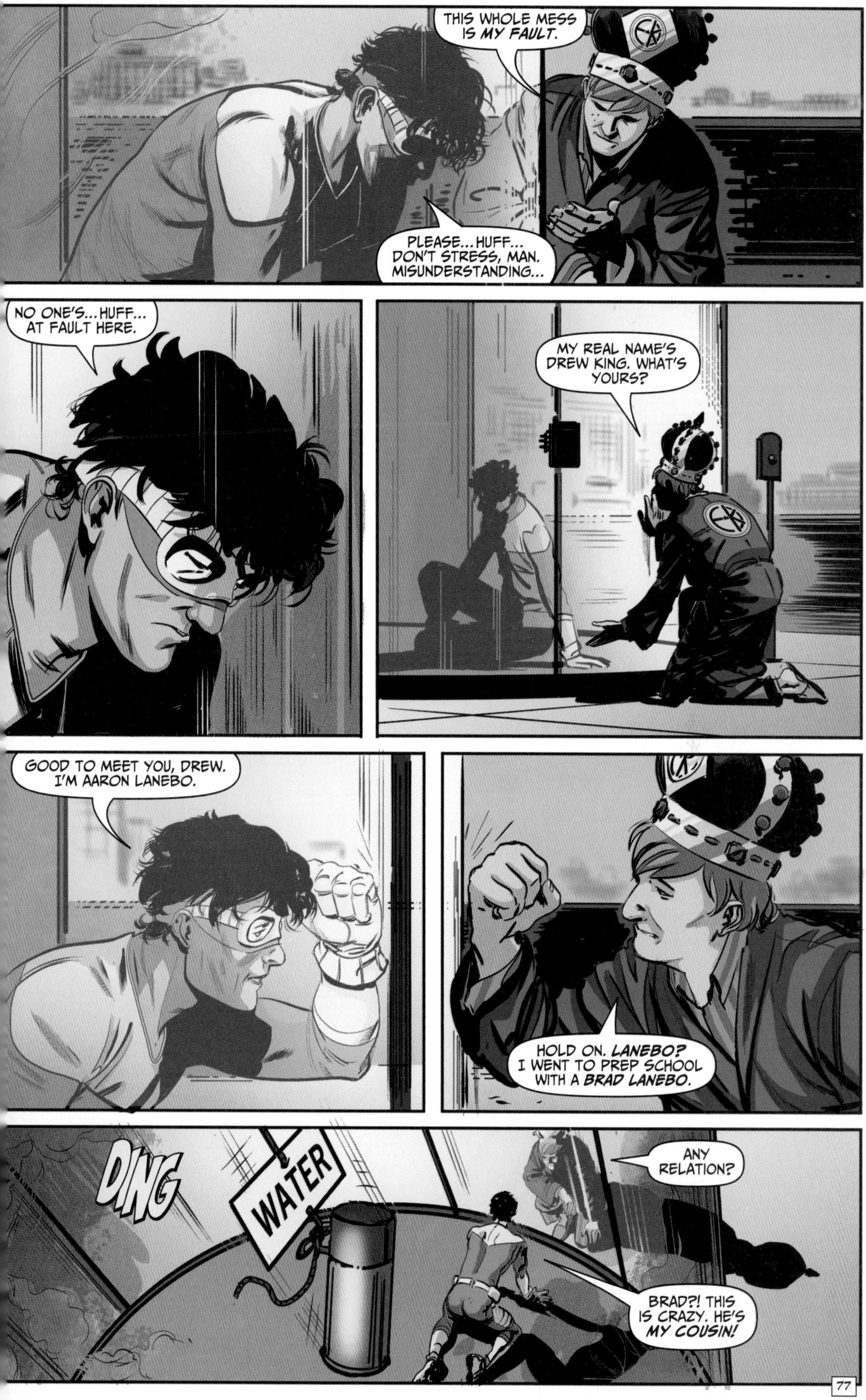
THIS WHOLE MESS IS MY FAULT.
PLEASE...HUFF... DON'T STRESS, MAN. MISUNDERSTANDING...
NO ONE'S...HUFF... AT FAULT HERE.
MY REAL NAME'S DREW KING. WHAT'S YOURS?
GOOD TO MEET YOU, DREW. I'M AARON LANEBO.
HOLD ON. LANEBO? I WENT TO PREP SCHOOL WITH A BRAD LANEBO.
DING
WATER
ANY RELATION?
BRAD?! THIS IS CRAZY. HE'S MY COUSIN!

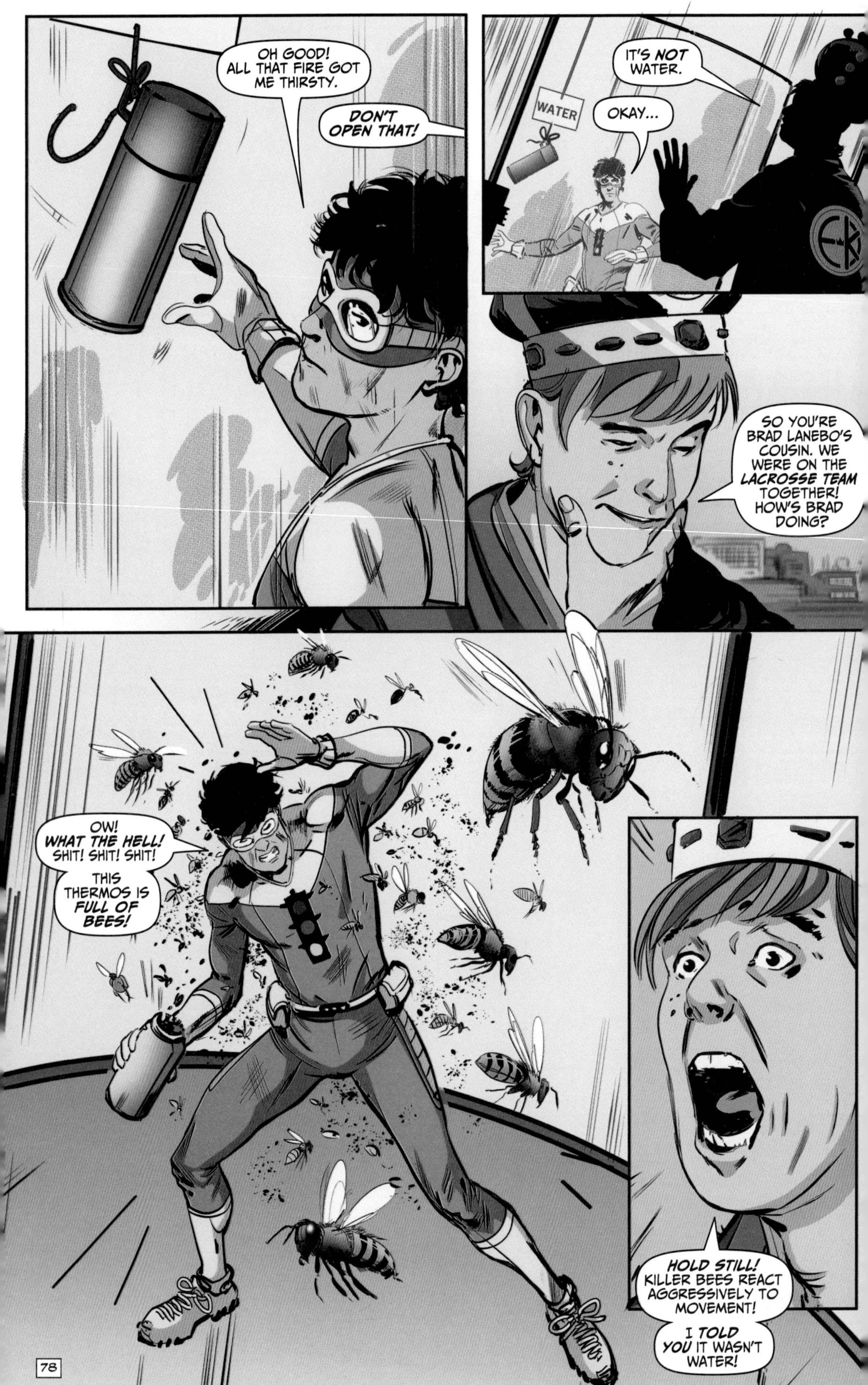
OH GOOD! ALL THAT FIRE GOT ME THIRSTY.
DON'T OPEN THAT!
IT'S *NOT* WATER.
WATER
OKAY...
SO YOU'RE BRAD LANEBO'S COUSIN. WE WERE ON THE *LACROSSE TEAM* TOGETHER! HOW'S BRAD DOING?
OW! *WHAT THE HELL!* SHIT! SHIT! SHIT!
THIS THERMOS IS *FULL OF BEES!*
HOLD STILL! KILLER BEES REACT AGGRESSIVELY TO MOVEMENT!
I *TOLD YOU* IT WASN'T WATER!

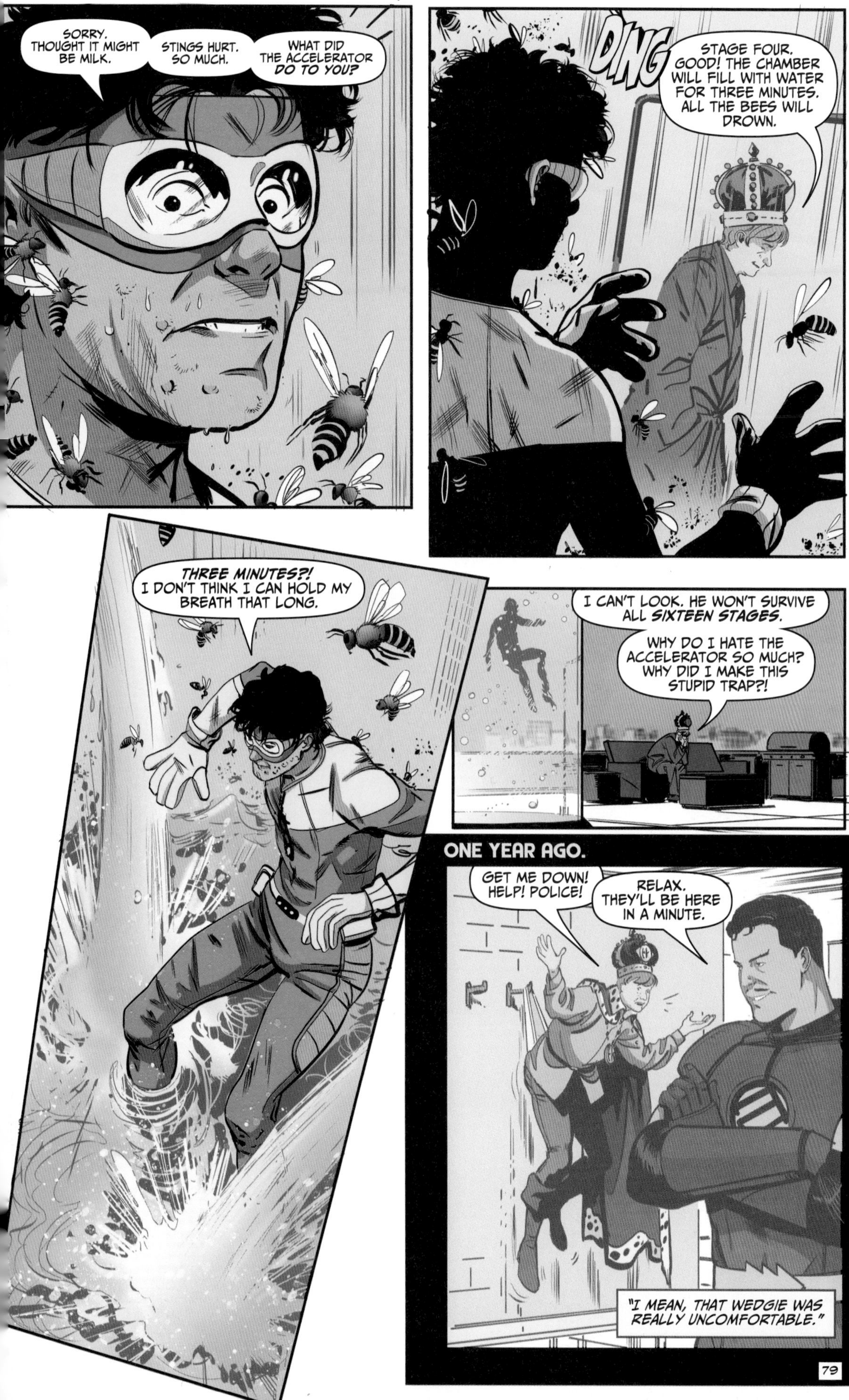
SORRY. THOUGHT IT MIGHT BE MILK.
STINGS HURT. SO MUCH.
WHAT DID THE ACCELERATOR *DO TO YOU?*
DING
STAGE FOUR. GOOD! THE CHAMBER WILL FILL WITH WATER FOR THREE MINUTES. ALL THE BEES WILL DROWN.
THREE MINUTES?! I DON'T THINK I CAN HOLD MY BREATH THAT LONG.
I CAN'T LOOK. HE WON'T SURVIVE ALL **SIXTEEN STAGES.**
WHY DO I HATE THE ACCELERATOR SO MUCH? WHY DID I MAKE THIS STUPID TRAP?!
ONE YEAR AGO.
GET ME DOWN! HELP! POLICE!
RELAX. THEY'LL BE HERE IN A MINUTE.
"I MEAN, THAT WEDGIE WAS REALLY UNCOMFORTABLE."

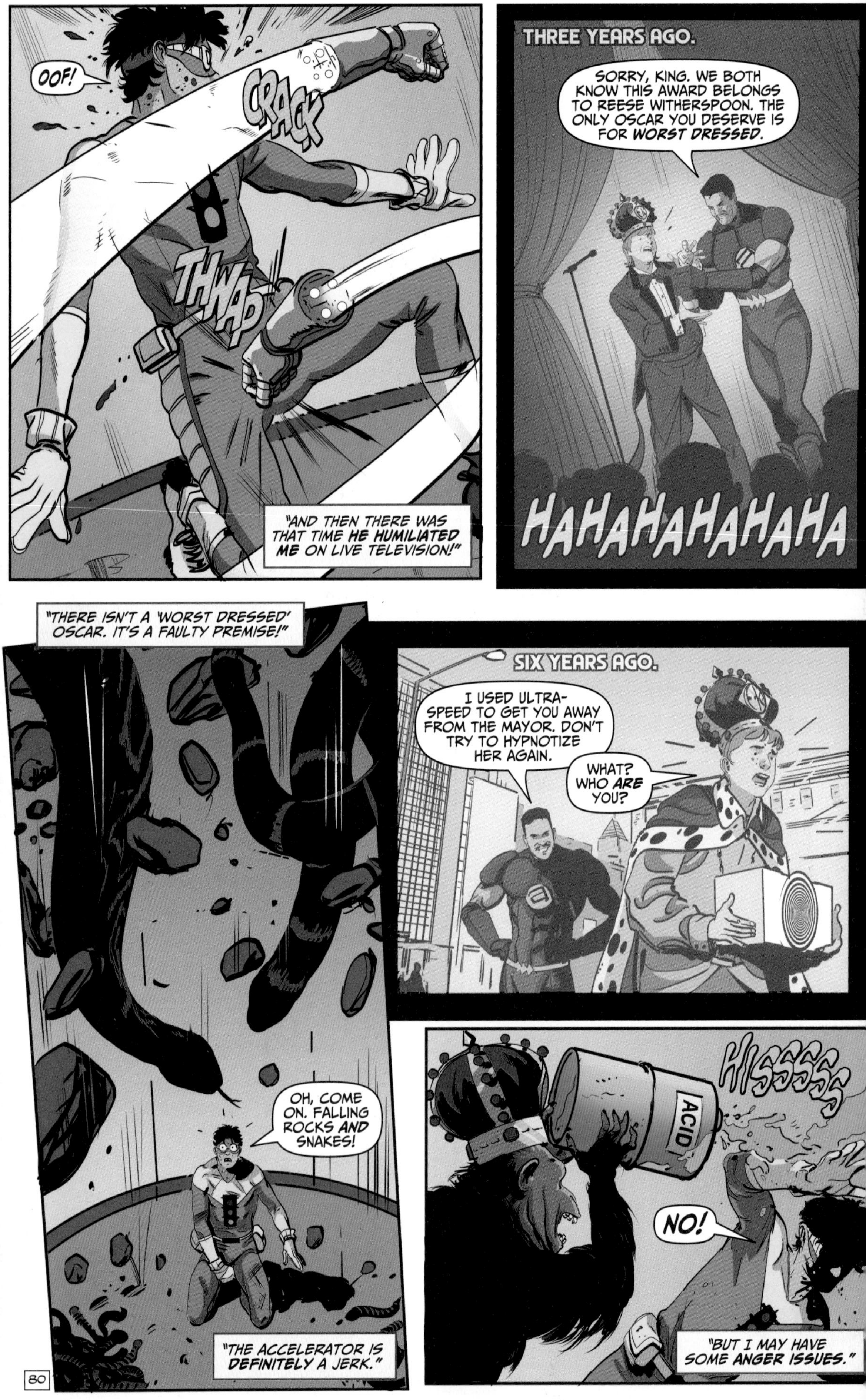
OOF!
CRACK
THWAP
"AND THEN THERE WAS THAT TIME HE HUMILIATED ME ON LIVE TELEVISION!"
THREE YEARS AGO.
SORRY, KING. WE BOTH KNOW THIS AWARD BELONGS TO REESE WITHERSPOON. THE ONLY OSCAR YOU DESERVE IS FOR WORST DRESSED.
HAHAHAHAHAHA
"THERE ISN'T A 'WORST DRESSED' OSCAR. IT'S A FAULTY PREMISE!"
OH, COME ON. FALLING ROCKS AND SNAKES!
"THE ACCELERATOR IS DEFINITELY A JERK."
SIX YEARS AGO.
I USED ULTRA-SPEED TO GET YOU AWAY FROM THE MAYOR. DON'T TRY TO HYPNOTIZE HER AGAIN.
WHAT? WHO ARE YOU?
ACID
HISSSSS
NO!
"BUT I MAY HAVE SOME ANGER ISSUES."

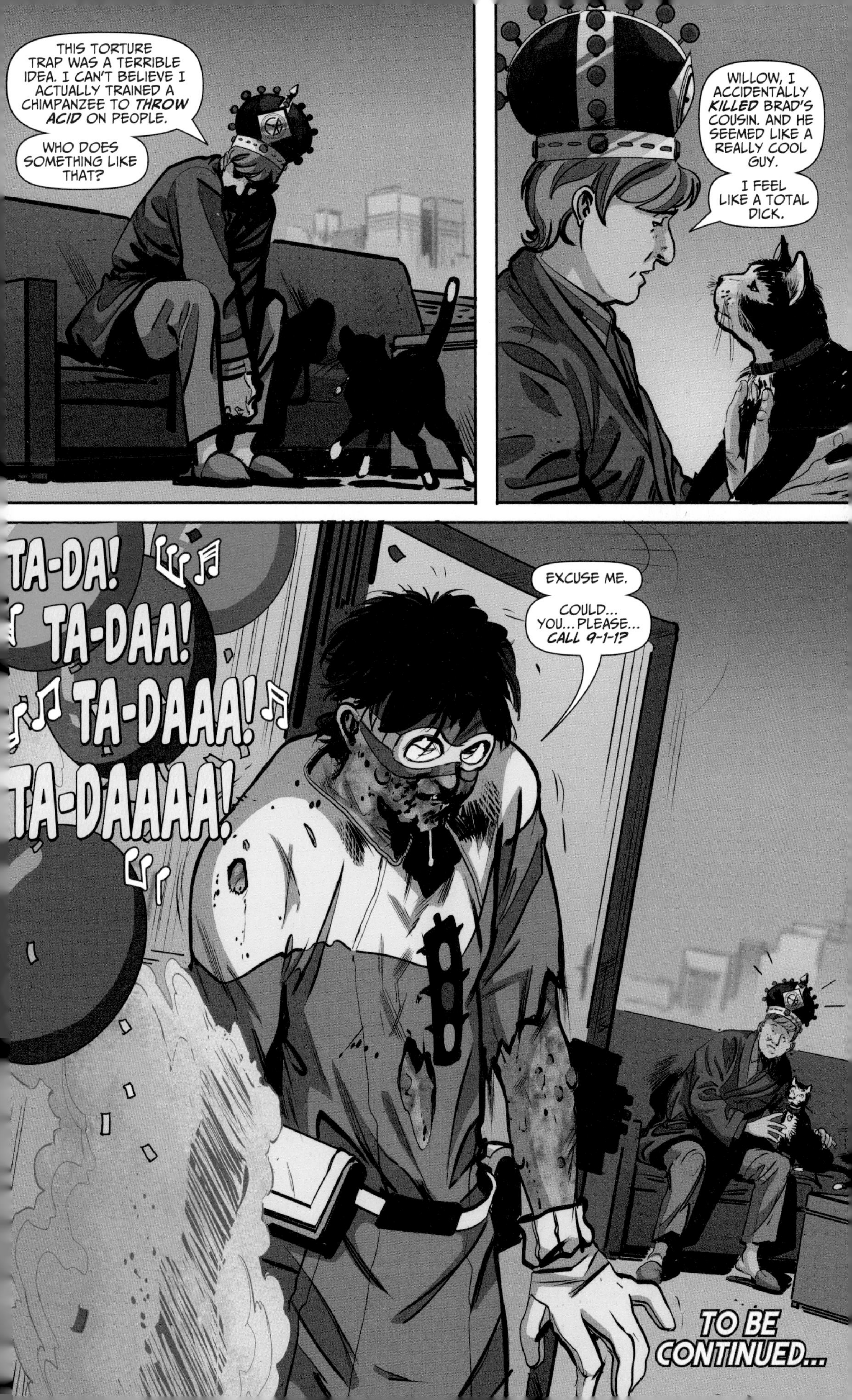
THIS TORTURE TRAP WAS A TERRIBLE IDEA. I CAN'T BELIEVE I ACTUALLY TRAINED A CHIMPANZEE TO *THROW ACID* ON PEOPLE.
WHO DOES SOMETHING LIKE THAT?
WILLOW, I ACCIDENTALLY *KILLED* BRAD'S COUSIN. AND HE SEEMED LIKE A REALLY COOL GUY.
I FEEL LIKE A TOTAL DICK.
TA-DA!
TA-DAA!
TA-DAAA!
TA-DAAAA!
EXCUSE ME.
COULD... YOU...PLEASE... *CALL 9-1-1?*
TO BE CONTINUED...

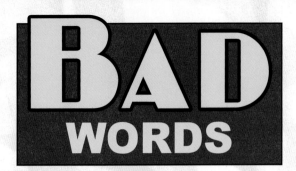

BAD WORDS

Welcome to BAD WORDS. I'm one of MY BAD's co-creators, Bouncing Baby Bryce Ingman. Mark and Peter are extremely busy men with thriving careers, so I'll be answering your emails and letters once again this month. That's totally cool. And they don't even need to thank me. You see, we're a team. And teammates don't need to thank other teammates for answering all of their stupid emails and letters. Even if that teammate is only getting paid a pitiful sixty bucks apiece for his really good letter answers. No thanks are necessary.

You readers are another matter altogether though. You all better start acknowledging the grueling labor that's required to ensure BAD WORDS is insightful, heartwarming, and informative each and every month. I'm pouring my heart and soul into this letter column, you ungrateful jerks! And my knee hurts, too.

Let's see what you have to bother me with this time.

Mark and Bryce,

Every time I spin around in circles and read MY BAD I get nauseous and throw up. Your comic book seems really entertaining but I can never make it past page three. Help!

Sheree
Happy Valley, OR

It's pretty obvious what the problem is here, Sheree. You're starting over on page one every time you spin and read! Begin spin-reading MY BAD with page four next time. From now on, each time you have to stop and vomit, put the comic book down on the couch and leave it open to the current page. When your stomach recovers it'll be right there waiting for another spin and read. I guarantee you'll get to the end of an issue of MY BAD after seven or eight vomits.

***

Peter, Bryce, and Mark,

I'm interested in paying you with cryptocurrency to purchase MY BAD's intellectual property rights so I may produce a major motion picture based on your comic book superheroes.

Harvey Weinstein
Wende Correctional Facility

P.S. I'm not the famous, abusive movie producer and convicted sex offender Harvey Weinstein. That guy sounds like a real asshole. I'm a completely different Harvey Weinstein and you can totally trust me.

Well, Harvey, I should probably talk to Mark and Peter first, but you seem like a trustworthy person, and I've been hearing a lot about these newfangled crypto-coins, so let's do it! Hollywood, here we come! (Quick question, do I need a special wallet or will the crypto-coins fit in my old leather one?)

***

Humans,

I am an alien. I live in outer space.

I am slightly taller than most other aliens.

Alien
Outer Space

Hey, it's last month's "Letter of the Month" winner, Alien! Great to hear from you again, dude. And, although it's hard to believe, this letter is even better than last month's missive! We've never done this before but, Alien, you're the "Letter of the Month" winner here at BAD WORDS for the second straight issue in a row! Remarkable. Stay gold, Alien.

***

Gentlemen,

My all-time favorite superhero is Manchild. He's been my favorite since even before he debuted in MY BAD #1, so I think my opinion counts for something here. I was really excited when I saw him on MY BAD #2's cover, but when I read the issue Manchild was nowhere to be found!

I've been buying comic books for almost fifty years and this is the first time I've encountered a blatant bait-and-switch like this. What a rip-off! I demand answers.

Anderson
Dewitt, NY

There's a funny story behind Manchild's mysterious issue #2 cover appearance, Anderson. And if you buy the MY BAD limited, signed, hardcover, gold-stamped slipcase collection when it's released in 2023, I think you'll enjoy reading that funny story in my foreword. It's a doozy!

***

Bryce and Mark,

Writers are magical people. I appreciate that.

Maxwell
Richmond, VA

Wow. That actually brought tears to my eyes, Maxwell. Your kindness makes me feel ashamed of some of the harsh things I said about readers earlier in this column. You've inspired me. I'll try to be better in the future. And if I struggle in my attempts to be better, I'll think of Maxwell from Richmond and try to be more like you.

Hey, it looks like you sent a follow-up email, Maxwell! What a nice way to end this month's column.

***

Bryce and Mark,

I will have your ears. I will put them in my bag of ears. I will have all the ears of all the writers and I will put them in my bag of ears. And when all the writers' ears are in my bag of ears I will sing the song and light the fire and the world will begin anew.

I will have your ears.

Maxwell
Richmond, VA

I'm going to have to rethink this whole "be like Maxwell" thing.

TOM'S TOOLBOX!

Fall in line, AHOYniks! Trustworthy Tom here! As promised in last month's truth-tellin' Toolbox, I'm back to answer the big, burning question that has set reader against reader, fan against fan! Namely, what the heck is The AHOY Philosophy? What values, virtues, and—unavoidably—vices are you unleashing upon the waiting world when you hand over your hard-earned fifteen quarters, two dimes, and four pennies for one of our museum-bound masterpieces? Are we all about love? Liberty? Licentious license? Well, here at last are the awesome answers! So sit up straight, clear your mind of critical thought, and start memorizing . . .

. . . THE AHOY PHILOSOPHY!

RESOLVED! Despite its reputation as disposable, mind-rotting junk, the red-hot medium unfortunately called "comics" should be revered and respected! You know what would help? A more contemporary-sounding name! We at AHOY call them *Rockin' Pop Litforms*, and you should, too! We'll also accept "Dramazines"! But "comics" is a slur!

RESOLVED! From the days of the cave dwellers, stories and pictures have been the most important things that ever existed! The *only* important things, most reasonable people would say! The world owes those of us who make Rockin' Pop Litforms nothing less than *all the attention and a really nice living!*

RESOLVED! To achieve a just society, it is necessary to publish Dramazines that occasionally make reference to "relevance" and "sticking it to The Man"! These should also feature editorials that politely plead for "brotherhood"!

RESOLVED! Real AHOYniks buy our collected editions even when they already have all the issues! Because that's what best friends do!

RESOLVED! The other comic book companies are really mean to AHOY, and that's unfair! Giving a dollar to them is like throwing a knife at us! Why would you ever do that? Why would you?

RESOLVED! We're here for *you*, AHOYnik! Never, ever, ever make us regret that! Do you understand?

Oh! And **RESOLVED!** America must preserve and extend its position of global leadership by maintaining the preeminence of U.S. military forces, pussycat!

Well, there you have it, AHOY Polloi: Our philosophy—and yours—in a nice, neat nutshell! We can't wait to hear how much you love it, so get lickin' those pasty, perforated postage stamps!

Occupare omnes terras,

Tom

COMING AHOY-TRACTIONS

EDGAR ALLAN POE'S SNIFTER OF DEATH #4 Special Sinister Slogan Issue! *MASK UP & VAX UP* for "A Tale of the Great Plague"! *VOTE GRUE NO MATTER WHO* in "Edgar Allan Poe's Werewolf of Washington"! All this plus a heaping treasure of AHOY illustrated prose! Join yours truly, a.k.a. Bouncing Baby Bryce—along with Rick Geary, Ryan Kelly, and Richard Williams—***January 19!***

BLACK'S MYTH—Collecting the series that introduced Janie Jones "Strummer" Mercado—an ordinary werewolf PI trying to make it on the mean streets of LA! It's by writer Eric Palicki, artist Wendell Cavalcanti, and cover artist Liana Kangas! In stores ***February 16!***

NEXT: An unexpected superpower! An unforgettable sandwich! AND: Acid Chimp! ***February 16!***

—Bryce

Write to MY BAD—or any AHOY Rockin' Pop Litform—at letters@comicsahoy.com. Snail mail: PO Box 189, DeWitt, NY 13214. Mark "OK to print" if it is.

AND! Subscribe to the free, funny-as-anything AHOY Newsletter at bit.ly/newsahoy.

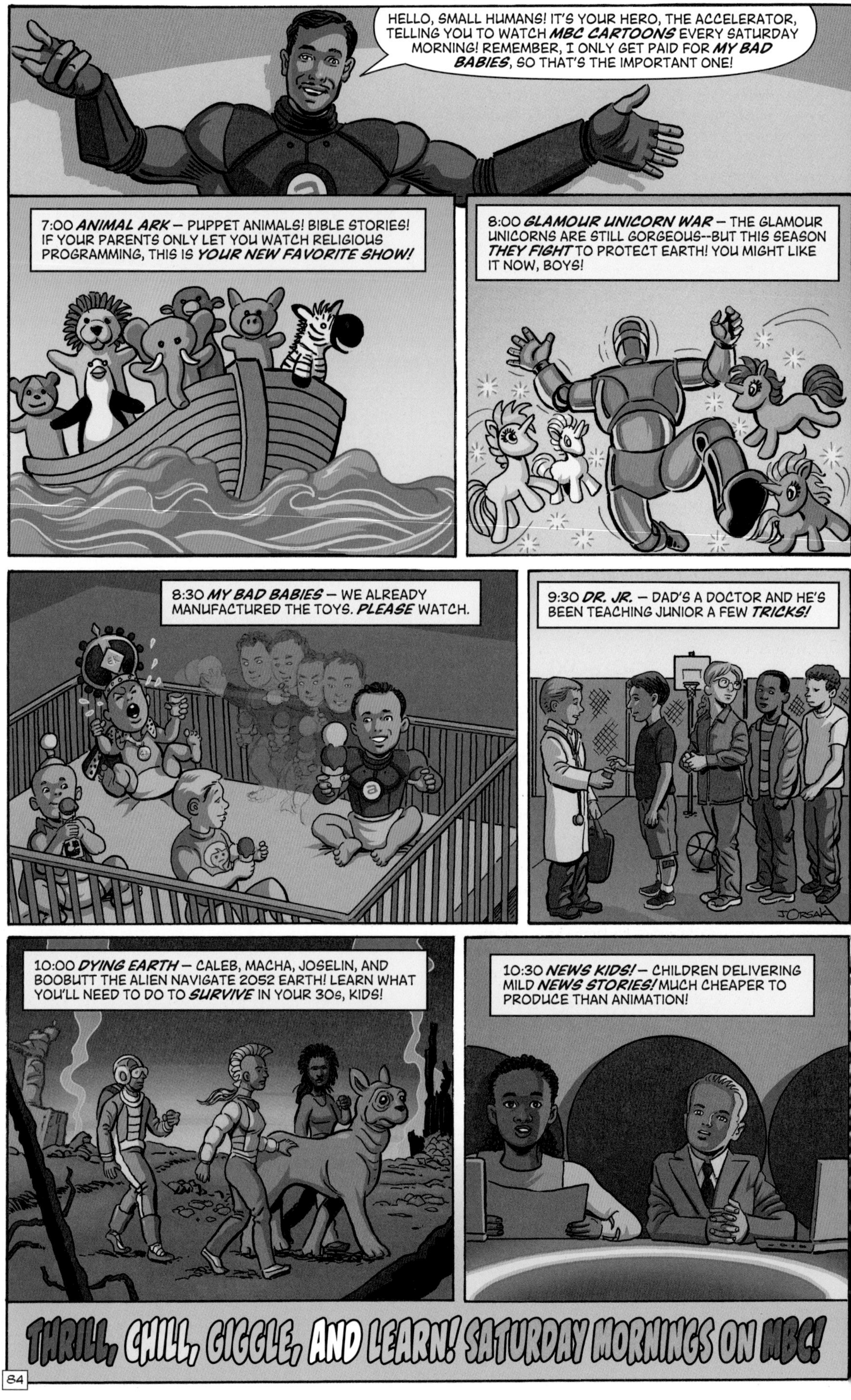
HELLO, SMALL HUMANS! IT'S YOUR HERO, THE ACCELERATOR, TELLING YOU TO WATCH *MBC CARTOONS* EVERY SATURDAY MORNING! REMEMBER, I ONLY GET PAID FOR *MY BAD BABIES*, SO THAT'S THE IMPORTANT ONE!
7:00 *ANIMAL ARK* — PUPPET ANIMALS! BIBLE STORIES! IF YOUR PARENTS ONLY LET YOU WATCH RELIGIOUS PROGRAMMING, THIS IS *YOUR NEW FAVORITE SHOW!*
8:00 *GLAMOUR UNICORN WAR* — THE GLAMOUR UNICORNS ARE STILL GORGEOUS--BUT THIS SEASON *THEY FIGHT* TO PROTECT EARTH! YOU MIGHT LIKE IT NOW, BOYS!
8:30 *MY BAD BABIES* — WE ALREADY MANUFACTURED THE TOYS. *PLEASE* WATCH.
9:30 *DR. JR.* — DAD'S A DOCTOR AND HE'S BEEN TEACHING JUNIOR A FEW *TRICKS!*
JORSAK
10:00 *DYING EARTH* — CALEB, MACHA, JOSELIN, AND BOOBUTT THE ALIEN NAVIGATE 2052 EARTH! LEARN WHAT YOU'LL NEED TO DO TO *SURVIVE* IN YOUR 30s, KIDS!
10:30 *NEWS KIDS!* — CHILDREN DELIVERING MILD *NEWS STORIES!* MUCH CHEAPER TO PRODUCE THAN ANIMATION!
THRILL, CHILL, GIGGLE, AND LEARN! SATURDAY MORNINGS ON MBC!

The Winthrop Family

This article is about the family. For information on Winthrop Lamps, see Winthrop Lamp Company. Also, fashion lamps.

The Winthrop (/win-thröp/) family is an American lamp-making dynasty that owns one of the nation's largest fortunes. Starting as a small mining lantern concern in the 1850s, the family grew to national prominence during the Civil War upon securing a contract to provide the Union Army with head lamps to be used in a daring initiative to introduce night-fighting. Though the initiative was scrapped once it became apparent that the lamps simply made those who wore them easier targets, the fortunes of the family were established.

The Winthrop Family and servants, 1890s. Seated, right to left: patriarch Sebastian Winthrop; his wife, Henrietta. Upon leopard rug: their young son, Augustus.

Contents [hide]

Family Background

The Winthrop Lamp Company was founded in 1852 by two brothers, Moses and J. Sebastian Winthrop, who made a meager living as traveling lantern repairmen/Shakespearean actors, often repairing the head-lanterns of coal miners in the morning while performing monologues from Othello and Julius Caesar for the same miners at night. The partnership suffered a setback when, in 1857, Moses Winthrop joined the millennial cult The Sacred Ascenders. The Sacred Ascenders believed that angels would carry the faithful up to Heaven at midnight on the 4th of July, 1858, but only if they could find them. To make himself easy to find, Moses decided to await the rapture atop a tall barn, though confused about whether the prediction meant he would be raptured in the very early morning of July 4th, or late that night as midnight approached. Moses thought it best to be atop the barn for both possibilities and, after being awake for thirty-six hours, fell asleep, rolled off the roof, and died.

Inheriting his brother's half of the company allowed J. Sebastian Winthrop to set his sights on greater ambitions. At an impromptu meeting with General Joseph Hooker in a hotel lobby, J. Sebastian convinced the general over several whiskeys that lamps and night-fighting represented the future of warfare. When appointed to the command of the Army of the Potomac in January 1863, General Hooker placed an order for forty thousand "fighting lamps" from the Winthrop Lamp Company, providing J. Sebastian with the seed for what would become his lamp-based empire.

Soon after the war, J. Sebastian married Henrietta Spofford, a handsome socialite, and the pair settled down in Gravel City, due to the regular supply of cheap labor the nearby quarry brought into the town. It was in Gravel City that they built their lamp factory, Winthrop Lampworks, and established their family estate. In 1884, J. Sebastian Winthrop died, leaving the Lampworks and control of the family fortune to his ten-year-old son and sole heir, Augustus Winthrop.

Legacy

The construction of the Winthrop Lampworks in 1872 doubled the size of Gravel City as workers and aspiring lamp designers arrived from all over the nation. As electricity became more common in homes and businesses, the lamp industry exploded and, by 1912, the Lampworks had replaced the quarry as Gravel City's largest employer.

It was soon after that hundreds of residents began coming down with what doctors then identified as "Filament poisoning." Thousands of angry townspeople descended on the Lampworks, determined to tar and feather Augustus Winthrop. After being repelled by National Guardsmen and Pinkerton agents, the townspeople laid siege to the factory. The siege was lifted only after Augustus promised to build the St. Olaf's Hospital for Victims of Lamp-Related Poisoning. Most of the cost of its construction was paid for by donations from the townspeople.

Popularity of Winthrop Lamps

By 1925, Winthrop Lamps were the best-selling lighting accessories in the world.

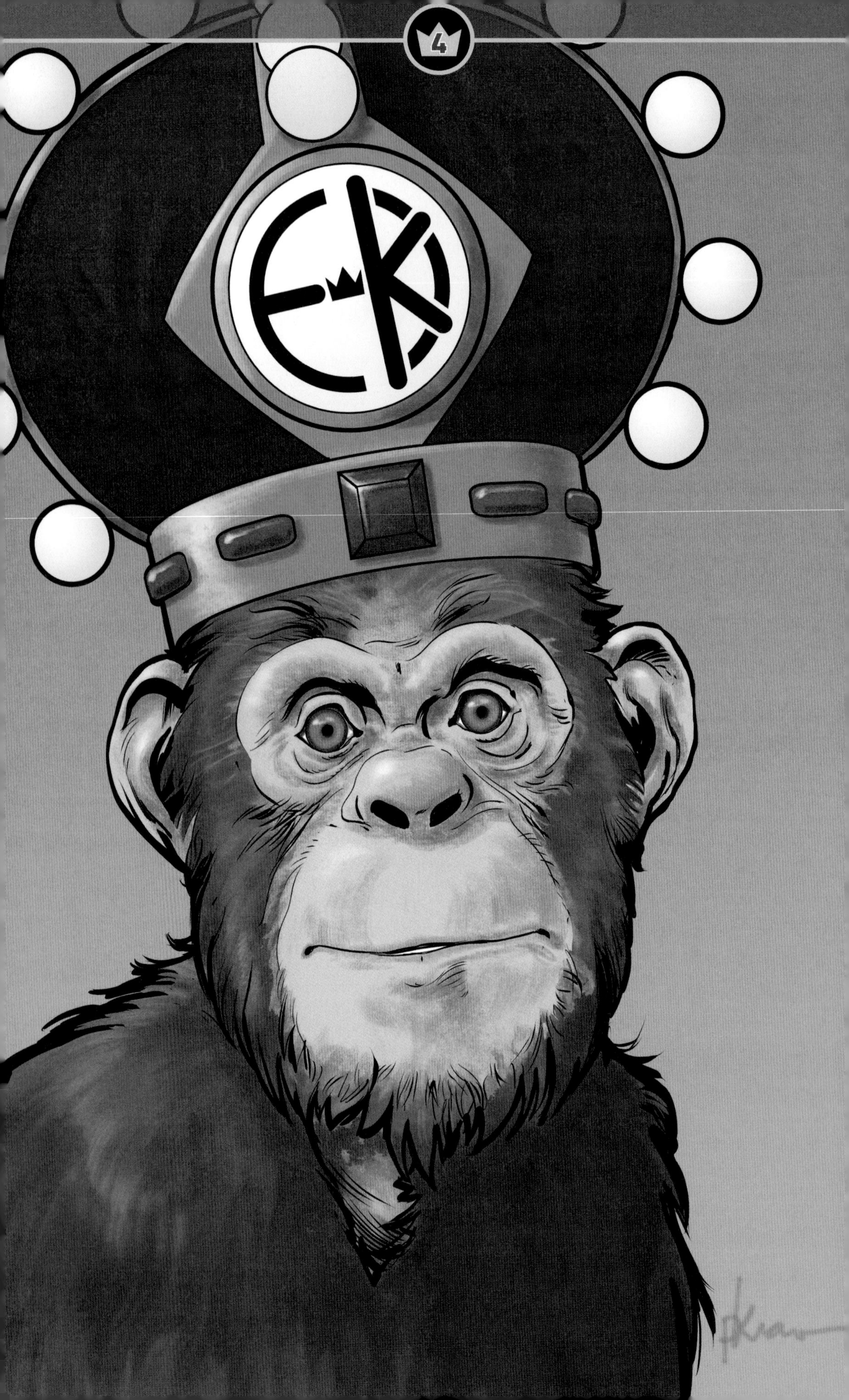

"THE POWER OF LOVE
IS A CURIOUS THING
MAKE ONE MAN WEEP,
MAKE ANOTHER MAN SING"

-SOCRATES

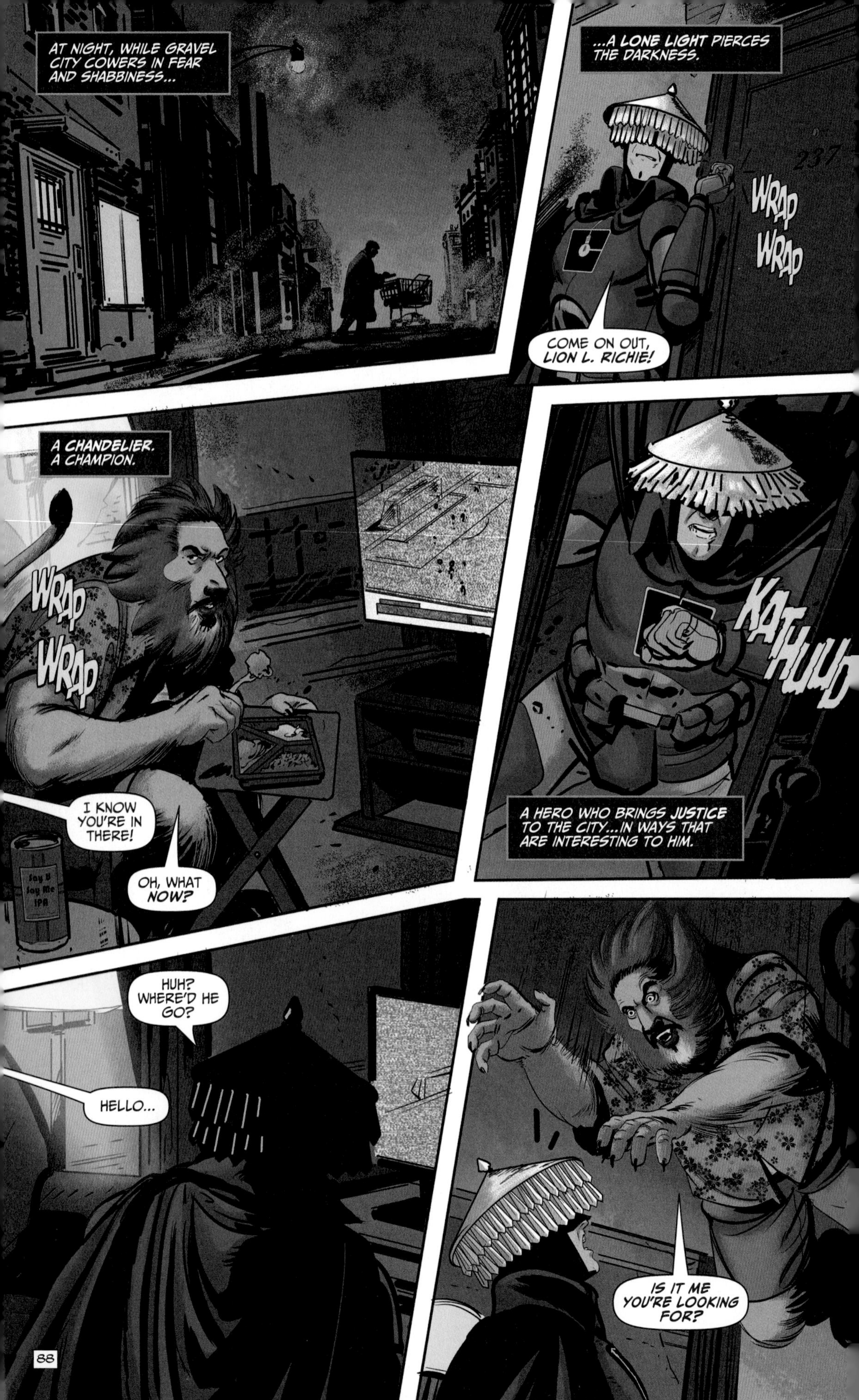

AT NIGHT, WHILE GRAVEL CITY COWERS IN FEAR AND SHABBINESS...
...A LONE LIGHT PIERCES THE DARKNESS.
237
WRAP WRAP
COME ON OUT, LION L. RICHIE!
A CHANDELIER. A CHAMPION.
WRAP WRAP
I KNOW YOU'RE IN THERE!
OH, WHAT NOW?
Say U Say Me IPA
KATHUUD
A HERO WHO BRINGS JUSTICE TO THE CITY...IN WAYS THAT ARE INTERESTING TO HIM.
HUH? WHERE'D HE GO?
HELLO...
IS IT ME YOU'RE LOOKING FOR?

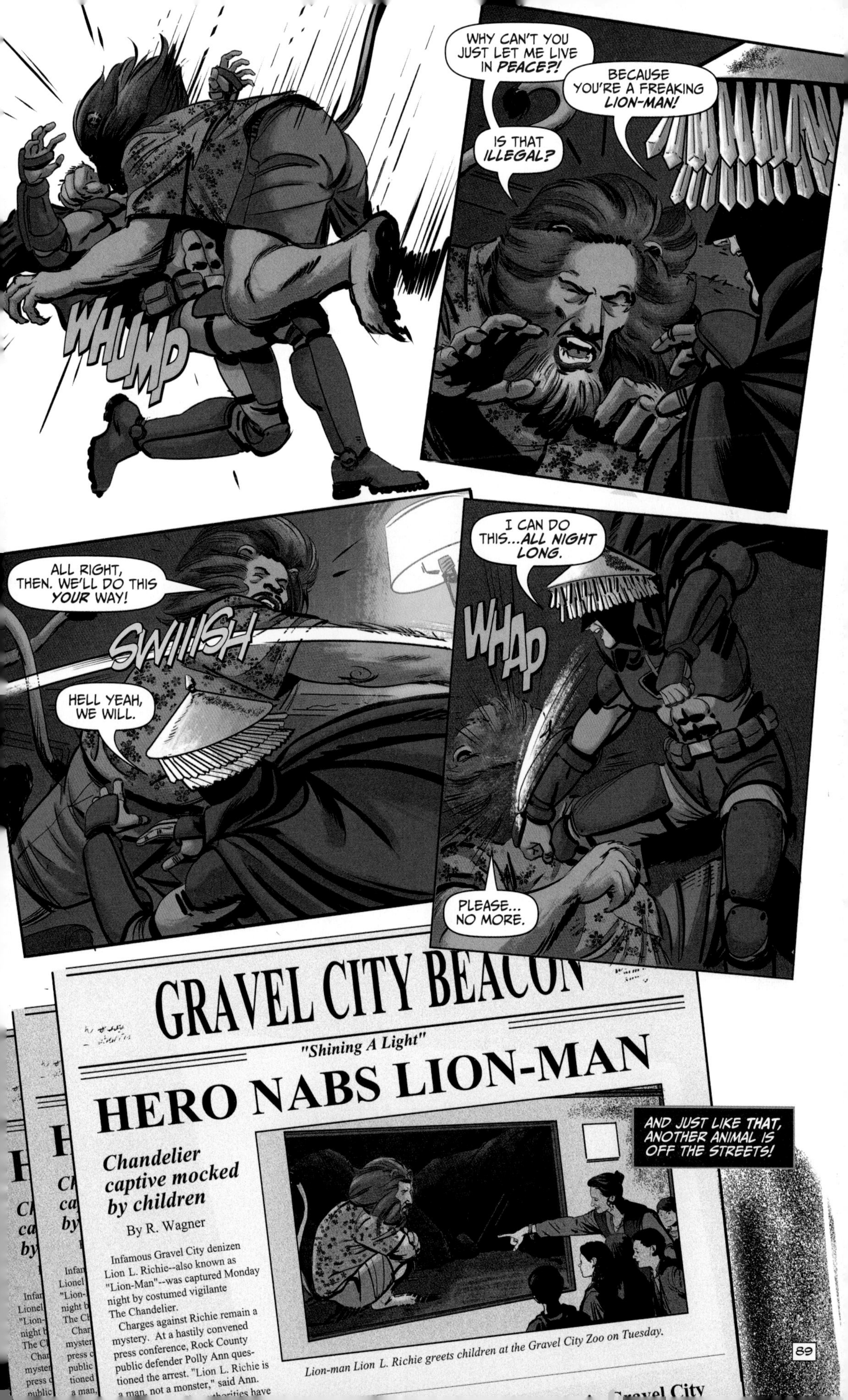
WHUMP
WHY CAN'T YOU JUST LET ME LIVE IN PEACE?!
BECAUSE YOU'RE A FREAKING LION-MAN!
IS THAT ILLEGAL?
ALL RIGHT, THEN. WE'LL DO THIS YOUR WAY!
SWIIISH
HELL YEAH, WE WILL.
I CAN DO THIS...ALL NIGHT LONG.
WHAP
PLEASE... NO MORE.
GRAVEL CITY BEACON
"Shining A Light"
HERO NABS LION-MAN
Chandelier captive mocked by children
By R. Wagner
Infamous Gravel City denizen Lion L. Richie--also known as "Lion-Man"--was captured Monday night by costumed vigilante The Chandelier.
Charges against Richie remain a mystery. At a hastily convened press conference, Rock County public defender Polly Ann questioned the arrest. "Lion L. Richie is a man, not a monster," said Ann.
Lion-man Lion L. Richie greets children at the Gravel City Zoo on Tuesday.
AND JUST LIKE THAT, ANOTHER ANIMAL IS OFF THE STREETS!

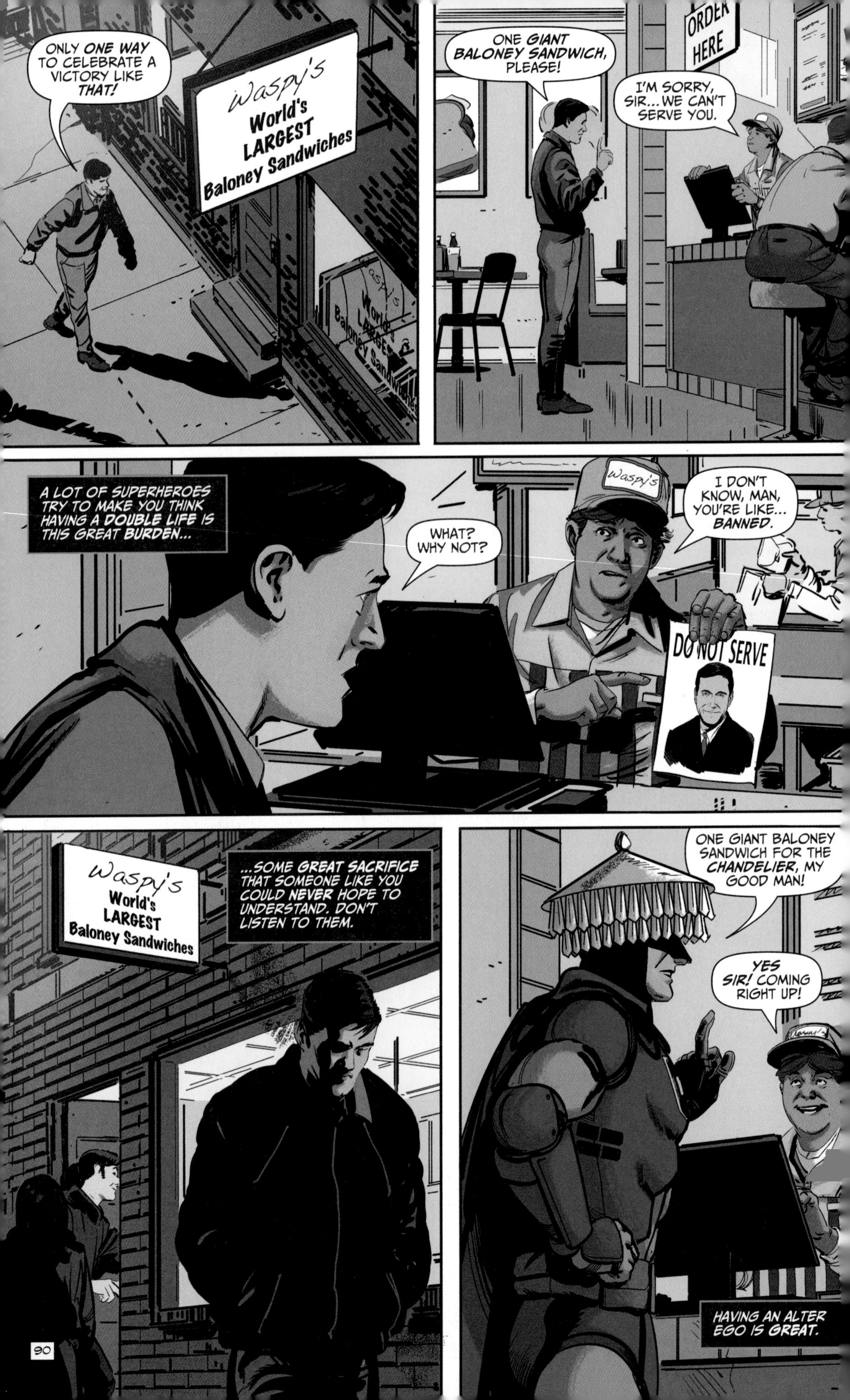
ONLY ONE WAY TO CELEBRATE A VICTORY LIKE THAT!
Waspy's World's LARGEST Baloney Sandwiches
ONE GIANT BALONEY SANDWICH, PLEASE!
ORDER HERE
I'M SORRY, SIR... WE CAN'T SERVE YOU.
A LOT OF SUPERHEROES TRY TO MAKE YOU THINK HAVING A DOUBLE LIFE IS THIS GREAT BURDEN...
Waspy's
WHAT? WHY NOT?
I DON'T KNOW, MAN, YOU'RE LIKE... BANNED.
DO NOT SERVE
Waspy's World's LARGEST Baloney Sandwiches
...SOME GREAT SACRIFICE THAT SOMEONE LIKE YOU COULD NEVER HOPE TO UNDERSTAND. DON'T LISTEN TO THEM.
ONE GIANT BALONEY SANDWICH FOR THE CHANDELIER, MY GOOD MAN!
YES SIR! COMING RIGHT UP!
HAVING AN ALTER EGO IS GREAT.

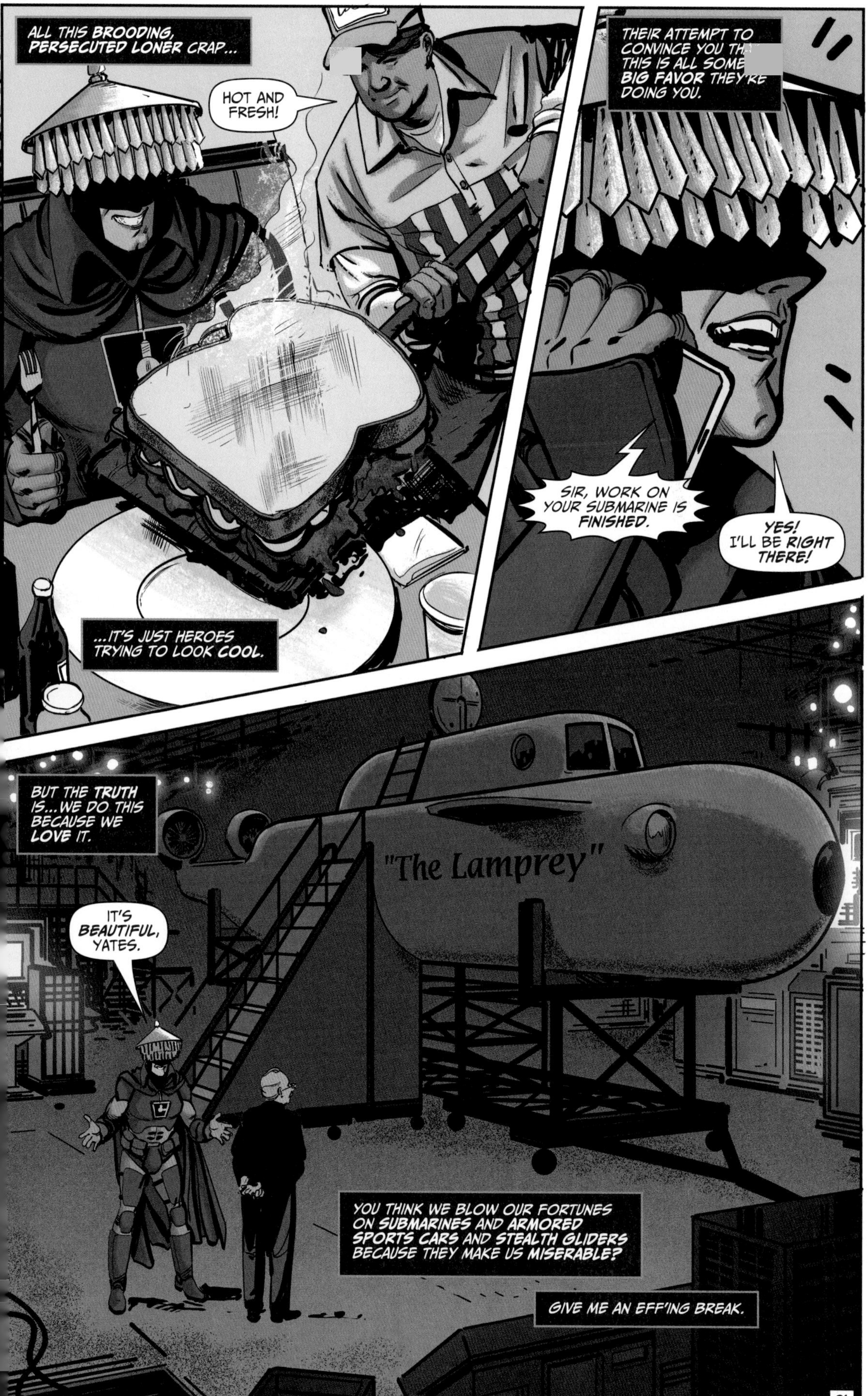

ALL THIS BROODING, PERSECUTED LONER CRAP...
HOT AND FRESH!
...IT'S JUST HEROES TRYING TO LOOK COOL.
THEIR ATTEMPT TO CONVINCE YOU TH THIS IS ALL SOME BIG FAVOR THEY'RE DOING YOU.
SIR, WORK ON YOUR SUBMARINE IS FINISHED.
YES! I'LL BE RIGHT THERE!
BUT THE TRUTH IS...WE DO THIS BECAUSE WE LOVE IT.
"The Lamprey"
IT'S BEAUTIFUL, YATES.
YOU THINK WE BLOW OUR FORTUNES ON SUBMARINES AND ARMORED SPORTS CARS AND STEALTH GLIDERS BECAUSE THEY MAKE US MISERABLE?
GIVE ME AN EFF'ING BREAK.

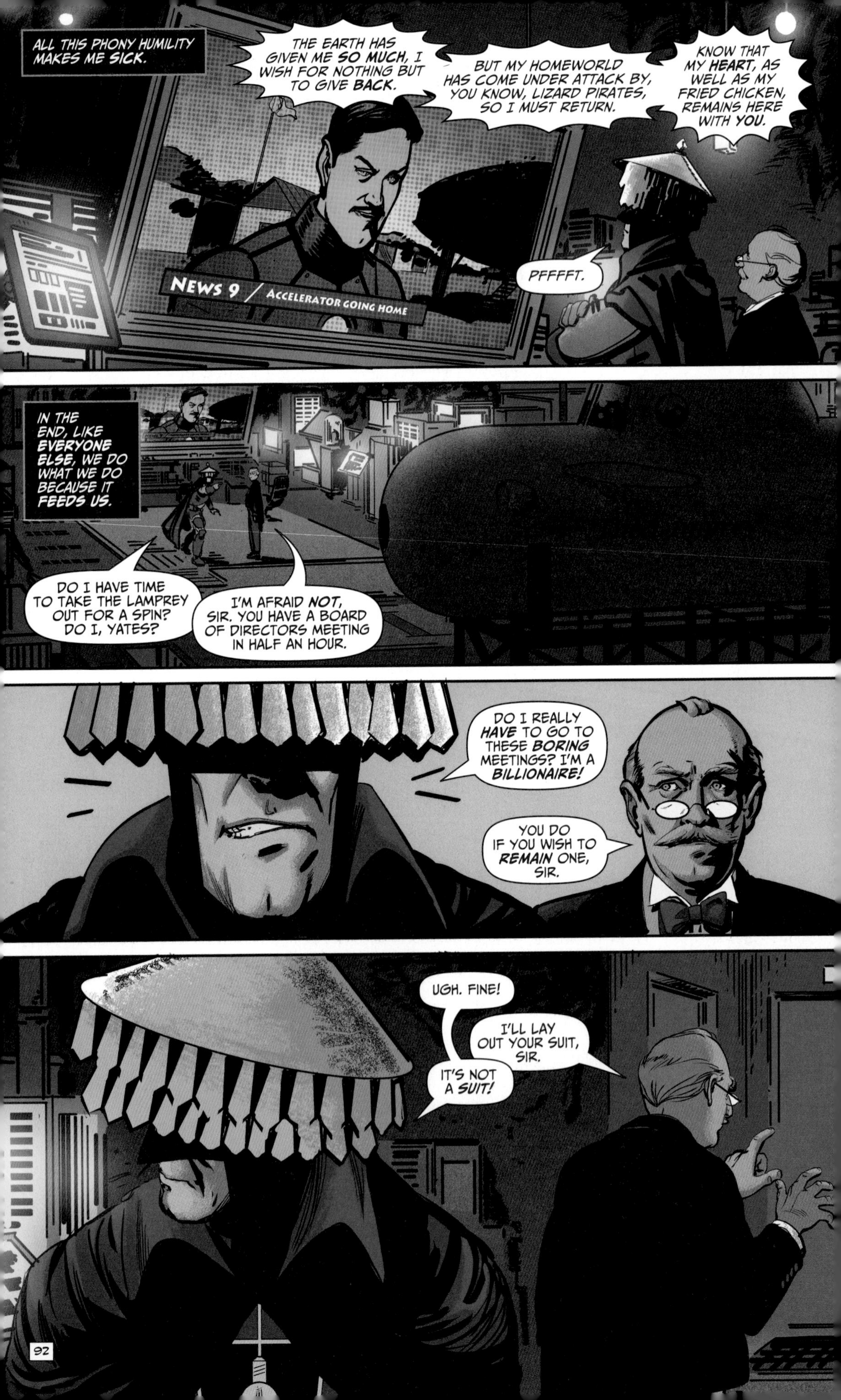
ALL THIS PHONY HUMILITY MAKES ME SICK.
THE EARTH HAS GIVEN ME SO MUCH, I WISH FOR NOTHING BUT TO GIVE BACK.
BUT MY HOMEWORLD HAS COME UNDER ATTACK BY, YOU KNOW, LIZARD PIRATES, SO I MUST RETURN.
KNOW THAT MY HEART, AS WELL AS MY FRIED CHICKEN, REMAINS HERE WITH YOU.
NEWS 9 / ACCELERATOR GOING HOME
PFFFFT.
IN THE END, LIKE EVERYONE ELSE, WE DO WHAT WE DO BECAUSE IT FEEDS US.
DO I HAVE TIME TO TAKE THE LAMPREY OUT FOR A SPIN? DO I, YATES?
I'M AFRAID NOT, SIR. YOU HAVE A BOARD OF DIRECTORS MEETING IN HALF AN HOUR.
DO I REALLY HAVE TO GO TO THESE BORING MEETINGS? I'M A BILLIONAIRE!
YOU DO IF YOU WISH TO REMAIN ONE, SIR.
UGH. FINE!
I'LL LAY OUT YOUR SUIT, SIR.
IT'S NOT A SUIT!

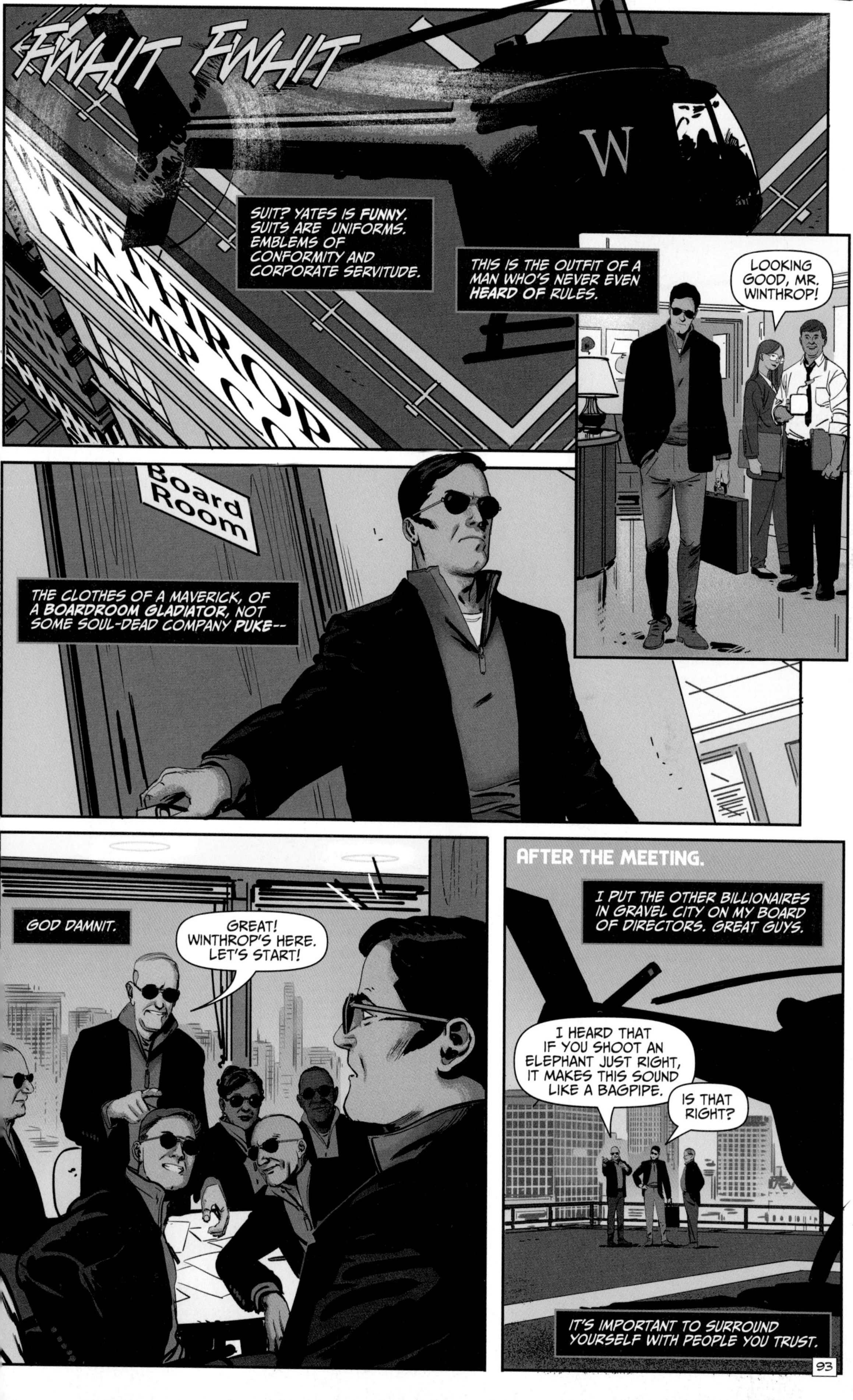

FWHIT FWHIT
W
SUIT? YATES IS FUNNY. SUITS ARE UNIFORMS. EMBLEMS OF CONFORMITY AND CORPORATE SERVITUDE.
THIS IS THE OUTFIT OF A MAN WHO'S NEVER EVEN HEARD OF RULES.
LOOKING GOOD, MR. WINTHROP!
Board Room
THE CLOTHES OF A MAVERICK, OF A BOARDROOM GLADIATOR, NOT SOME SOUL-DEAD COMPANY PUKE--
GOD DAMNIT.
GREAT! WINTHROP'S HERE. LET'S START!
AFTER THE MEETING.
I PUT THE OTHER BILLIONAIRES IN GRAVEL CITY ON MY BOARD OF DIRECTORS. GREAT GUYS.
I HEARD THAT IF YOU SHOOT AN ELEPHANT JUST RIGHT, IT MAKES THIS SOUND LIKE A BAGPIPE.
IS THAT RIGHT?
IT'S IMPORTANT TO SURROUND YOURSELF WITH PEOPLE YOU TRUST.

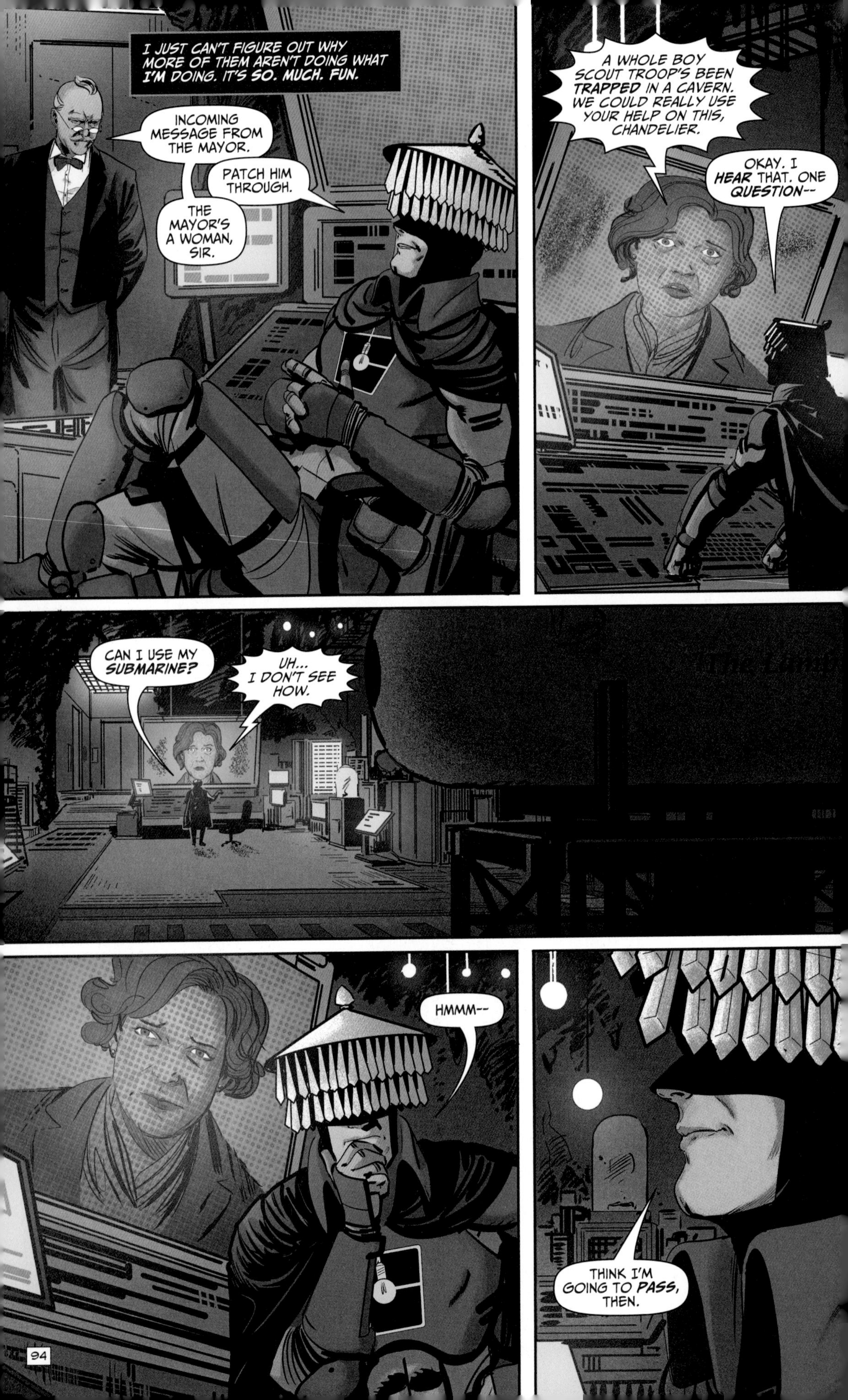
I JUST CAN'T FIGURE OUT WHY MORE OF THEM AREN'T DOING WHAT I'M DOING. IT'S SO. MUCH. FUN.
INCOMING MESSAGE FROM THE MAYOR.
PATCH HIM THROUGH.
THE MAYOR'S A WOMAN, SIR.
A WHOLE BOY SCOUT TROOP'S BEEN TRAPPED IN A CAVERN. WE COULD REALLY USE YOUR HELP ON THIS, CHANDELIER.
OKAY. I HEAR THAT. ONE QUESTION--
CAN I USE MY SUBMARINE?
UH... I DON'T SEE HOW.
HMMM--
THINK I'M GOING TO PASS, THEN.

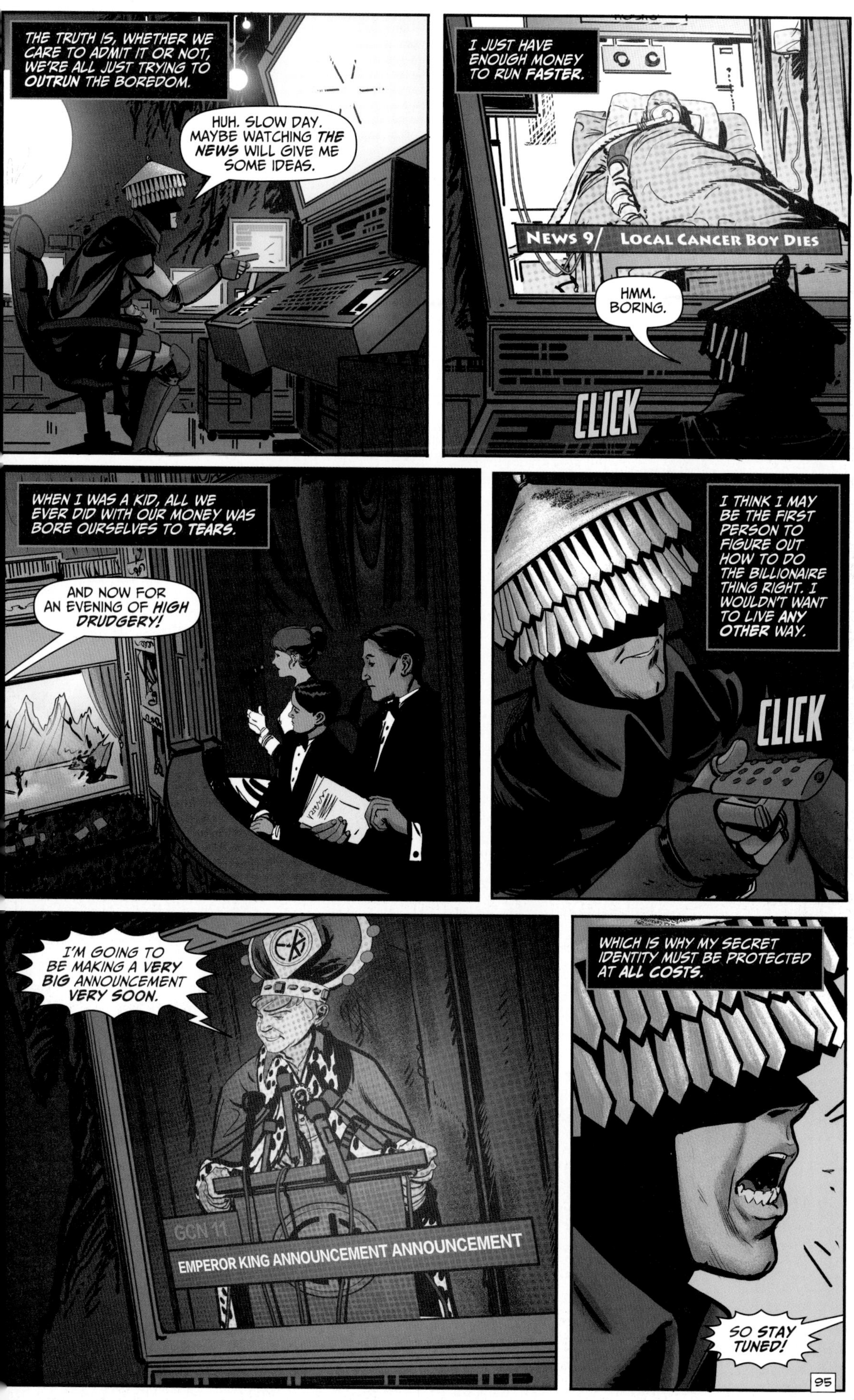
THE TRUTH IS, WHETHER WE CARE TO ADMIT IT OR NOT, WE'RE ALL JUST TRYING TO OUTRUN THE BOREDOM.
HUH. SLOW DAY. MAYBE WATCHING THE NEWS WILL GIVE ME SOME IDEAS.
I JUST HAVE ENOUGH MONEY TO RUN FASTER.
NEWS 9/ LOCAL CANCER BOY DIES
HMM. BORING.
CLICK
WHEN I WAS A KID, ALL WE EVER DID WITH OUR MONEY WAS BORE OURSELVES TO TEARS.
AND NOW FOR AN EVENING OF HIGH DRUDGERY!
I THINK I MAY BE THE FIRST PERSON TO FIGURE OUT HOW TO DO THE BILLIONAIRE THING RIGHT. I WOULDN'T WANT TO LIVE ANY OTHER WAY.
CLICK
I'M GOING TO BE MAKING A VERY BIG ANNOUNCEMENT VERY SOON.
GCN 11
EMPEROR KING ANNOUNCEMENT ANNOUNCEMENT
WHICH IS WHY MY SECRET IDENTITY MUST BE PROTECTED AT ALL COSTS.
SO STAY TUNED!

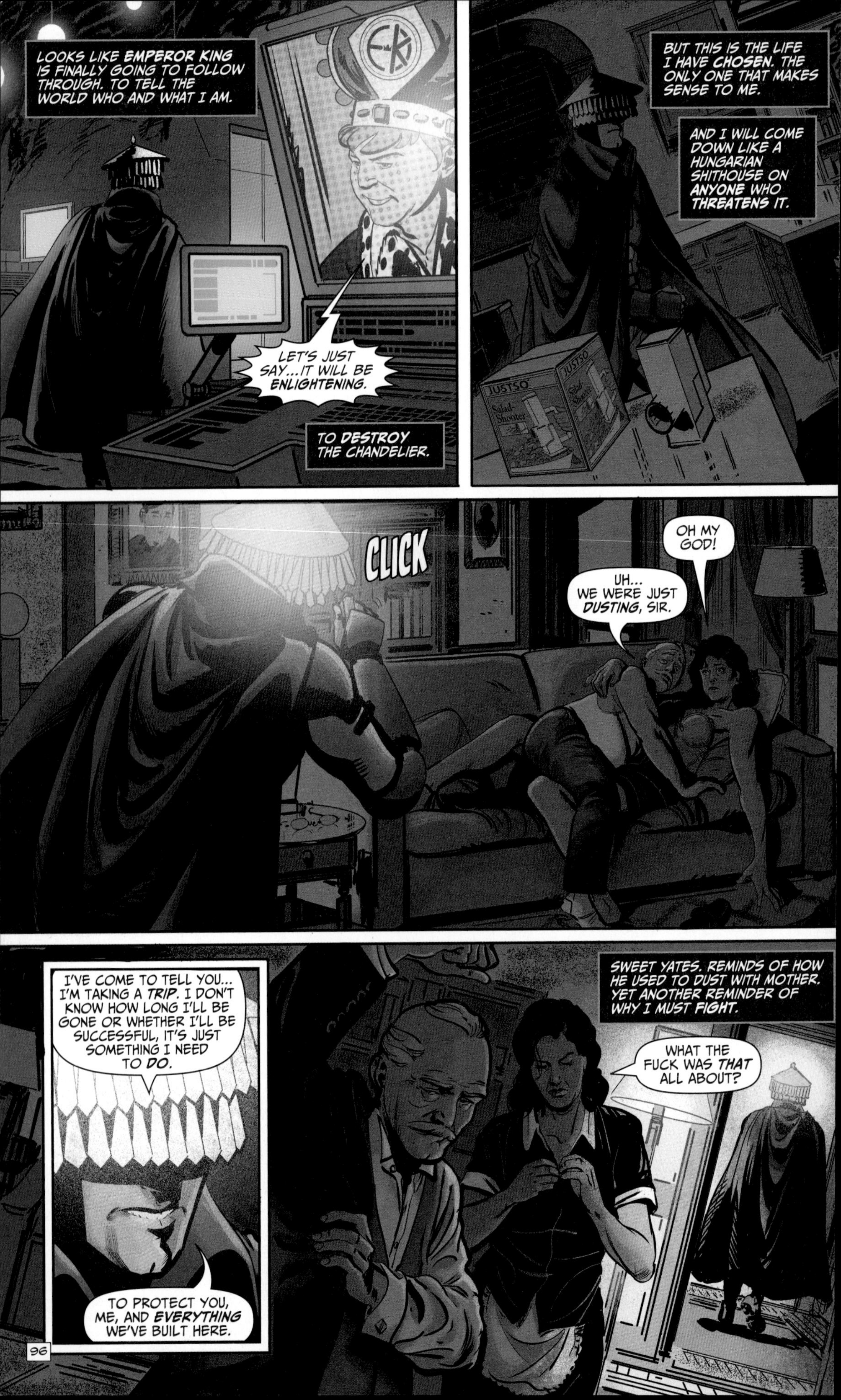
LOOKS LIKE EMPEROR KING IS FINALLY GOING TO FOLLOW THROUGH. TO TELL THE WORLD WHO AND WHAT I AM.
LET'S JUST SAY...IT WILL BE ENLIGHTENING.
TO DESTROY THE CHANDELIER.
BUT THIS IS THE LIFE I HAVE CHOSEN. THE ONLY ONE THAT MAKES SENSE TO ME.
AND I WILL COME DOWN LIKE A HUNGARIAN SHITHOUSE ON ANYONE WHO THREATENS IT.
JUSTSO Salad-Shooter
CLICK
UH... WE WERE JUST DUSTING, SIR.
OH MY GOD!
I'VE COME TO TELL YOU... I'M TAKING A TRIP. I DON'T KNOW HOW LONG I'LL BE GONE OR WHETHER I'LL BE SUCCESSFUL, IT'S JUST SOMETHING I NEED TO DO.
TO PROTECT YOU, ME, AND EVERYTHING WE'VE BUILT HERE.
SWEET YATES. REMINDS OF HOW HE USED TO DUST WITH MOTHER. YET ANOTHER REMINDER OF WHY I MUST FIGHT.
WHAT THE FUCK WAS THAT ALL ABOUT?

EMPEROR KING...
I'M COMING FOR YOU.
HEADING:
LOS ANGELES.
WINTHROP
LAMP CO.
TO BE CONTINUED.

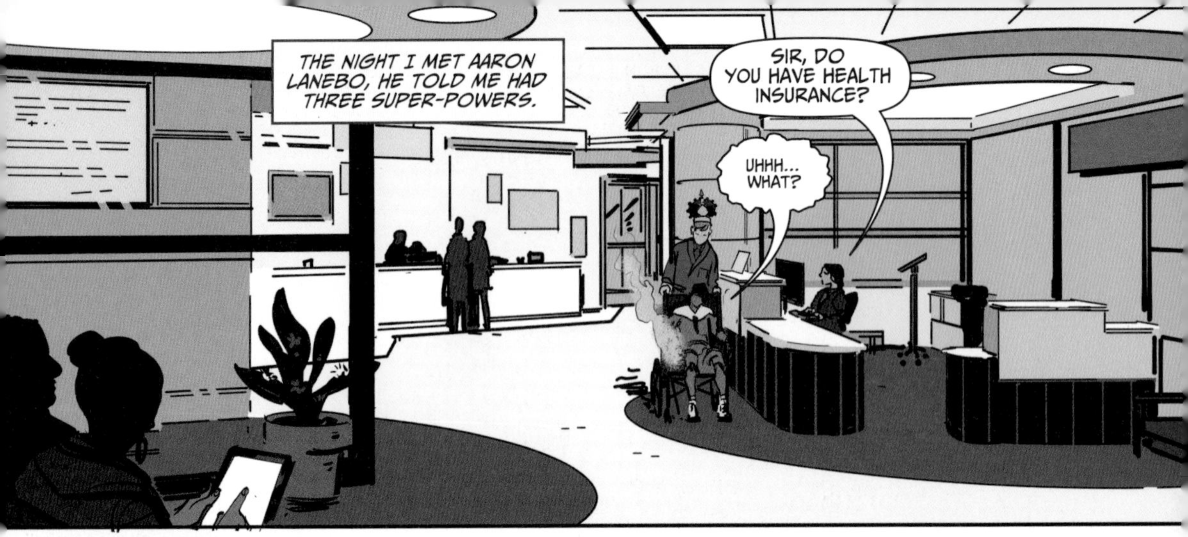
THE NIGHT I MET AARON LANEBO, HE TOLD ME HAD THREE SUPER-POWERS.
SIR, DO YOU HAVE HEALTH INSURANCE?
UHHH... WHAT?

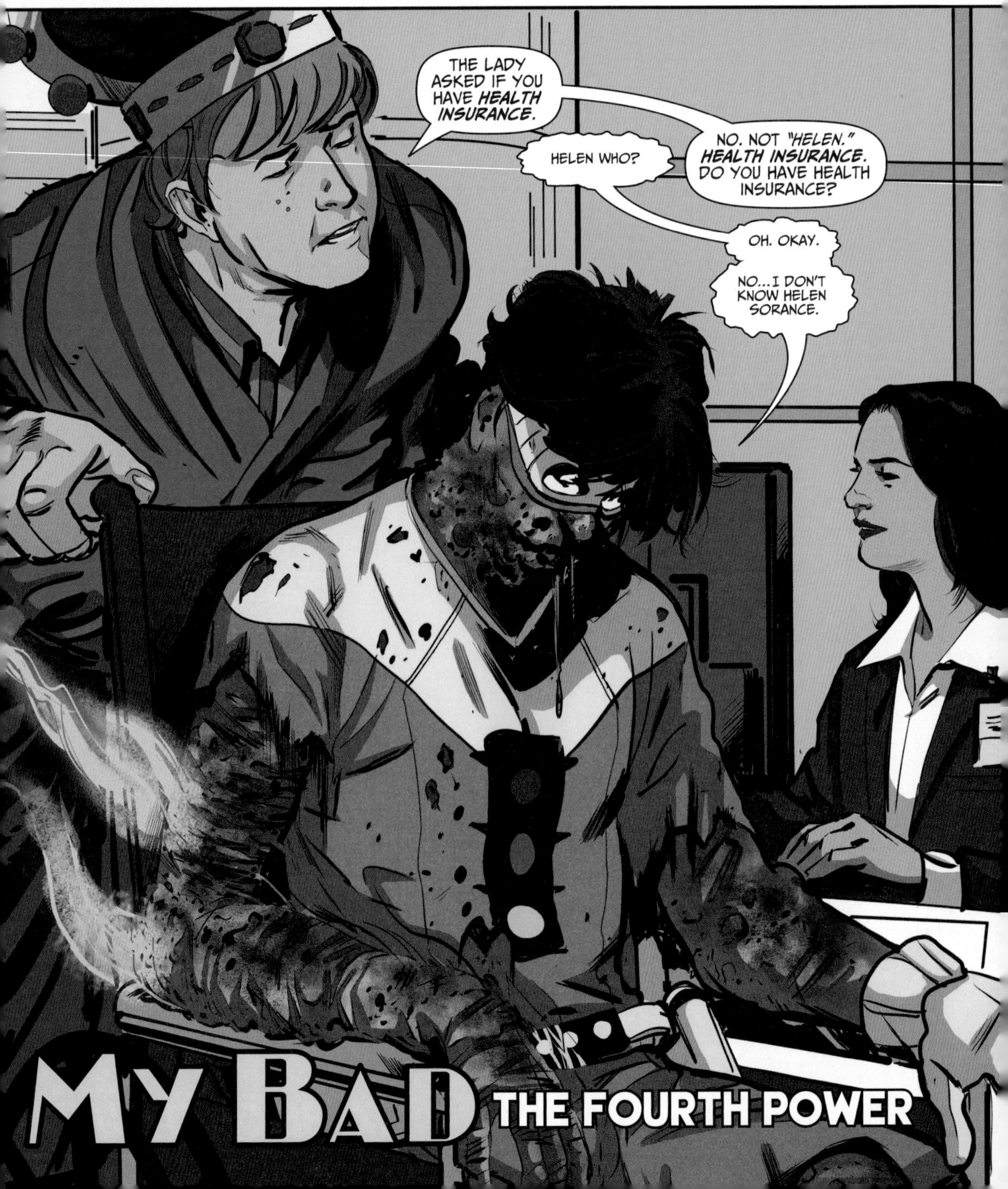
THE LADY ASKED IF YOU HAVE HEALTH INSURANCE.
HELEN WHO?
NO. NOT "HELEN." HEALTH INSURANCE. DO YOU HAVE HEALTH INSURANCE?
OH. OKAY.
NO...I DON'T KNOW HELEN SORANCE.
MY BAD THE FOURTH POWER

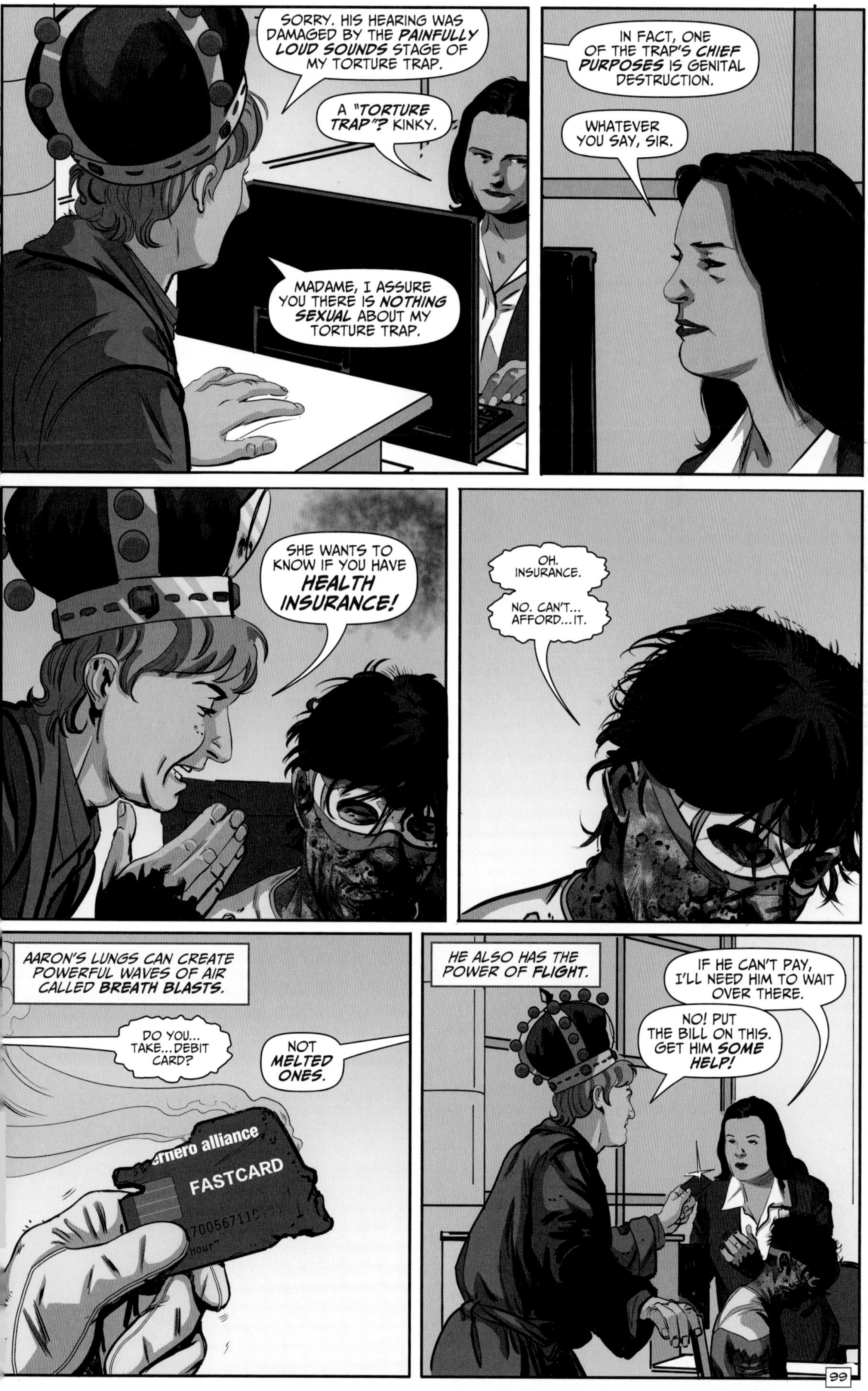
SORRY. HIS HEARING WAS DAMAGED BY THE PAINFULLY LOUD SOUNDS STAGE OF MY TORTURE TRAP.
A "TORTURE TRAP"? KINKY.
MADAME, I ASSURE YOU THERE IS NOTHING SEXUAL ABOUT MY TORTURE TRAP.
IN FACT, ONE OF THE TRAP'S CHIEF PURPOSES IS GENITAL DESTRUCTION.
WHATEVER YOU SAY, SIR.
SHE WANTS TO KNOW IF YOU HAVE HEALTH INSURANCE!
OH. INSURANCE.
NO. CAN'T... AFFORD... IT.
AARON'S LUNGS CAN CREATE POWERFUL WAVES OF AIR CALLED BREATH BLASTS.
DO YOU... TAKE... DEBIT CARD?
NOT MELTED ONES.
ernero alliance
FASTCARD
HE ALSO HAS THE POWER OF FLIGHT.
IF HE CAN'T PAY, I'LL NEED HIM TO WAIT OVER THERE.
NO! PUT THE BILL ON THIS. GET HIM SOME HELP!

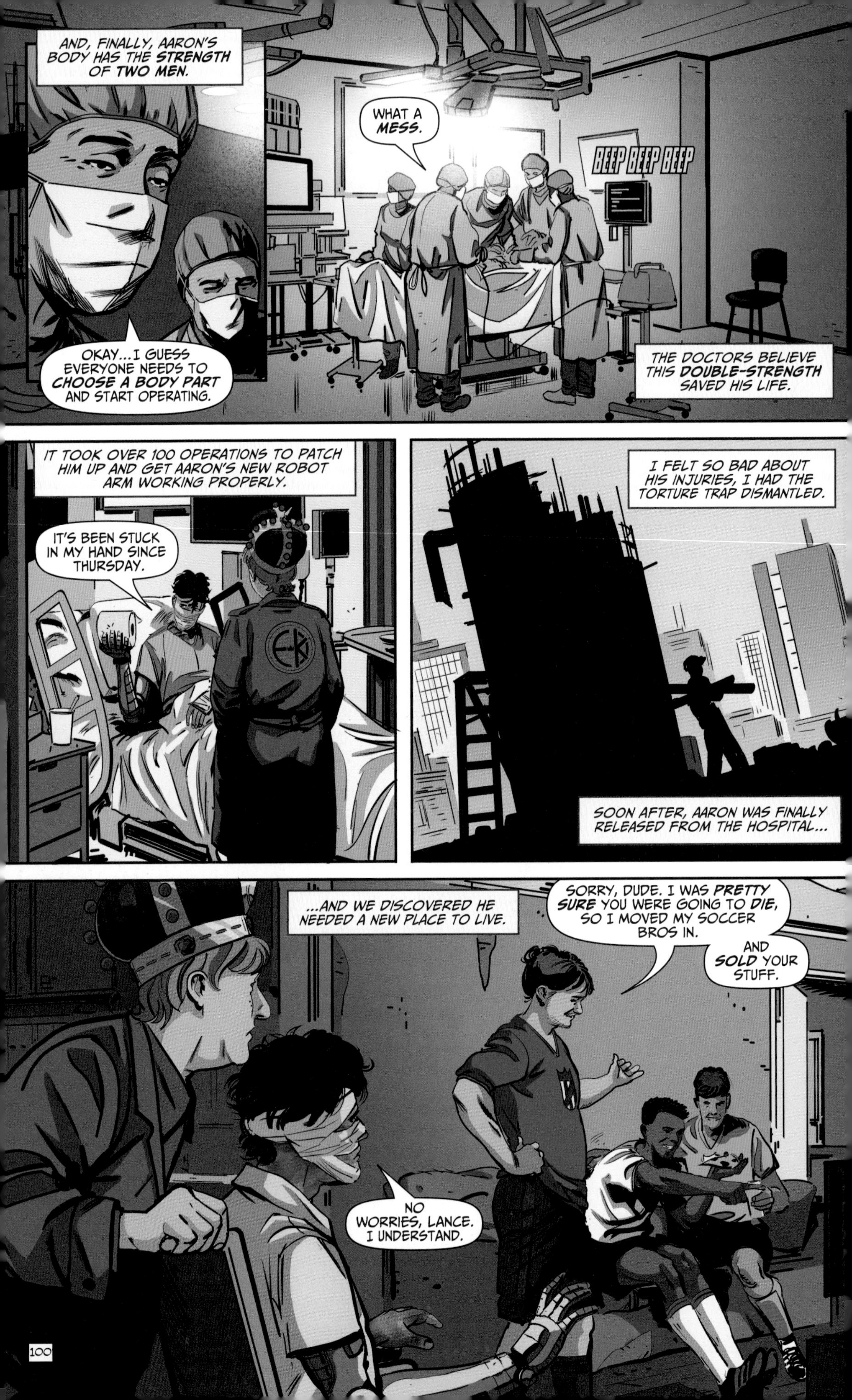
AND, FINALLY, AARON'S BODY HAS THE **STRENGTH** OF **TWO MEN**.
OKAY...I GUESS EVERYONE NEEDS TO **CHOOSE A BODY PART** AND START OPERATING.
WHAT A **MESS**.
BEEP BEEP BEEP
THE DOCTORS BELIEVE THIS **DOUBLE-STRENGTH** SAVED HIS LIFE.
IT TOOK OVER 100 OPERATIONS TO PATCH HIM UP AND GET AARON'S NEW ROBOT ARM WORKING PROPERLY.
IT'S BEEN STUCK IN MY HAND SINCE THURSDAY.
I FELT SO BAD ABOUT HIS INJURIES, I HAD THE TORTURE TRAP DISMANTLED.
SOON AFTER, AARON WAS FINALLY RELEASED FROM THE HOSPITAL...
...AND WE DISCOVERED HE NEEDED A NEW PLACE TO LIVE.
SORRY, DUDE. I WAS **PRETTY SURE** YOU WERE GOING TO **DIE**, SO I MOVED MY SOCCER BROS IN.
AND **SOLD** YOUR STUFF.
NO WORRIES, LANCE. I UNDERSTAND.

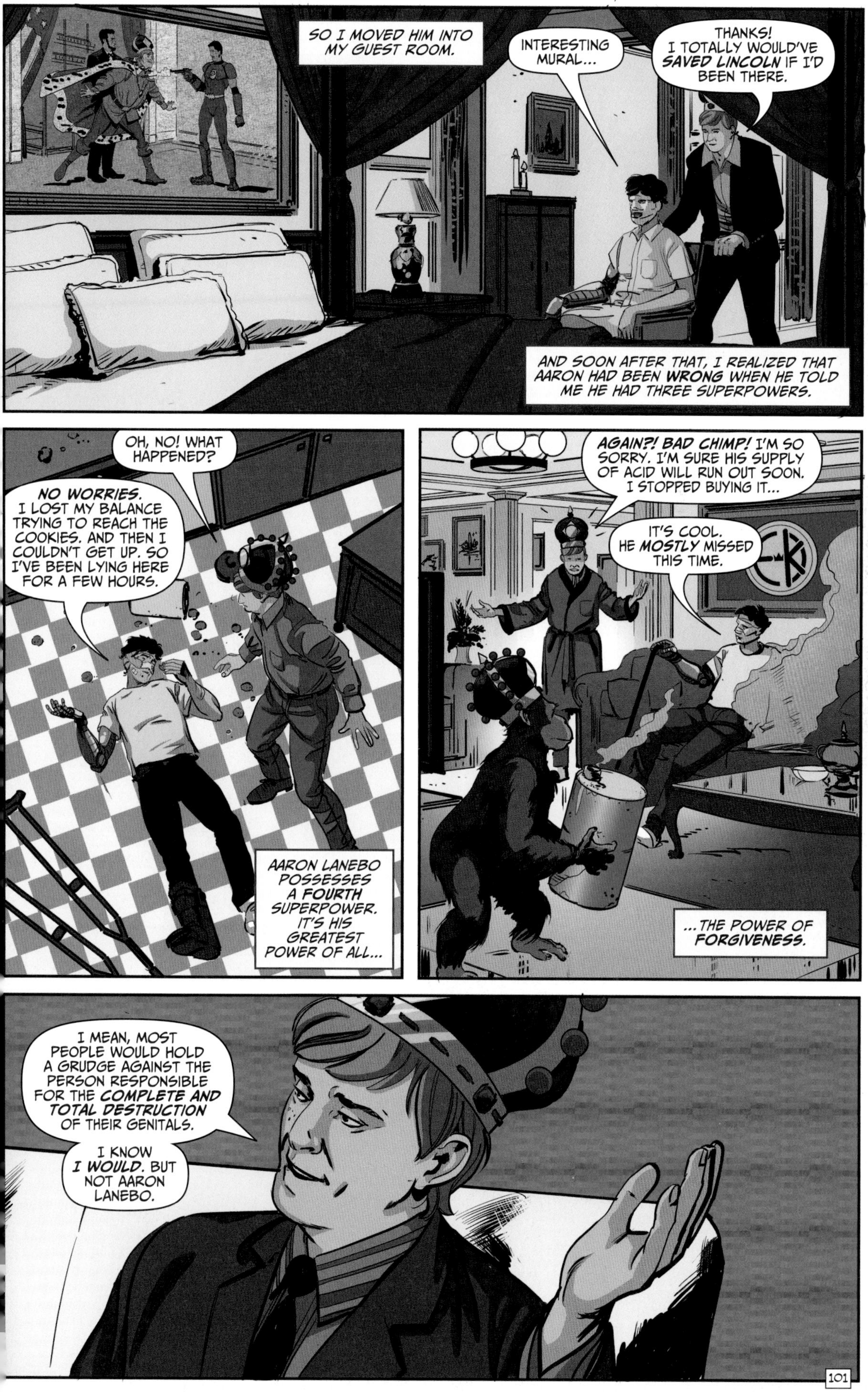
SO I MOVED HIM INTO MY GUEST ROOM.
INTERESTING MURAL...
THANKS! I TOTALLY WOULD'VE SAVED LINCOLN IF I'D BEEN THERE.
AND SOON AFTER THAT, I REALIZED THAT AARON HAD BEEN WRONG WHEN HE TOLD ME HE HAD THREE SUPERPOWERS.
OH, NO! WHAT HAPPENED?
NO WORRIES. I LOST MY BALANCE TRYING TO REACH THE COOKIES. AND THEN I COULDN'T GET UP. SO I'VE BEEN LYING HERE FOR A FEW HOURS.
AARON LANEBO POSSESSES A FOURTH SUPERPOWER. IT'S HIS GREATEST POWER OF ALL...
AGAIN?! BAD CHIMP! I'M SO SORRY. I'M SURE HIS SUPPLY OF ACID WILL RUN OUT SOON. I STOPPED BUYING IT...
IT'S COOL. HE MOSTLY MISSED THIS TIME.
...THE POWER OF FORGIVENESS.
I MEAN, MOST PEOPLE WOULD HOLD A GRUDGE AGAINST THE PERSON RESPONSIBLE FOR THE COMPLETE AND TOTAL DESTRUCTION OF THEIR GENITALS.
I KNOW I WOULD. BUT NOT AARON LANEBO.

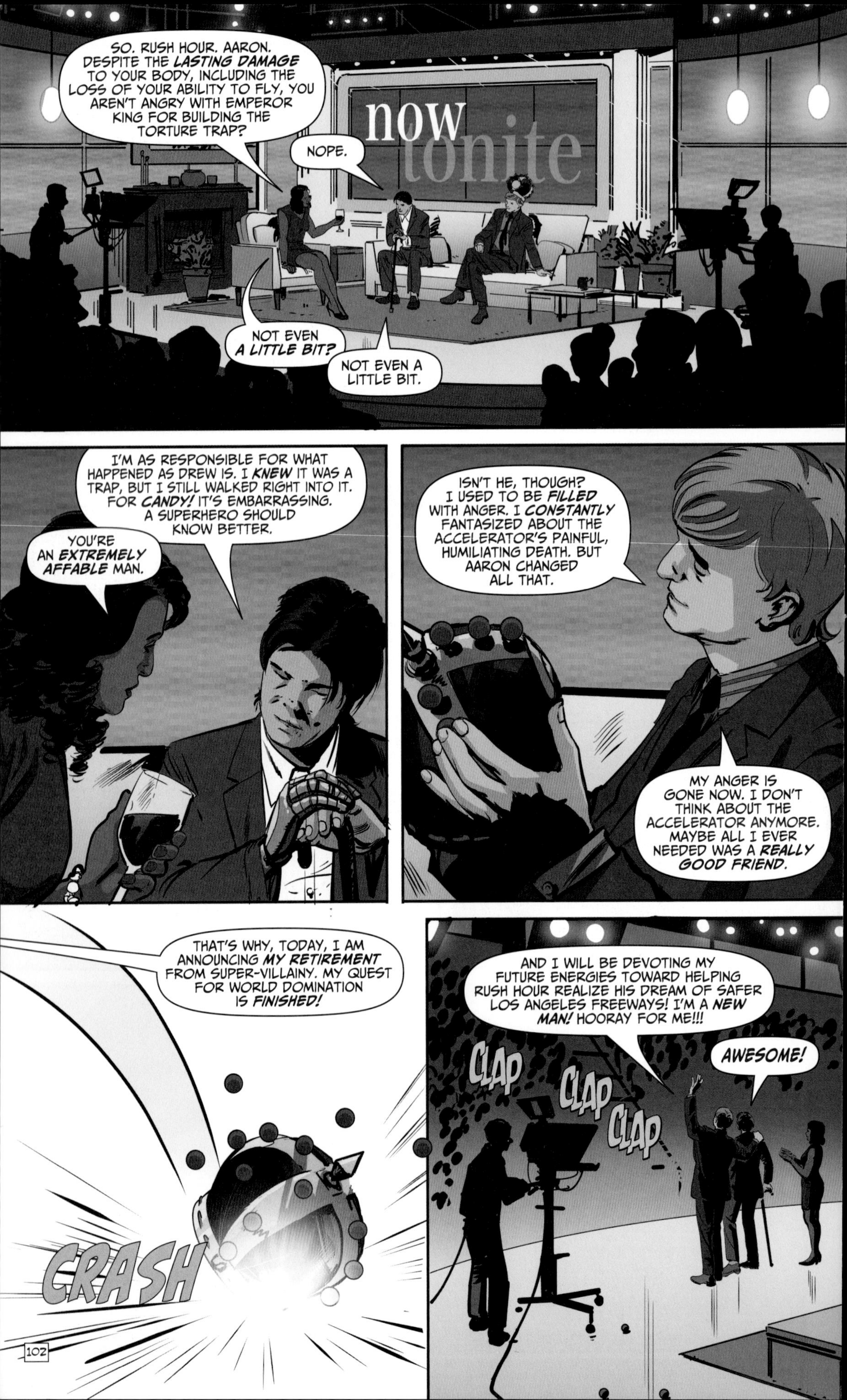

SO. RUSH HOUR. AARON. DESPITE THE LASTING DAMAGE TO YOUR BODY, INCLUDING THE LOSS OF YOUR ABILITY TO FLY, YOU AREN'T ANGRY WITH EMPEROR KING FOR BUILDING THE TORTURE TRAP?
NOPE.
now
tonite
NOT EVEN A LITTLE BIT?
NOT EVEN A LITTLE BIT.
I'M AS RESPONSIBLE FOR WHAT HAPPENED AS DREW IS. I KNEW IT WAS A TRAP, BUT I STILL WALKED RIGHT INTO IT. FOR CANDY! IT'S EMBARRASSING. A SUPERHERO SHOULD KNOW BETTER.
YOU'RE AN EXTREMELY AFFABLE MAN.
ISN'T HE, THOUGH? I USED TO BE FILLED WITH ANGER. I CONSTANTLY FANTASIZED ABOUT THE ACCELERATOR'S PAINFUL, HUMILIATING DEATH. BUT AARON CHANGED ALL THAT.
MY ANGER IS GONE NOW. I DON'T THINK ABOUT THE ACCELERATOR ANYMORE. MAYBE ALL I EVER NEEDED WAS A REALLY GOOD FRIEND.
THAT'S WHY, TODAY, I AM ANNOUNCING MY RETIREMENT FROM SUPER-VILLAINY. MY QUEST FOR WORLD DOMINATION IS FINISHED!
CRASH
AND I WILL BE DEVOTING MY FUTURE ENERGIES TOWARD HELPING RUSH HOUR REALIZE HIS DREAM OF SAFER LOS ANGELES FREEWAYS! I'M A NEW MAN! HOORAY FOR ME!!!
CLAP
CLAP
CLAP
AWESOME!

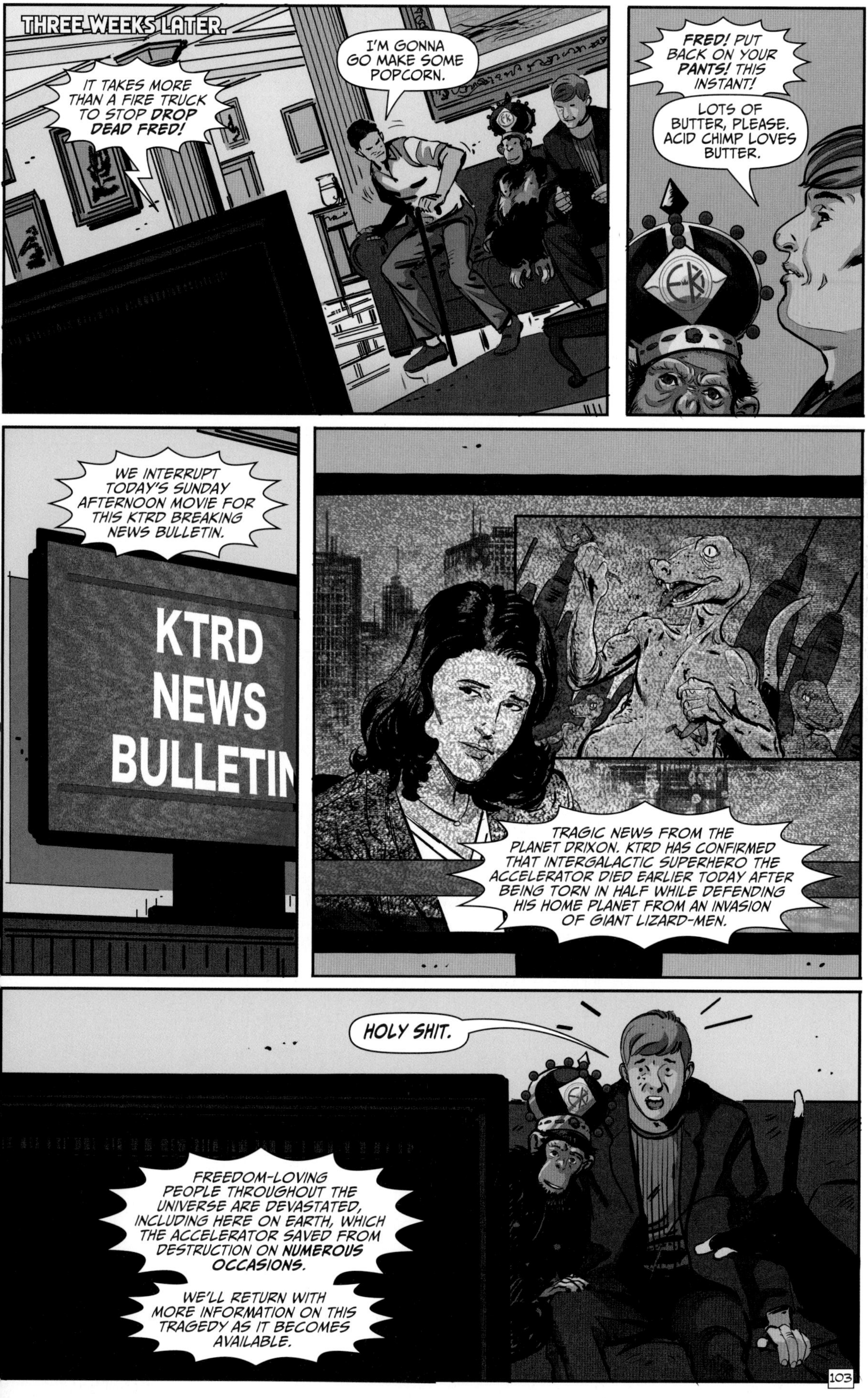
THREE WEEKS LATER.
IT TAKES MORE THAN A FIRE TRUCK TO STOP DROP DEAD FRED!
I'M GONNA GO MAKE SOME POPCORN.
FRED! PUT BACK ON YOUR PANTS! THIS INSTANT!
LOTS OF BUTTER, PLEASE. ACID CHIMP LOVES BUTTER.
WE INTERRUPT TODAY'S SUNDAY AFTERNOON MOVIE FOR THIS KTRD BREAKING NEWS BULLETIN.
KTRD NEWS BULLETIN
TRAGIC NEWS FROM THE PLANET DRIXON. KTRD HAS CONFIRMED THAT INTERGALACTIC SUPERHERO THE ACCELERATOR DIED EARLIER TODAY AFTER BEING TORN IN HALF WHILE DEFENDING HIS HOME PLANET FROM AN INVASION OF GIANT LIZARD-MEN.
HOLY SHIT.
FREEDOM-LOVING PEOPLE THROUGHOUT THE UNIVERSE ARE DEVASTATED, INCLUDING HERE ON EARTH, WHICH THE ACCELERATOR SAVED FROM DESTRUCTION ON NUMEROUS OCCASIONS.
WE'LL RETURN WITH MORE INFORMATION ON THIS TRAGEDY AS IT BECOMES AVAILABLE.

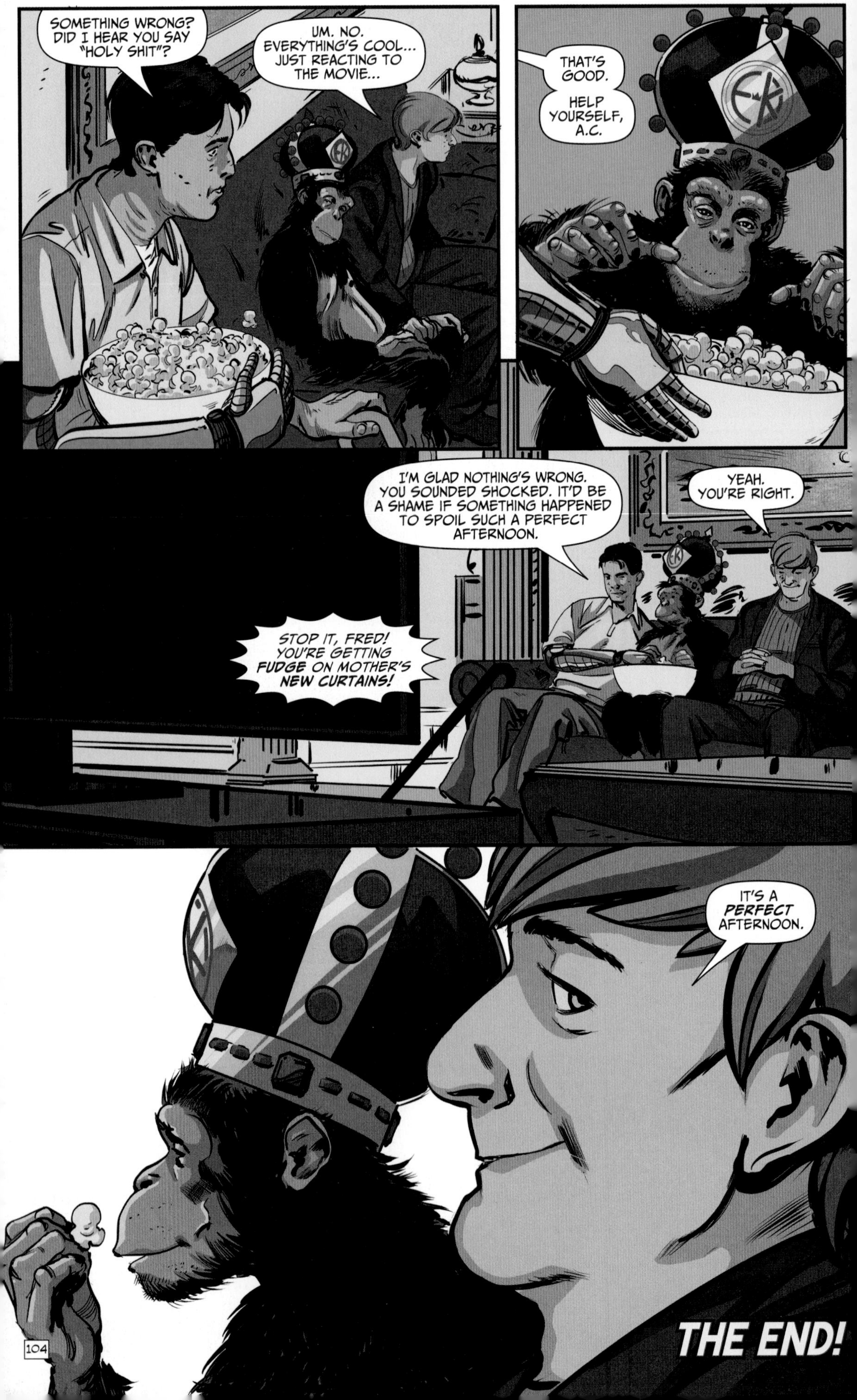
SOMETHING WRONG? DID I HEAR YOU SAY "HOLY SHIT"?
UM. NO. EVERYTHING'S COOL... JUST REACTING TO THE MOVIE...
THAT'S GOOD.
HELP YOURSELF, A.C.
I'M GLAD NOTHING'S WRONG. YOU SOUNDED SHOCKED. IT'D BE A SHAME IF SOMETHING HAPPENED TO SPOIL SUCH A PERFECT AFTERNOON.
YEAH. YOU'RE RIGHT.
STOP IT, FRED! YOU'RE GETTING *FUDGE* ON MOTHER'S *NEW CURTAINS!*
IT'S A *PERFECT* AFTERNOON.
THE END!

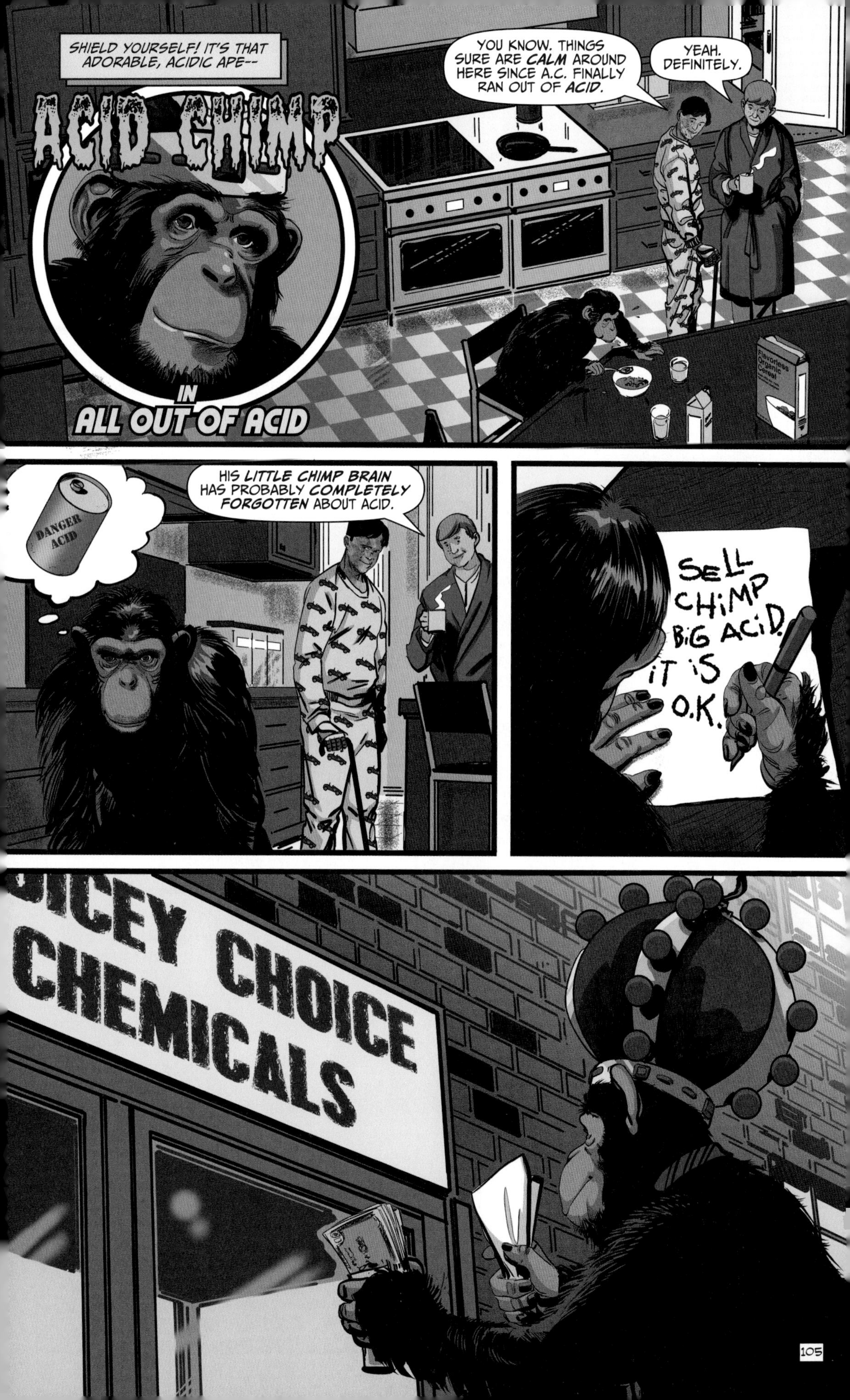
SHIELD YOURSELF! IT'S THAT ADORABLE, ACIDIC APE--
ACID CHIMP
IN
ALL OUT OF ACID
YOU KNOW. THINGS SURE ARE CALM AROUND HERE SINCE A.C. FINALLY RAN OUT OF ACID.
YEAH. DEFINITELY.
Flavorless Organic Cereal
DANGER ACID
HIS LITTLE CHIMP BRAIN HAS PROBABLY COMPLETELY FORGOTTEN ABOUT ACID.
SELL CHIMP BIG ACID. IT IS O.K.
ICEY CHOICE
CHEMICALS

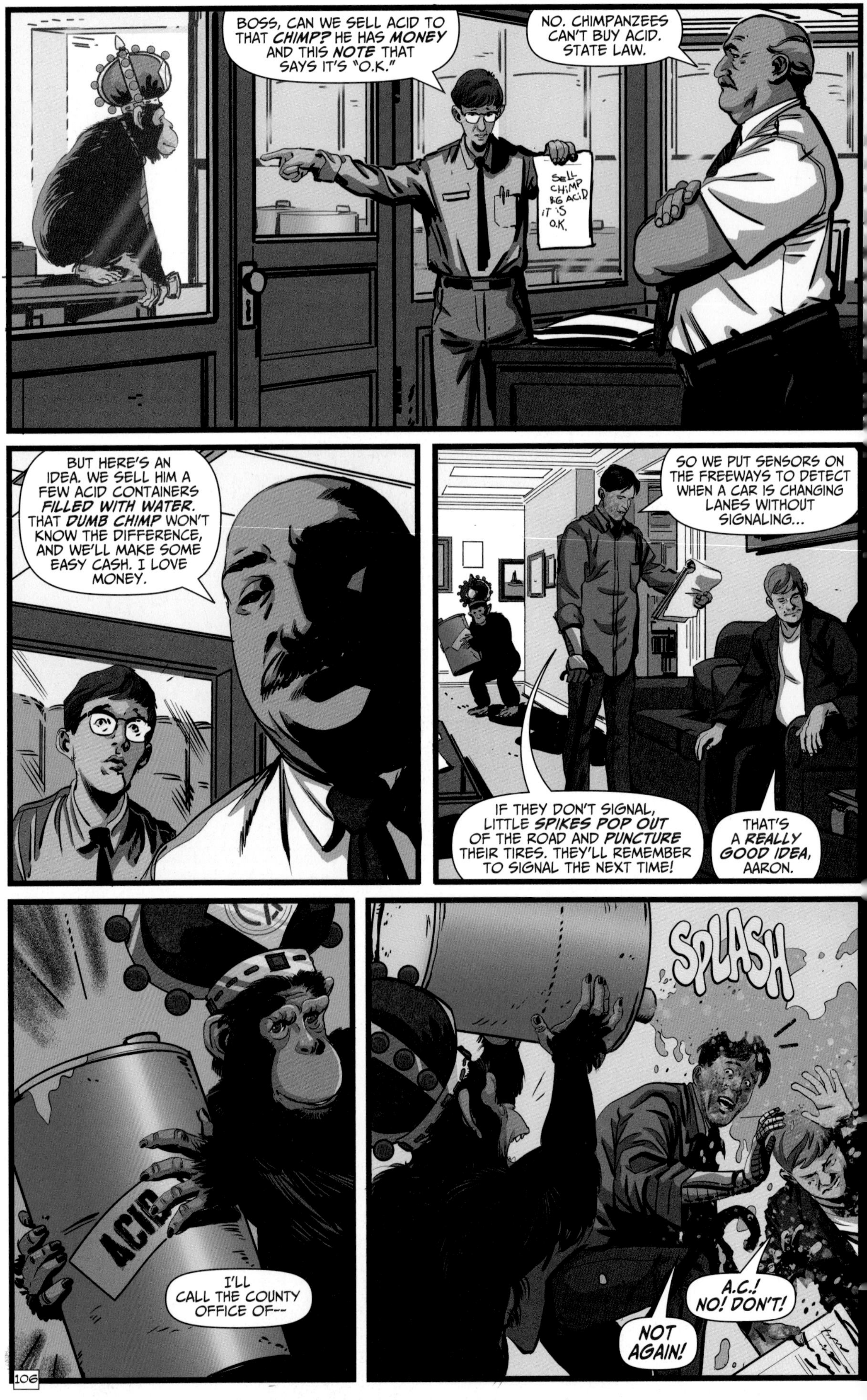
BOSS, CAN WE SELL ACID TO THAT CHIMP? HE HAS MONEY AND THIS NOTE THAT SAYS IT'S "O.K."
SELL CHIMP BIG ACID IT IS O.K.
NO. CHIMPANZEES CAN'T BUY ACID. STATE LAW.
BUT HERE'S AN IDEA. WE SELL HIM A FEW ACID CONTAINERS FILLED WITH WATER. THAT DUMB CHIMP WON'T KNOW THE DIFFERENCE, AND WE'LL MAKE SOME EASY CASH. I LOVE MONEY.
SO WE PUT SENSORS ON THE FREEWAYS TO DETECT WHEN A CAR IS CHANGING LANES WITHOUT SIGNALING...
IF THEY DON'T SIGNAL, LITTLE SPIKES POP OUT OF THE ROAD AND PUNCTURE THEIR TIRES. THEY'LL REMEMBER TO SIGNAL THE NEXT TIME!
THAT'S A REALLY GOOD IDEA, AARON.
ACID
I'LL CALL THE COUNTY OFFICE OF--
SPLASH
A.C.! NO! DON'T!
NOT AGAIN!

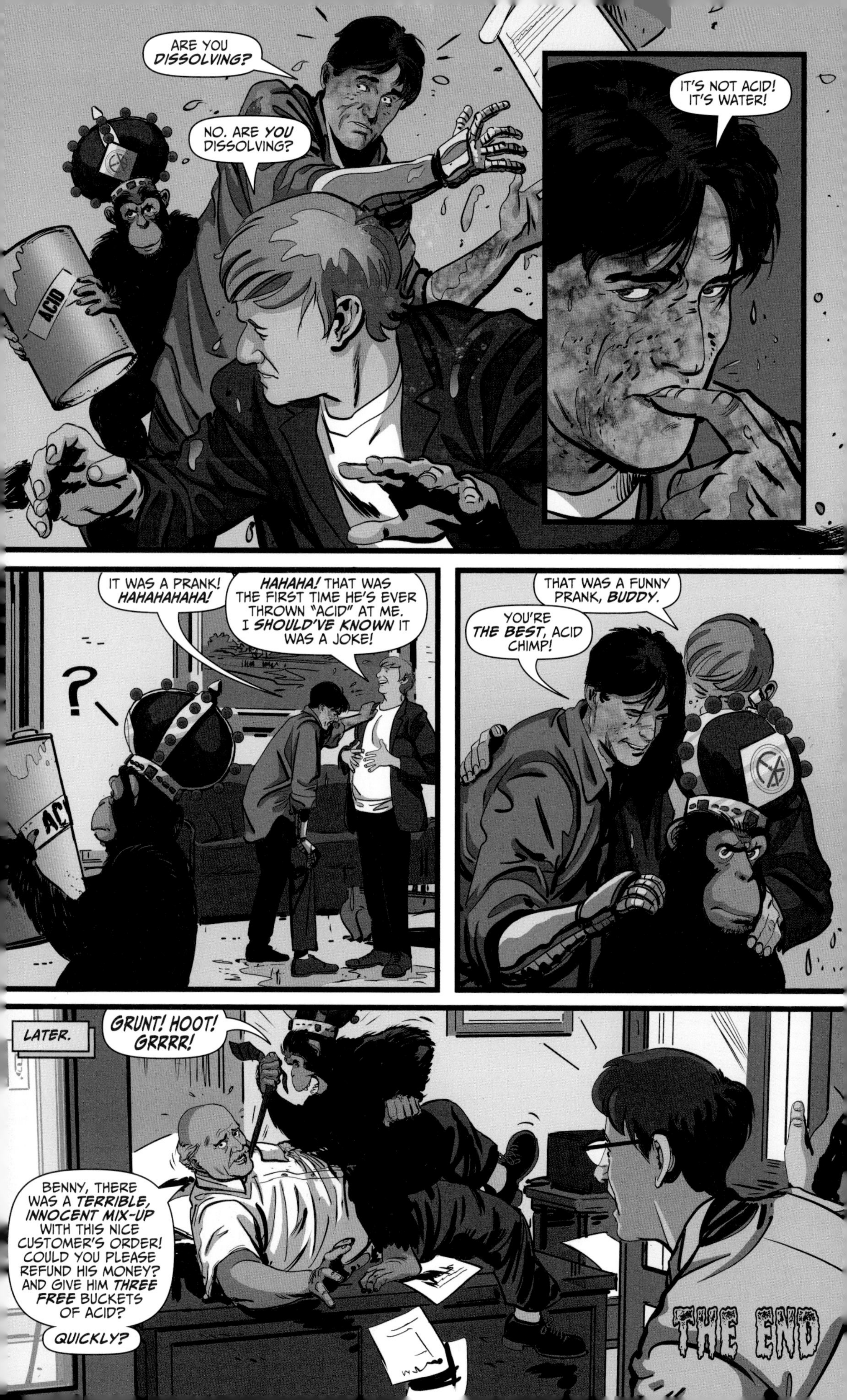
ARE YOU DISSOLVING?
NO. ARE YOU DISSOLVING?
ACID
IT'S NOT ACID! IT'S WATER!
IT WAS A PRANK! HAHAHAHAHA!
HAHAHA! THAT WAS THE FIRST TIME HE'S EVER THROWN "ACID" AT ME. I SHOULD'VE KNOWN IT WAS A JOKE!
?
THAT WAS A FUNNY PRANK, BUDDY.
YOU'RE THE BEST, ACID CHIMP!
LATER.
GRUNT! HOOT! GRRRR!
BENNY, THERE WAS A TERRIBLE, INNOCENT MIX-UP WITH THIS NICE CUSTOMER'S ORDER! COULD YOU PLEASE REFUND HIS MONEY? AND GIVE HIM THREE FREE BUCKETS OF ACID?
QUICKLY?
THE END

BAD WORDS

Welcome, valued reader. It's Bouncing Baby Bryce here with another installment of your thoughtful letters and my respectful responses. Right off the top let me say that, over the last few months, my behavior here in the Bad Words column has been a bit erratic. Frankly, I'd let the massive, worldwide success of MY BAD go to my head. Let me tell you, friends, it's hard to keep your feet on the ground when you're regularly hobnobbing with Hollywood superstars like Kevin Spacey and Lori Loughlin. Yes, MY BAD has opened a lot of doors for me. But that's no excuse for acting like a rude jerk. That's on me. My bad.

I had a lot of time to think over the two days Mark and I were imprisoned in an electrified cage by that serial killer who wanted to cut off our ears and use them to start some sort of dark magic apocalypse. I'm sure you're tired of hearing about it. It seemed like it was all the networks could talk about that week! (BTW, I think that Maxwell guy who wrote into Bad Words last month saying he wanted our ears might be the same guy who kidnapped us.) Anyway, while we were waiting for the FBI to rescue us, I vowed to be a better Bryce. No more rudeness! I will behave like a gentleman at all times. No exceptions. That's the Bouncing Baby Bryce Pledge!

Let's see what you wonderful readers have to say this month.

Bryce and Mark,

Your comic book is not believable. It's some fake-ass fake shit. The Chandelier is definitely not a real person. And Drixon Fried Chicken doesn't exist either! Not one person I know has even heard of DFC. How stupid do you think I am? Nice try, assholes.

Brent
Chico, CA

Wow. This is harder than I thought. It's not easy being a gentleman when someone calls you an asshole. I'd better quickly move on to the next email.

***

MARK, PETER, KELLY, ROB & bryce,

I love MY BAD. It's the best new comic book in years. MARK, your scripts sparkle with wit and thoughtful humanism. PETER, your renderings are ridiculously expressive and imaginative. And, KELLY, your exquisite colors forge a bold but welcome harmony with those renderings! But let's not forget ROB; ROB provides some of the finest, most innovative lettering I've ever laid eyes upon. Kudos to MARK, PETER, KELLY and ROB! TOM and HART too!

What's it like to work with all these talented people, bryce?

Marjorie
Pierre, SD

Marjorie, I feel like you are purposefully trying to get me to break my pledge with this one. But I will meet your cruelty with love, Marjorie! I will meet your cruelty with love.

Thank you for reading and enjoying MY BAD. It's a wonderful experience working with all those talented people. Have a beautiful day, Marjorie. Drop by Bad Words anytime. See? I'm a gentleman!

***

Humans,

I am an alien. I live in outer space.

I know how to do three skateboard tricks.

Alien
Outer Space

It's so good to hear from you each month, Alien. The first two letters today were... challenging, and your delightful words are the perfect tonic. Not one. Not two. But "three skateboard tricks"! Amazing. Alien, you are truly a fascinating fellow.

Tom Peyer warned me not to do this again, but I think he'll understand considering the circumstances. Alien, you are now a three-time "Bad Words Letter of the Month" award winner! Thank you for everything you do.

***

Bouncing Baby Bryce,

My name is Paul. I am an actor. I've been performing the popular role of "Alien" in this letter column for the past three months. I presented myself to Bad Words as "Alien" for two reasons. First, I wanted the world to see how brilliant I am at acting. I think that went rather well, didn't it? And second, I wanted to prove to everyone that Bouncing Baby Bryce is as dumb as a bucket of spit.

And I think that went rather well too, didn't it?

Paul
Outer Space

My heart doesn't want to believe you, Paul. But your address is the same as "Alien" so my head tells me what you're saying must be true. You have wrecked me, Paul. I have never felt so low. So hopeless. The power of your masterful acting has left me broken and teetering on the edge of despair. But I will keep my pledge, Paul! I will remain a gentleman! You won't take that from me, Paul. Even if you have taken everything else I hold dear in this cold, dark world...

***

Okay. Best to move on. Let's try another email.

Bryce and Mark,

You guys are brilliant writers. Especially you, Bryce!

I love carrots. I was wondering - does Emperor King like carrots?

Tina
New York City, NY

Stop attacking me! I hate you, Tina! I hate you so much! I hope you die, Tina! I hope you die and rot!

Shit. Now that I've taken a breath and reread your email, I'm starting to wonder if you actually deserved that response, Tina. I may have overreacted a bit. If I offended you, please accept my apology. I used to be a rude person, but that's not who I am anymore.

Okay, that's enough for me this month. It's time for another enlightening edition of Tom's Toolbox!

TOM'S TOOLBOX!

Aloha, AHOYdom assembled! Timeless Tom here, typin' atcha from the Red Roof Inn Guest Lounge on sunny Waikiki Beach!

Y'know, it's a darn good thing some anonymous mega-genius invented portable typewriters, or I'd never be able to get the ol' Toolbox out to you, my peerless public, promptly! What with all the writing, editing, speaking, traveling, voiceovers, cameos, and mixed-up modeling our pushy publisher expects of me, it's a wonder my ticker's still ticking! Half the time I don't even know what day it is, and my autograph-signing hand is developing a truly terrifying tremor!

But don't cry for me, AHOYniks! My life is great! I mean it! There's nothing like galivanting around this gorgeous globe to rub elbows with you rollickin' readers—as if our dynamic dramazines weren't a big enough bargain for your money, and we somehow owe you my body and soul on top of it! Anyway, I gotta go; the bartender finally decided to show up! It's like nobody wants to work anymore! Sheesh!

Occupare omnes terras,

Tom

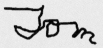

COMING AHOY-TRACTIONS

EDGAR ALLAN POE'S SNIFTER OF DEATH #5—Obsession, guilt, murder, and drugs: it's just another day in Poe's snifter! Stories by Kirk Vanderbeek, art by Jon Proctor and Shane Oakley, cover by Richard Williams! ***February 23!***

THE WRONG EARTH: TRAPPED ON TEEN PLANET #1—Gritty Dragonfly is whisked to a planet of typical teens in this extra-sized one-shot by writer Gail Simone and artists Bill Morrison, Walter Geovani, and Rob Lean! Covers by Jamal Igle, Dan Parent, and Gene Ha! ***March 2!***

SNELSON: COMEDY IS DYING Collected Edition—A formerly edgy, past-his-prime standup comic flirts with some ugly ways of prolonging his career in this satire of white male entitlement and so-called "cancel culture." "The best satire in America is between these covers. So dark, so rich, and so beautifully, eerily rendered."—David Sedaris. ***March 16!***

NEXT: The livin' ending of the beginning of the important new superhero universe! ***February 16!***

—Bryce

Write to MY BAD—or any AHOY Rockin' Pop Litform—at letters@comicsahoy.com. Snail mail: PO Box 189, DeWitt, NY 13214. Mark "OK to print" if it is.

AND! Subscribe to the free, funny-as-anything AHOY Newsletter at bit.ly/newsahoy.

DRAW ME   DRAW ME

HEY KIDS! DO YOU HAVE WHAT IT TAKES TO BE A *REAL LIFE* COMIC BOOK ARTIST?

CAN YOU DRAW ON COMMAND? ARE YOU GOOD WITH DEADLINES? ARE YOU NOT OVERLY ATTACHED TO WEEKENDS?

TURTLE PIRATE THE RECKONING

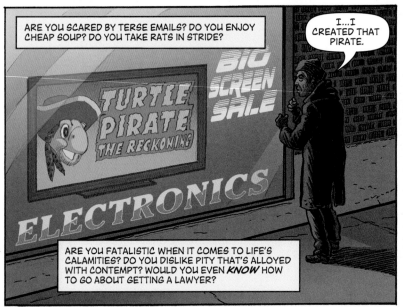

ARE YOU SCARED BY TERSE EMAILS? DO YOU ENJOY CHEAP SOUP? DO YOU TAKE RATS IN STRIDE?

BIG SCREEN SALE

TURTLE PIRATE THE RECKONING

ELECTRONICS

I...I CREATED THAT PIRATE.

ARE YOU FATALISTIC WHEN IT COMES TO LIFE'S CALAMITIES? DO YOU DISLIKE PITY THAT'S ALLOYED WITH CONTEMPT? WOULD YOU EVEN *KNOW* HOW TO GO ABOUT GETTING A LAWYER?

I CREATED THAT PIRATE!

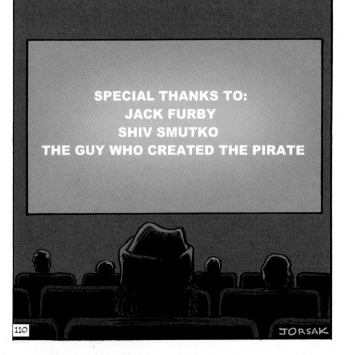

SPECIAL THANKS TO:
JACK FURBY
SHIV SMUTKO
THE GUY WHO CREATED THE PIRATE

NICE!

THEN TAKE THIS TEST TODAY! YOUR FUTURE AWAITS.

110

JORSAK

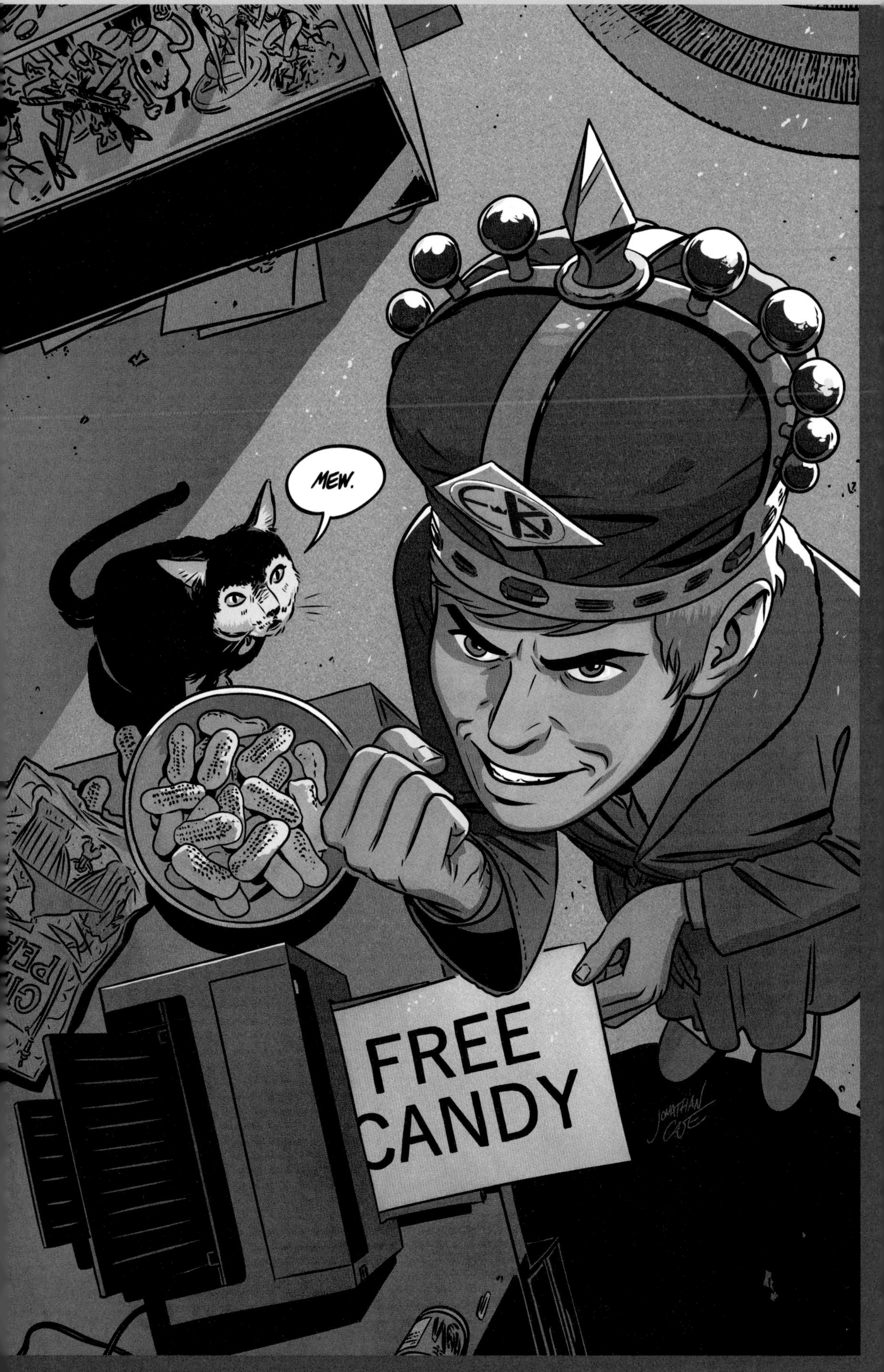
MEW.
FREE CANDY
JONATHAN CASE

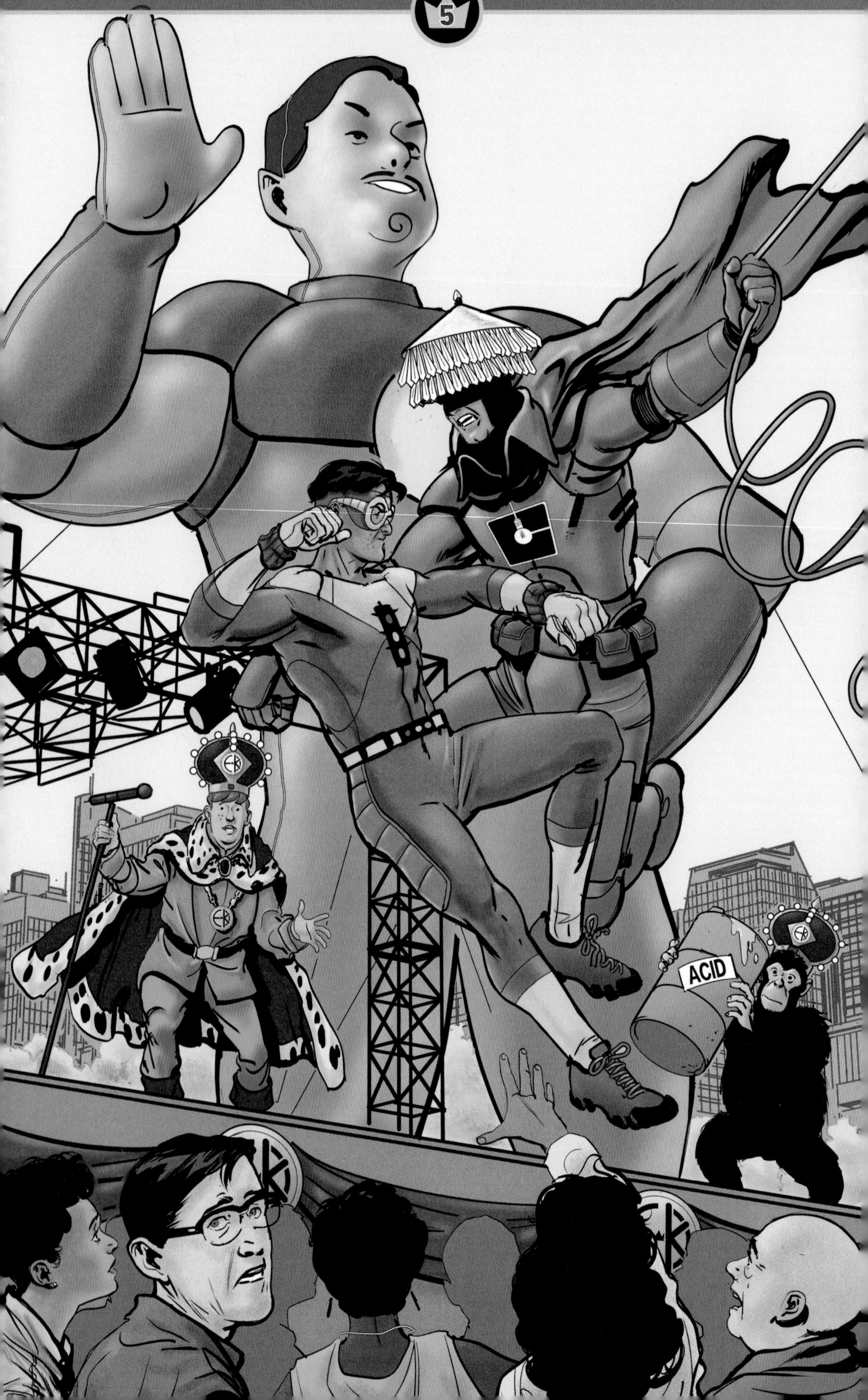
ACID

AN IMPORTANT WARNING

APPROVED BY THE COMICS CODE AUTHORITY®

Comics will ruin your life. Well, "ruin" is a strong word. Nothing ever really ruins your life so much as it unlocks something already deeply toxic within you and ***that*** ruins your life. But you get what I'm saying. You might think bringing some "hot flips" to school will help you fit in with the other outcasts or, at the very least, provide you with some solace in an otherwise sullen existence. But, in reality, comics are just one more force of emotional manipulation competing for your limited attention and even more limited money. To comics, you are just a thirsty man wandering deeper into the desert, not realizing those you meet along the way smile at you only because they know you're a dead man whose possessions will soon be theirs. And, I mean, the stories aren't even usually that good. Most of them were written by some middle-aged man hunched over a laptop, squeezing a living from it like the last drop of toothpaste from a spent tube, who nonetheless works seven days a week making fictional characters say and do things in lieu of producing actual children. Comics certainly didn't do ***his*** life any favors, did it?

Even more tragic is when one of these human parachute failures gets it into their head to create some ***art***, to try and say something meaningful about the world, like a clown riding a tiny bicycle. Imagine, just imagine, the sheer existential horror of an editor telling them they can put everything they've ever had to say about life into a comic book so long as it doesn't interfere with the drawing of someone getting punched out by a guy in an animal-themed sex mask. I mean, at least in my day comics were ***filthy***. This is just sad more than anything.

Look, I'm sure you're a decent person and all, I just think there are better things you could be doing with your time than reading comics. At any rate, you've been warned.

"WALK UPON THYSELF AS A PATH, FOR THEN YOU SHALL NEVER BE LOST."

-SILVANUS

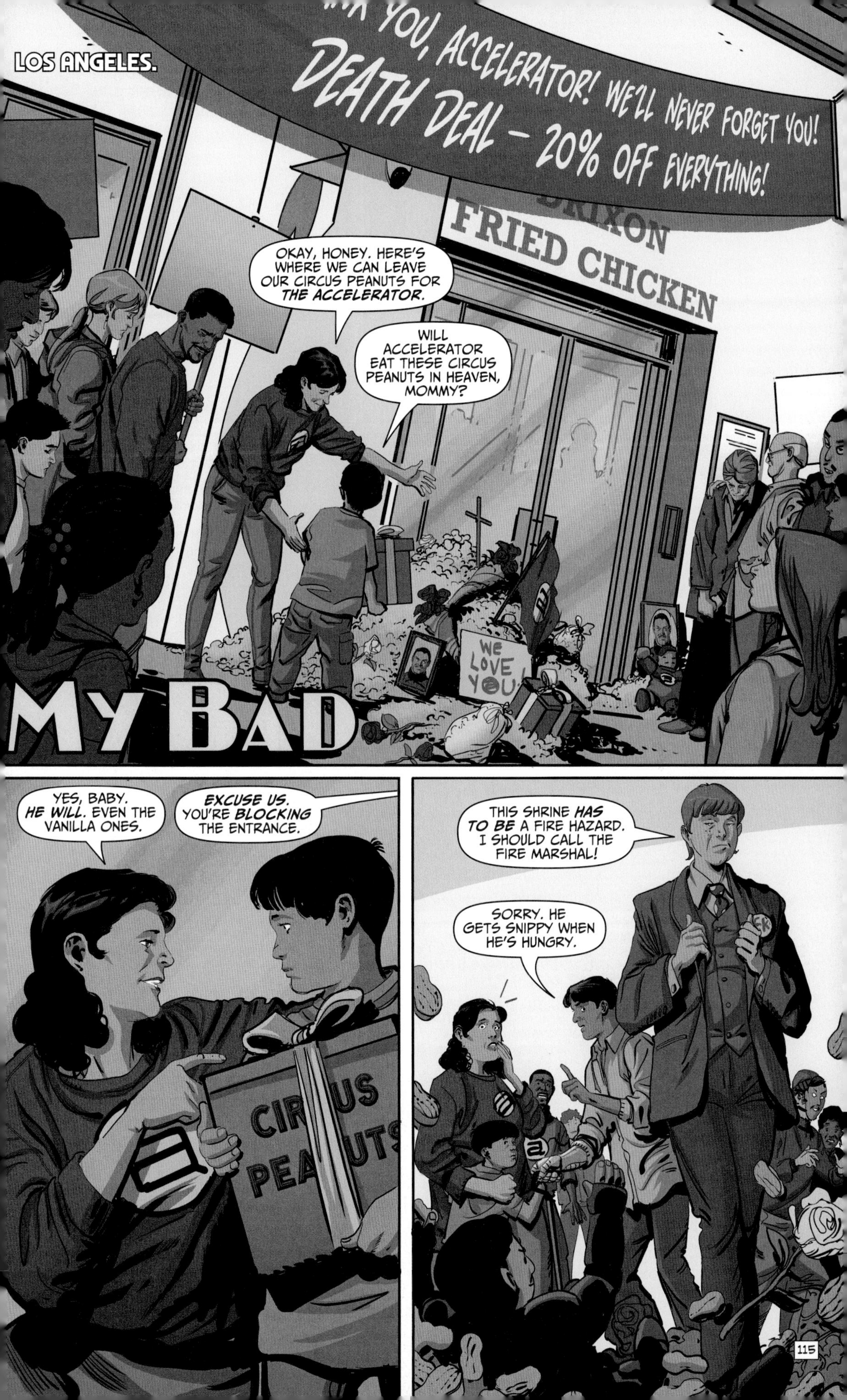

LOS ANGELES.
YOU, ACCELERATOR! WE'LL NEVER FORGET YOU!
DEATH DEAL — 20% OFF EVERYTHING!
FRIED CHICKEN
OKAY, HONEY. HERE'S WHERE WE CAN LEAVE OUR CIRCUS PEANUTS FOR *THE ACCELERATOR*.
WILL ACCELERATOR EAT THESE CIRCUS PEANUTS IN HEAVEN, MOMMY?
WE LOVE YOU
MY BAD
YES, BABY. *HE WILL*. EVEN THE VANILLA ONES.
EXCUSE US. YOU'RE *BLOCKING* THE ENTRANCE.
THIS SHRINE *HAS TO BE* A FIRE HAZARD. I SHOULD CALL THE FIRE MARSHAL!
SORRY. HE GETS SNIPPY WHEN HE'S HUNGRY.

I UNDERSTAND. THE ACCELERATOR WAS A POPULAR GUY. BUT HE DIED ON SUNDAY. IT'S TUESDAY NOW!!! IT'S BEEN *TWO DAYS*. WHAT ARE THEY STILL DOING HERE?

MOVE ON WITH YOUR LIVES, RABBLE!!

I'M EMPEROR KING! HE'S RUSH HOUR! WE WERE JUST ON *NOW TONITE!*

NO ONE CARES. IS ANYONE EVEN GOING TO SHOW UP DOWNTOWN FOR OUR BIG ANNOUNCEMENT? THE ACCELERATOR'S DEAD AND HE'S *STILL MORE POPULAR* THAN US! IT'S NOT FAIR!

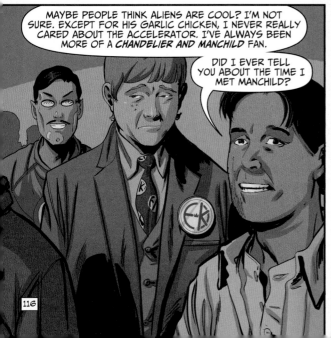

MAYBE PEOPLE THINK ALIENS ARE COOL? I'M NOT SURE. EXCEPT FOR HIS GARLIC CHICKEN, I NEVER REALLY CARED ABOUT THE ACCELERATOR. I'VE ALWAYS BEEN MORE OF A *CHANDELIER AND MANCHILD* FAN.

DID I EVER TELL YOU ABOUT THE TIME I MET MANCHILD?

WHAT?! HOLD ON. A *CHANDELIER FAN?!* YOU'RE KIDDING, RIGHT?

116

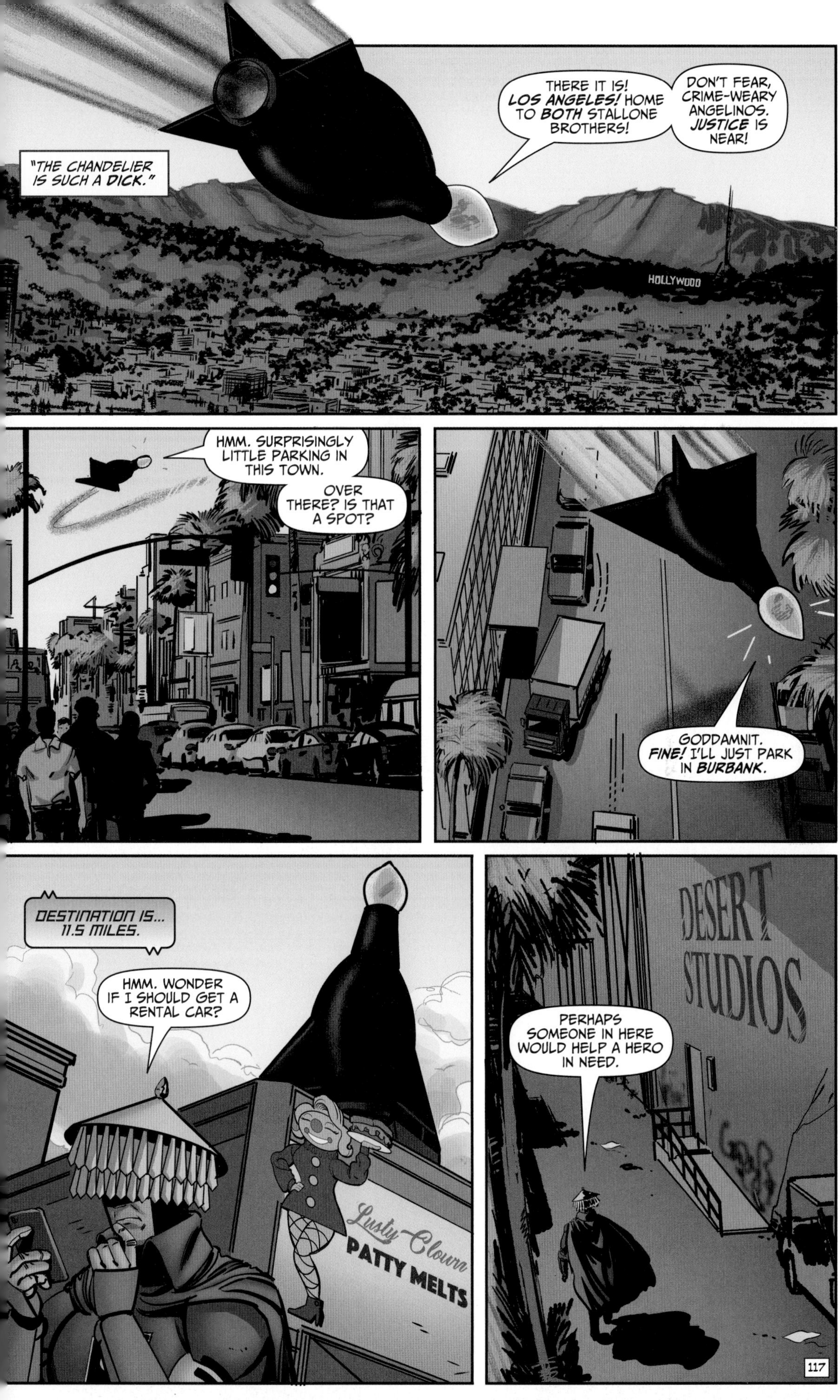
"THE CHANDELIER IS SUCH A DICK."
THERE IT IS! LOS ANGELES! HOME TO BOTH STALLONE BROTHERS!
DON'T FEAR, CRIME-WEARY ANGELINOS. JUSTICE IS NEAR!
HOLLYWOOD
HMM. SURPRISINGLY LITTLE PARKING IN THIS TOWN.
OVER THERE? IS THAT A SPOT?
GODDAMNIT. FINE! I'LL JUST PARK IN BURBANK.
DESTINATION IS... 11.5 MILES.
HMM. WONDER IF I SHOULD GET A RENTAL CAR?
Lusty Clown
PATTY MELTS
DESERT STUDIOS
PERHAPS SOMEONE IN HERE WOULD HELP A HERO IN NEED.

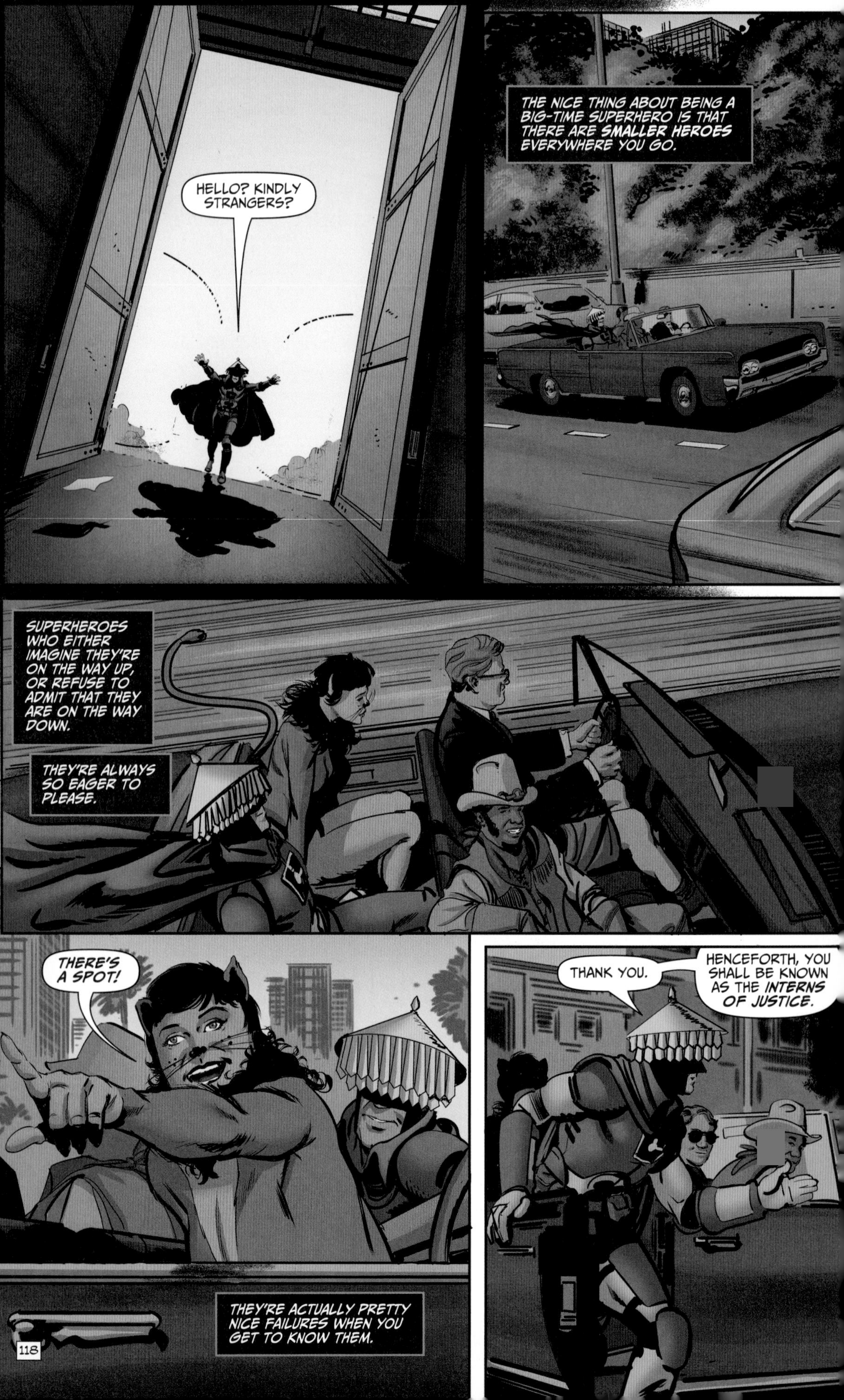
HELLO? KINDLY STRANGERS?
THE NICE THING ABOUT BEING A BIG-TIME SUPERHERO IS THAT THERE ARE SMALLER HEROES EVERYWHERE YOU GO.
SUPERHEROES WHO EITHER IMAGINE THEY'RE ON THE WAY UP, OR REFUSE TO ADMIT THAT THEY ARE ON THE WAY DOWN.
THEY'RE ALWAYS SO EAGER TO PLEASE.
THERE'S A SPOT!
THEY'RE ACTUALLY PRETTY NICE FAILURES WHEN YOU GET TO KNOW THEM.
THANK YOU.
HENCEFORTH, YOU SHALL BE KNOWN AS THE INTERNS OF JUSTICE.

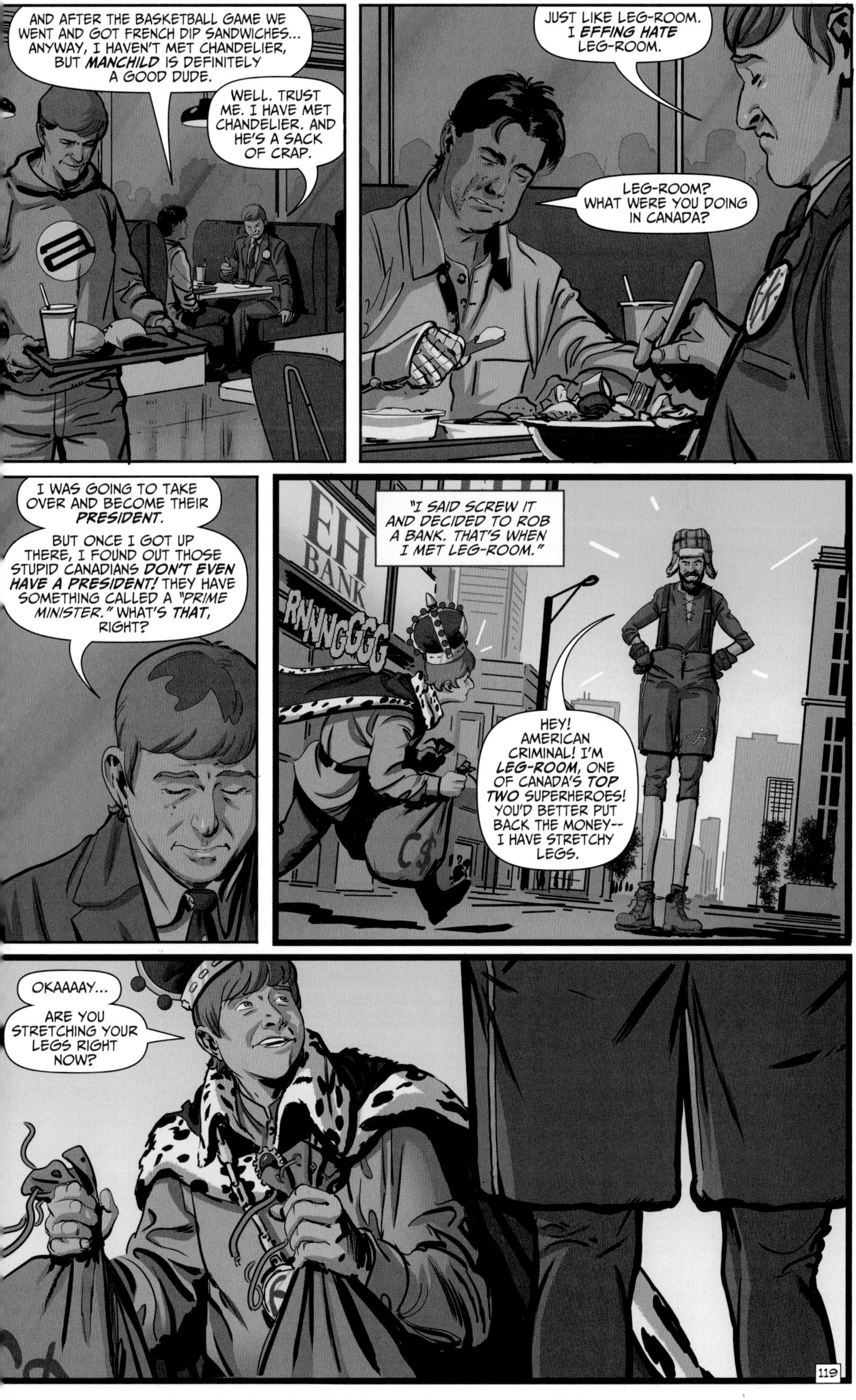
AND AFTER THE BASKETBALL GAME WE WENT AND GOT FRENCH DIP SANDWICHES... ANYWAY, I HAVEN'T MET CHANDELIER, BUT MANCHILD IS DEFINITELY A GOOD DUDE.
WELL. TRUST ME. I HAVE MET CHANDELIER. AND HE'S A SACK OF CRAP.
JUST LIKE LEG-ROOM. I EFFING HATE LEG-ROOM.
LEG-ROOM? WHAT WERE YOU DOING IN CANADA?
I WAS GOING TO TAKE OVER AND BECOME THEIR PRESIDENT.
BUT ONCE I GOT UP THERE, I FOUND OUT THOSE STUPID CANADIANS DON'T EVEN HAVE A PRESIDENT! THEY HAVE SOMETHING CALLED A "PRIME MINISTER." WHAT'S THAT, RIGHT?
"I SAID SCREW IT AND DECIDED TO ROB A BANK. THAT'S WHEN I MET LEG-ROOM."
EH BANK
RNNNGGGG
C$
HEY! AMERICAN CRIMINAL! I'M LEG-ROOM, ONE OF CANADA'S TOP TWO SUPERHEROES! YOU'D BETTER PUT BACK THE MONEY-- I HAVE STRETCHY LEGS.
OKAAAAY...
ARE YOU STRETCHING YOUR LEGS RIGHT NOW?

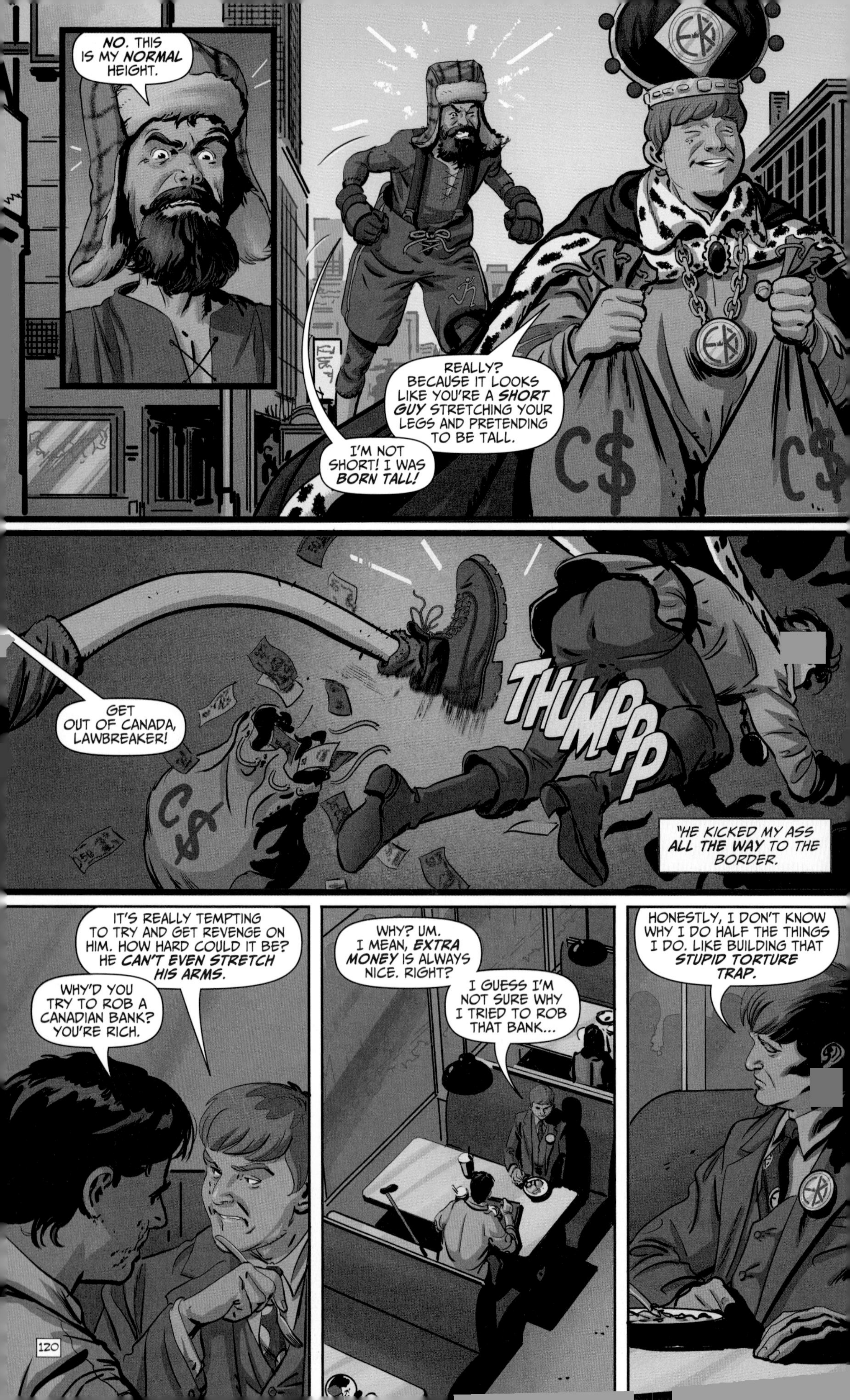
NO. THIS IS MY NORMAL HEIGHT.
REALLY? BECAUSE IT LOOKS LIKE YOU'RE A SHORT GUY STRETCHING YOUR LEGS AND PRETENDING TO BE TALL.
I'M NOT SHORT! I WAS BORN TALL!
GET OUT OF CANADA, LAWBREAKER!
THUMPPP
"HE KICKED MY ASS ALL THE WAY TO THE BORDER.
IT'S REALLY TEMPTING TO TRY AND GET REVENGE ON HIM. HOW HARD COULD IT BE? HE CAN'T EVEN STRETCH HIS ARMS.
WHY'D YOU TRY TO ROB A CANADIAN BANK? YOU'RE RICH.
WHY? UM. I MEAN, EXTRA MONEY IS ALWAYS NICE. RIGHT?
I GUESS I'M NOT SURE WHY I TRIED TO ROB THAT BANK...
HONESTLY, I DON'T KNOW WHY I DO HALF THE THINGS I DO. LIKE BUILDING THAT STUPID TORTURE TRAP.

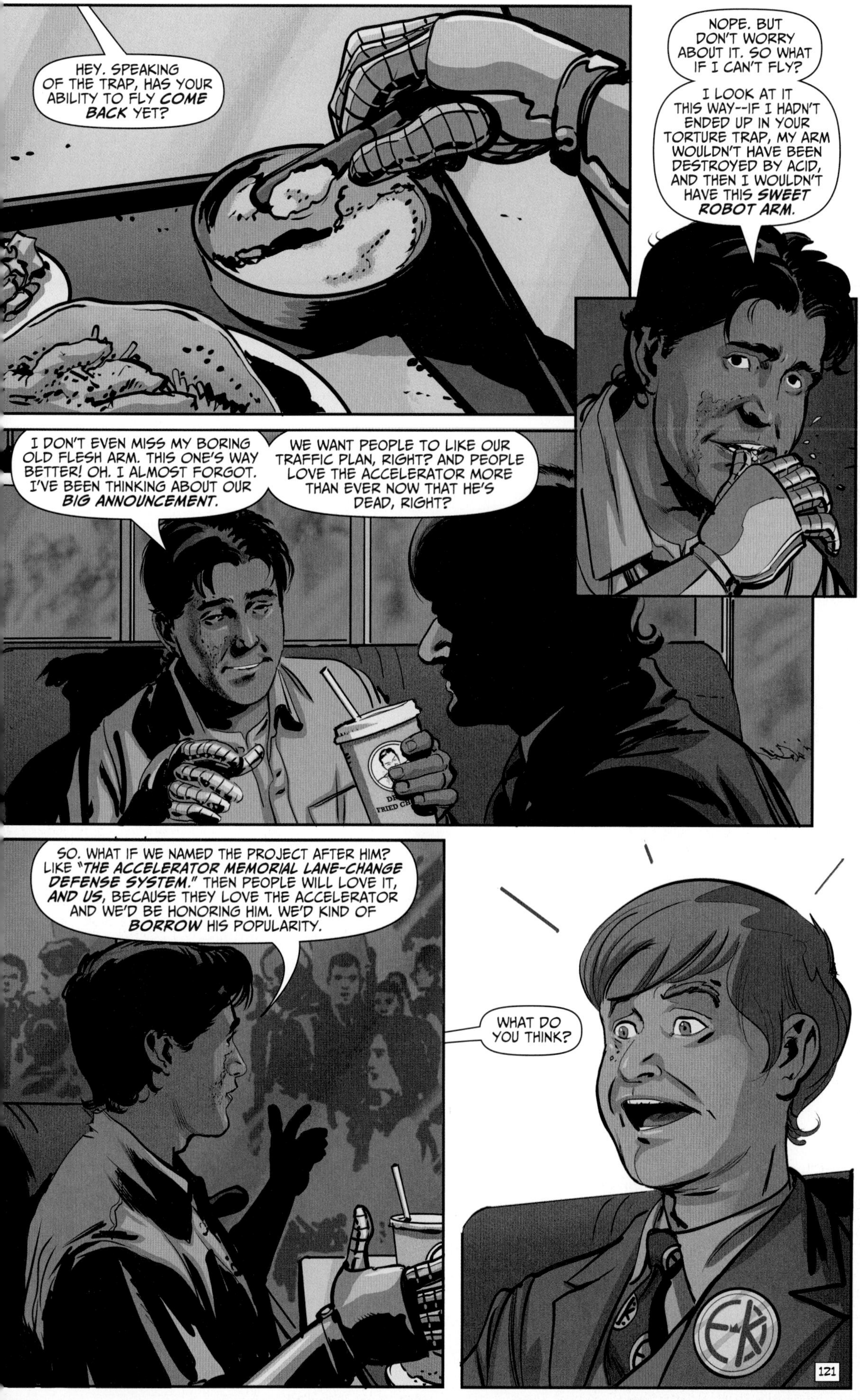
HEY. SPEAKING OF THE TRAP, HAS YOUR ABILITY TO FLY *COME BACK* YET?
NOPE. BUT DON'T WORRY ABOUT IT. SO WHAT IF I CAN'T FLY?
I LOOK AT IT THIS WAY--IF I HADN'T ENDED UP IN YOUR TORTURE TRAP, MY ARM WOULDN'T HAVE BEEN DESTROYED BY ACID, AND THEN I WOULDN'T HAVE THIS *SWEET ROBOT ARM*.
I DON'T EVEN MISS MY BORING OLD FLESH ARM. THIS ONE'S WAY BETTER! OH. I ALMOST FORGOT. I'VE BEEN THINKING ABOUT OUR *BIG ANNOUNCEMENT*.
WE WANT PEOPLE TO LIKE OUR TRAFFIC PLAN, RIGHT? AND PEOPLE LOVE THE ACCELERATOR MORE THAN EVER NOW THAT HE'S DEAD, RIGHT?
SO. WHAT IF WE NAMED THE PROJECT AFTER HIM? LIKE "*THE ACCELERATOR MEMORIAL LANE-CHANGE DEFENSE SYSTEM*." THEN PEOPLE WILL LOVE IT, *AND US*, BECAUSE THEY LOVE THE ACCELERATOR AND WE'D BE HONORING HIM. WE'D KIND OF *BORROW* HIS POPULARITY.
WHAT DO YOU THINK?

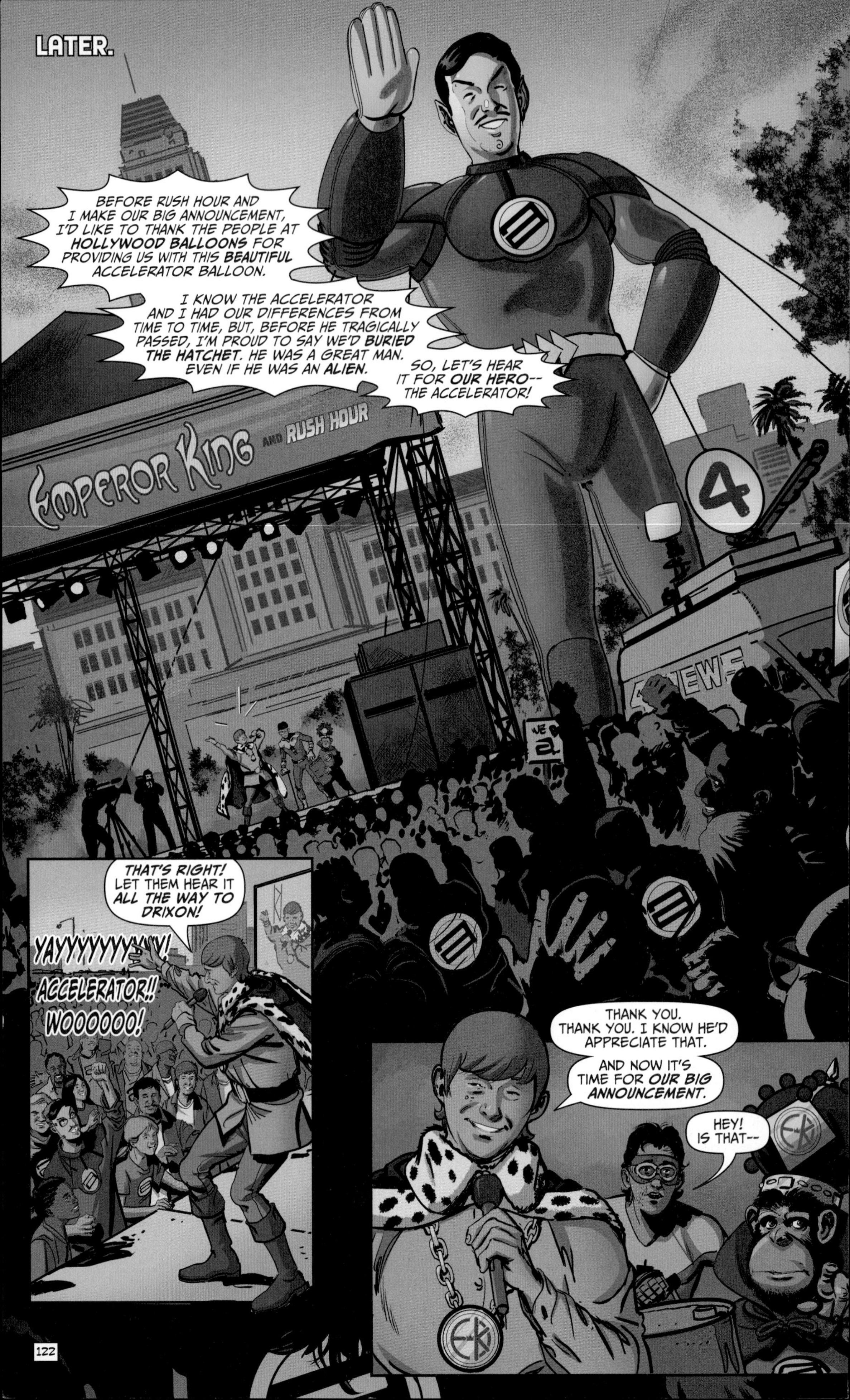
LATER.
BEFORE RUSH HOUR AND I MAKE OUR BIG ANNOUNCEMENT, I'D LIKE TO THANK THE PEOPLE AT **HOLLYWOOD BALLOONS** FOR PROVIDING US WITH THIS **BEAUTIFUL** ACCELERATOR BALLOON.
I KNOW THE ACCELERATOR AND I HAD OUR DIFFERENCES FROM TIME TO TIME, BUT, BEFORE HE TRAGICALLY PASSED, I'M PROUD TO SAY WE'D **BURIED THE HATCHET**. HE WAS A GREAT MAN. EVEN IF HE WAS AN **ALIEN**.
SO, LET'S HEAR IT FOR **OUR HERO**-- THE ACCELERATOR!
EMPEROR KING AND RUSH HOUR
4
NEWS
THAT'S RIGHT! LET THEM HEAR IT ***ALL THE WAY TO DRIXON!***
YAYYYYYYYYY!
ACCELERATOR!!
WOOOOOO!
THANK YOU. THANK YOU. I KNOW HE'D APPRECIATE THAT.
AND NOW IT'S TIME FOR ***OUR BIG ANNOUNCEMENT.***
HEY! IS THAT--

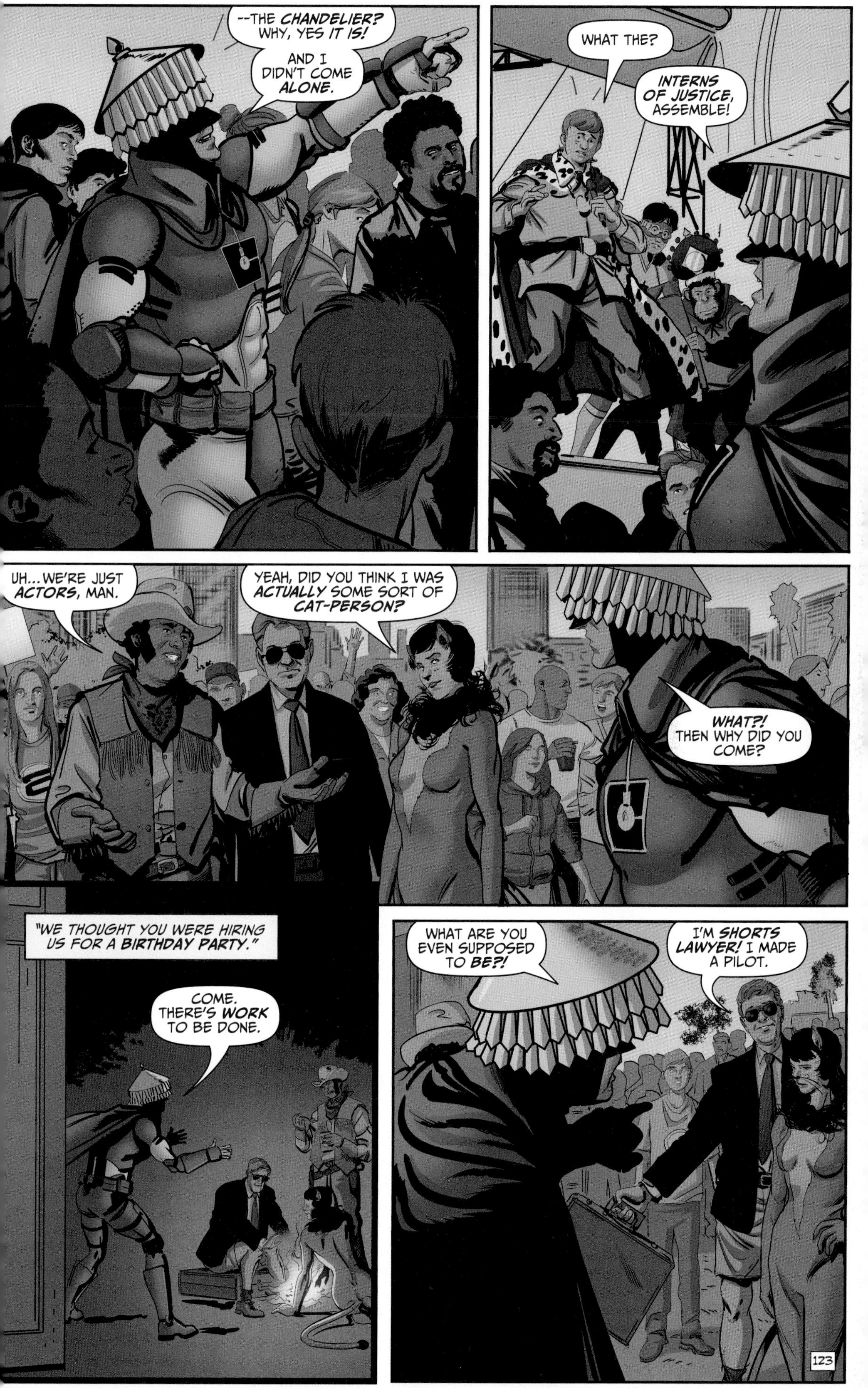
--THE CHANDELIER? WHY, YES IT IS!
AND I DIDN'T COME ALONE.
WHAT THE?
INTERNS OF JUSTICE, ASSEMBLE!
UH...WE'RE JUST ACTORS, MAN.
YEAH, DID YOU THINK I WAS ACTUALLY SOME SORT OF CAT-PERSON?
WHAT?! THEN WHY DID YOU COME?
"WE THOUGHT YOU WERE HIRING US FOR A BIRTHDAY PARTY."
COME. THERE'S WORK TO BE DONE.
WHAT ARE YOU EVEN SUPPOSED TO BE?!
I'M SHORTS LAWYER! I MADE A PILOT.

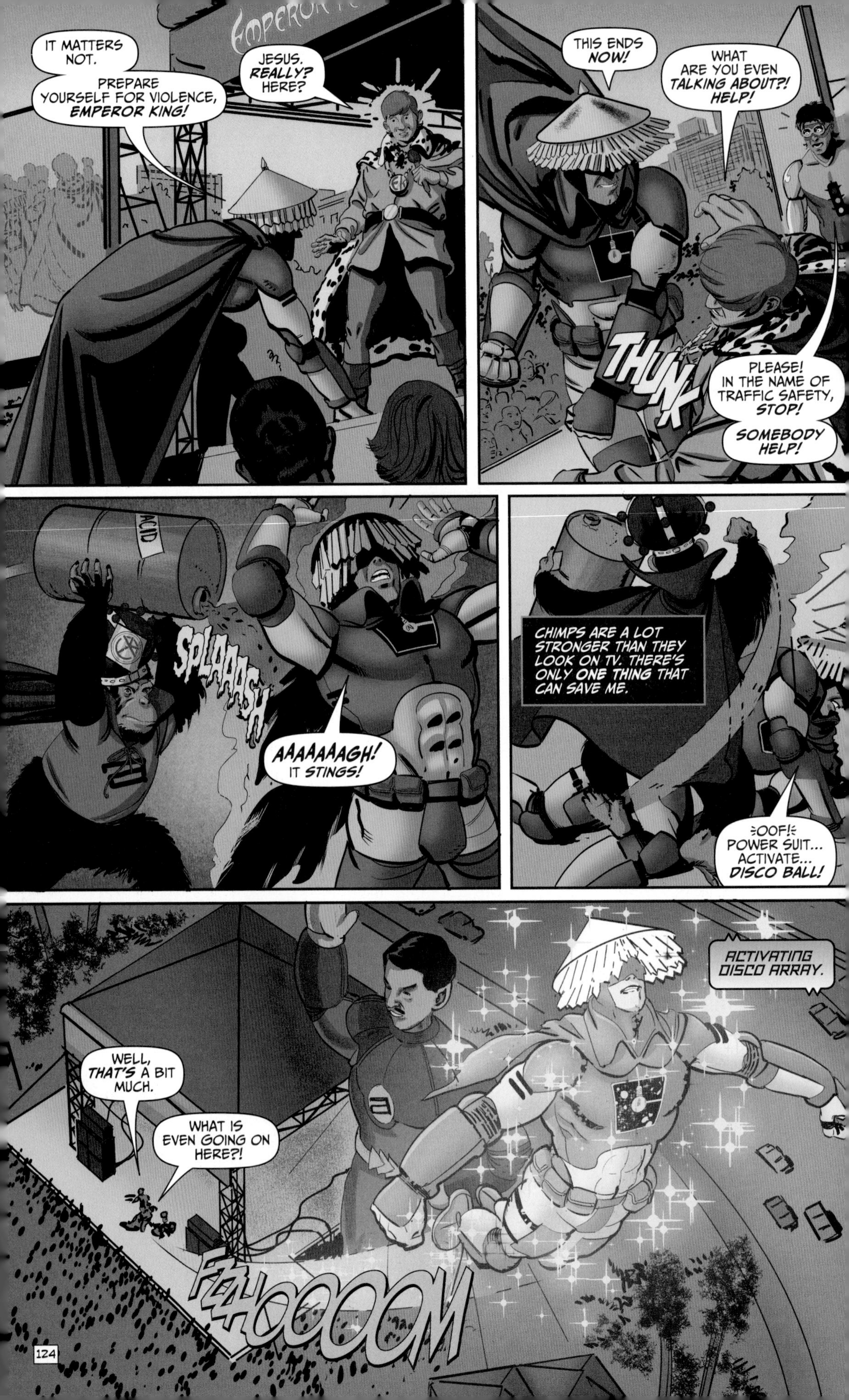
EMPEROR
IT MATTERS NOT.
PREPARE YOURSELF FOR VIOLENCE, EMPEROR KING!
JESUS. REALLY? HERE?
THIS ENDS NOW!
WHAT ARE YOU EVEN TALKING ABOUT?! HELP!
THUNK
PLEASE! IN THE NAME OF TRAFFIC SAFETY, STOP!
SOMEBODY HELP!
ACID
SPLAAASH
AAAAAAGH! IT STINGS!
CHIMPS ARE A LOT STRONGER THAN THEY LOOK ON TV. THERE'S ONLY ONE THING THAT CAN SAVE ME.
OOF! POWER SUIT... ACTIVATE... DISCO BALL!
ACTIVATING DISCO ARRAY.
WELL, THAT'S A BIT MUCH.
WHAT IS EVEN GOING ON HERE?!
FZZHOOOOM

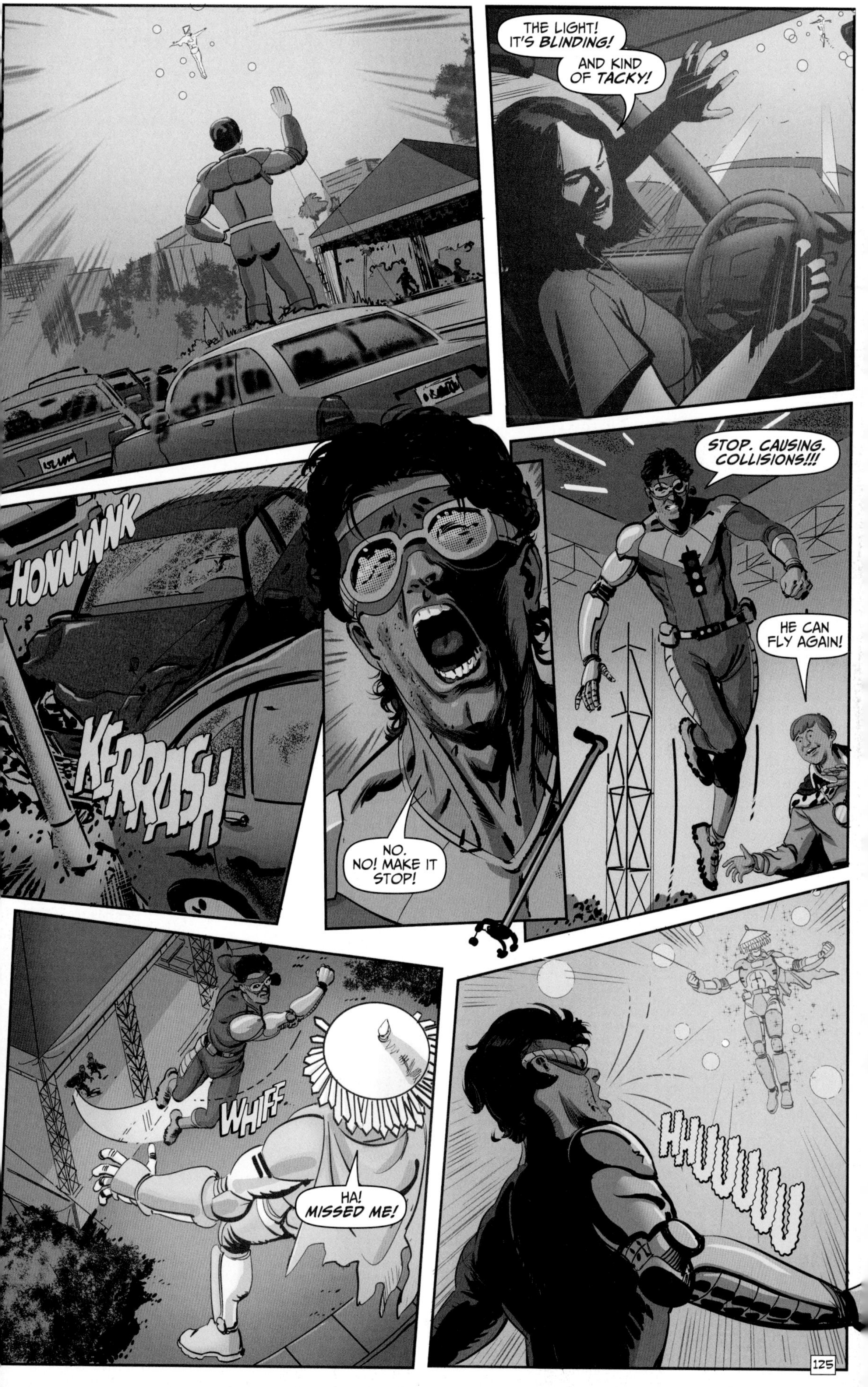

THE LIGHT! IT'S *BLINDING!*
AND KIND OF *TACKY!*
HONNNNNK
KERRASH
NO. NO! MAKE IT STOP!
STOP. CAUSING. COLLISIONS!!!
HE CAN FLY AGAIN!
WHIFF
HA! *MISSED ME!*
HHUUUUUU

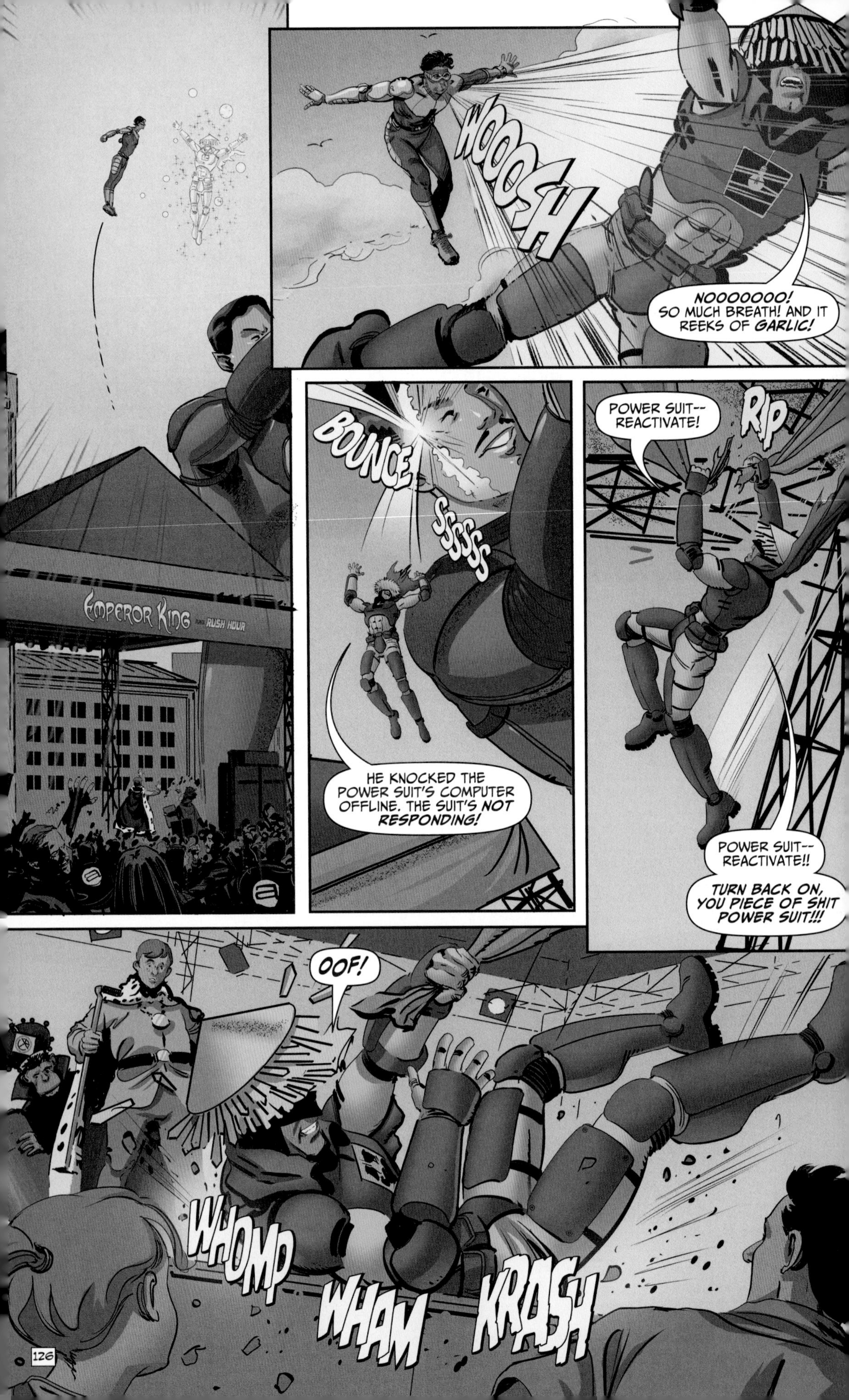
WOOOSH
NOOOOOOO! SO MUCH BREATH! AND IT REEKS OF GARLIC!
EMPEROR KING
RUSH HOUR
BOUNCE
SSSSS
HE KNOCKED THE POWER SUIT'S COMPUTER OFFLINE. THE SUIT'S NOT RESPONDING!
POWER SUIT-- REACTIVATE!
RIP
POWER SUIT-- REACTIVATE!!
TURN BACK ON, YOU PIECE OF SHIT POWER SUIT!!!
OOF!
WHOMP
WHAM
KRASH

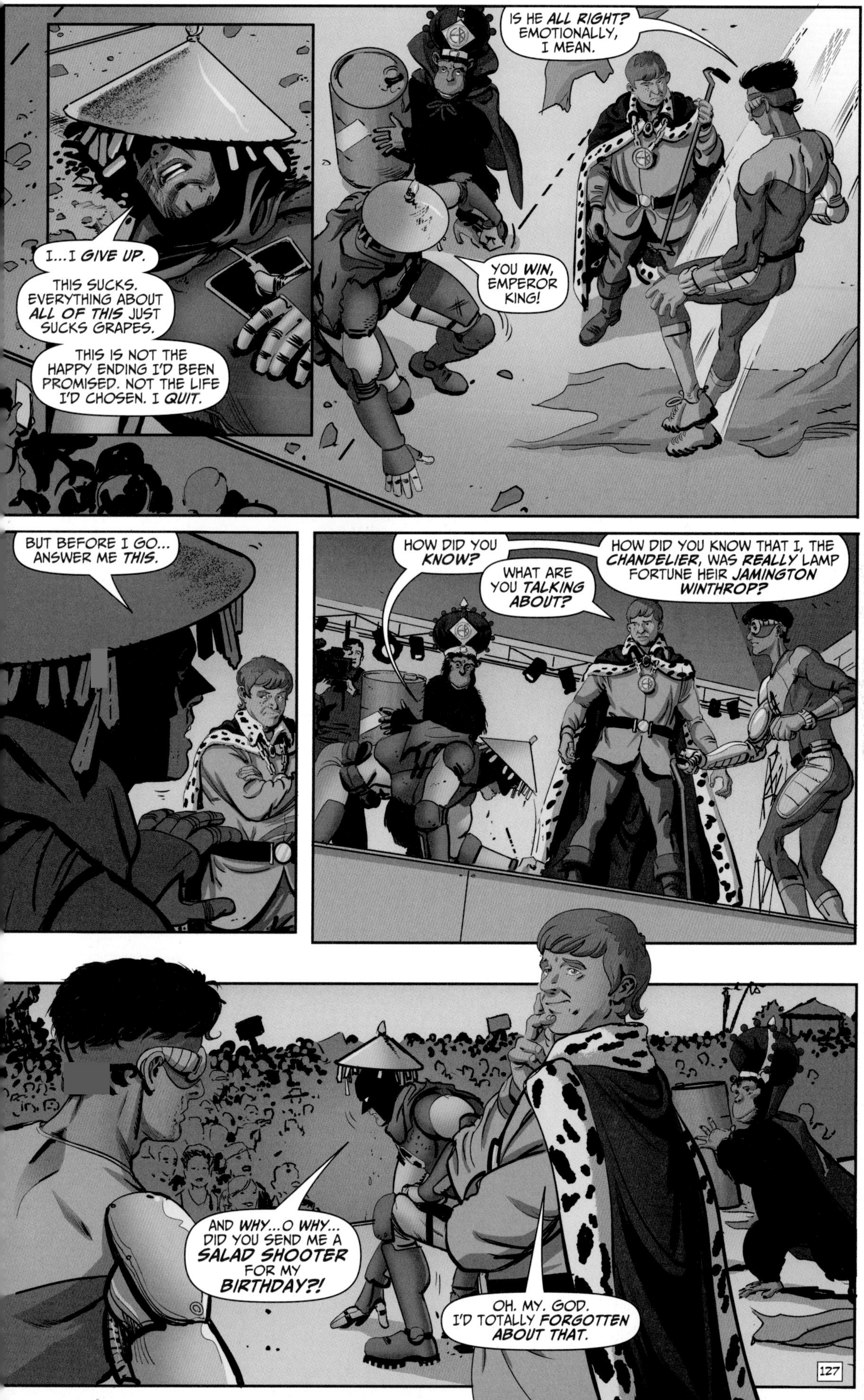
I...I *GIVE UP*.
THIS SUCKS. EVERYTHING ABOUT *ALL OF THIS* JUST SUCKS GRAPES.
THIS IS NOT THE HAPPY ENDING I'D BEEN PROMISED. NOT THE LIFE I'D CHOSEN. I *QUIT*.
IS HE *ALL RIGHT?* EMOTIONALLY, I MEAN.
YOU *WIN*, EMPEROR KING!
BUT BEFORE I GO... ANSWER ME *THIS*.
HOW DID YOU *KNOW?*
WHAT ARE YOU *TALKING ABOUT?*
HOW DID YOU KNOW THAT I, THE *CHANDELIER*, WAS *REALLY* LAMP FORTUNE HEIR *JAMINGTON WINTHROP?*
AND *WHY*...O *WHY*... DID YOU SEND ME A *SALAD SHOOTER* FOR MY *BIRTHDAY?!*
OH. MY. GOD. I'D TOTALLY *FORGOTTEN ABOUT THAT*.

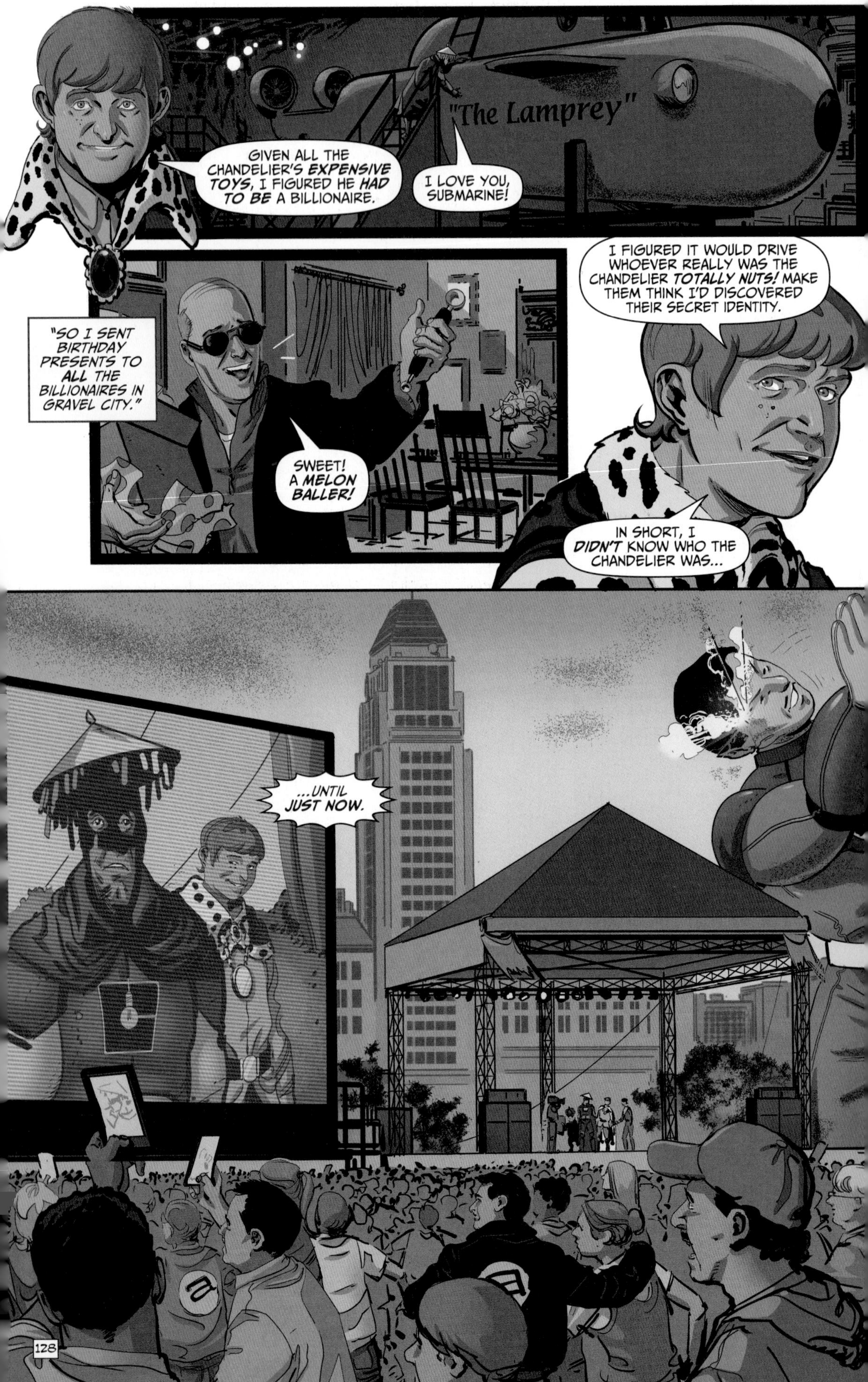
"The Lamprey"
GIVEN ALL THE CHANDELIER'S *EXPENSIVE TOYS,* I FIGURED HE *HAD TO BE* A BILLIONAIRE.
I LOVE YOU, SUBMARINE!
"SO I SENT BIRTHDAY PRESENTS TO **ALL** THE BILLIONAIRES IN GRAVEL CITY."
SWEET! A *MELON BALLER!*
I FIGURED IT WOULD DRIVE WHOEVER REALLY WAS THE CHANDELIER *TOTALLY NUTS!* MAKE THEM THINK I'D DISCOVERED THEIR SECRET IDENTITY.
IN SHORT, I *DIDN'T* KNOW WHO THE CHANDELIER WAS...
...UNTIL *JUST NOW.*

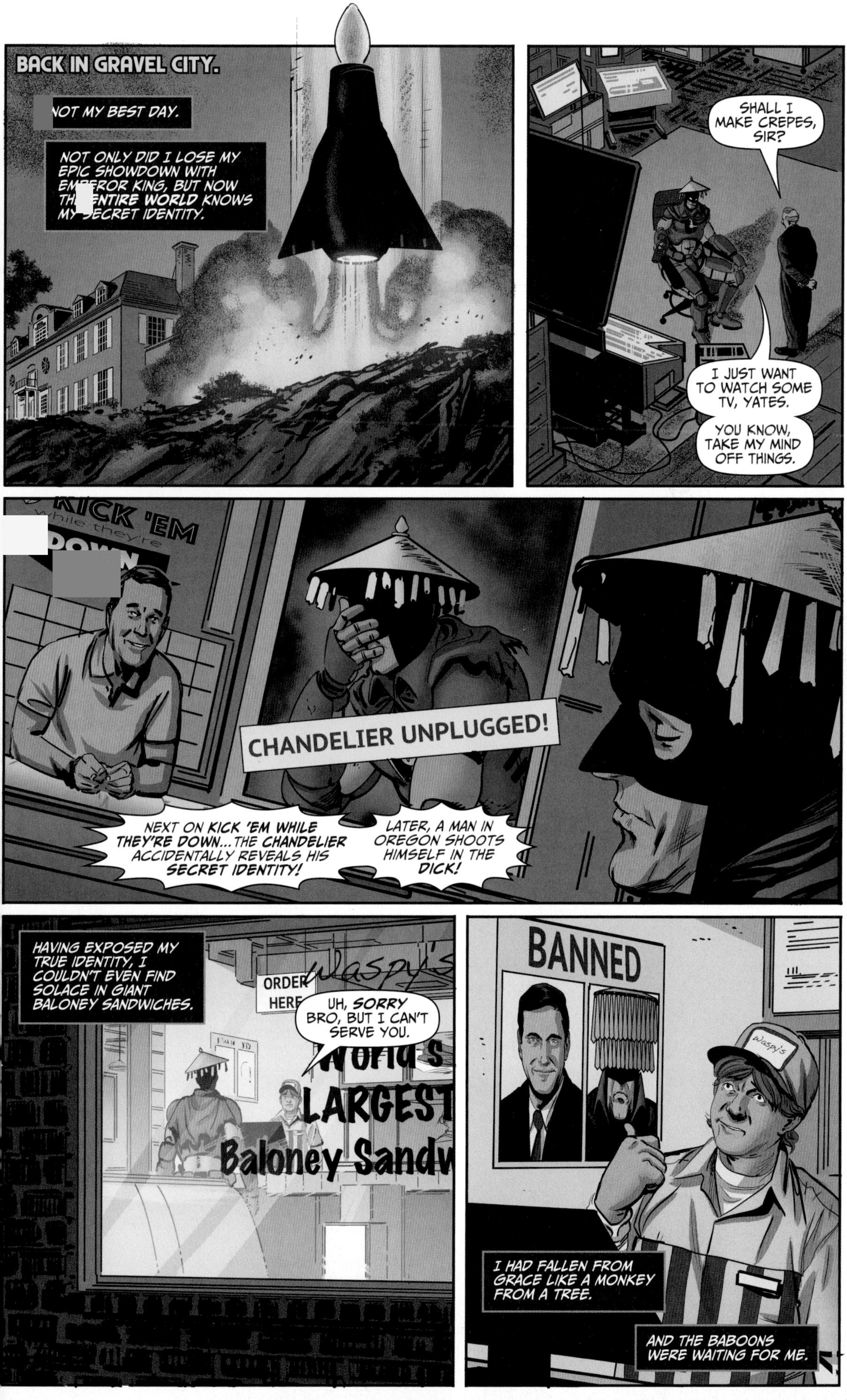
BACK IN GRAVEL CITY.
NOT MY BEST DAY.
NOT ONLY DID I LOSE MY EPIC SHOWDOWN WITH EMPEROR KING, BUT NOW THE ENTIRE WORLD KNOWS MY SECRET IDENTITY.
SHALL I MAKE CREPES, SIR?
I JUST WANT TO WATCH SOME TV, YATES.
YOU KNOW, TAKE MY MIND OFF THINGS.
KICK 'EM
while they're
CHANDELIER UNPLUGGED!
NEXT ON KICK 'EM WHILE THEY'RE DOWN...THE CHANDELIER ACCIDENTALLY REVEALS HIS SECRET IDENTITY!
LATER, A MAN IN OREGON SHOOTS HIMSELF IN THE DICK!
HAVING EXPOSED MY TRUE IDENTITY, I COULDN'T EVEN FIND SOLACE IN GIANT BALONEY SANDWICHES.
ORDER HERE
Waspy's
UH, SORRY BRO, BUT I CAN'T SERVE YOU.
LARGEST
Baloney Sandw
BANNED
Waspy's
I HAD FALLEN FROM GRACE LIKE A MONKEY FROM A TREE.
AND THE BABOONS WERE WAITING FOR ME.

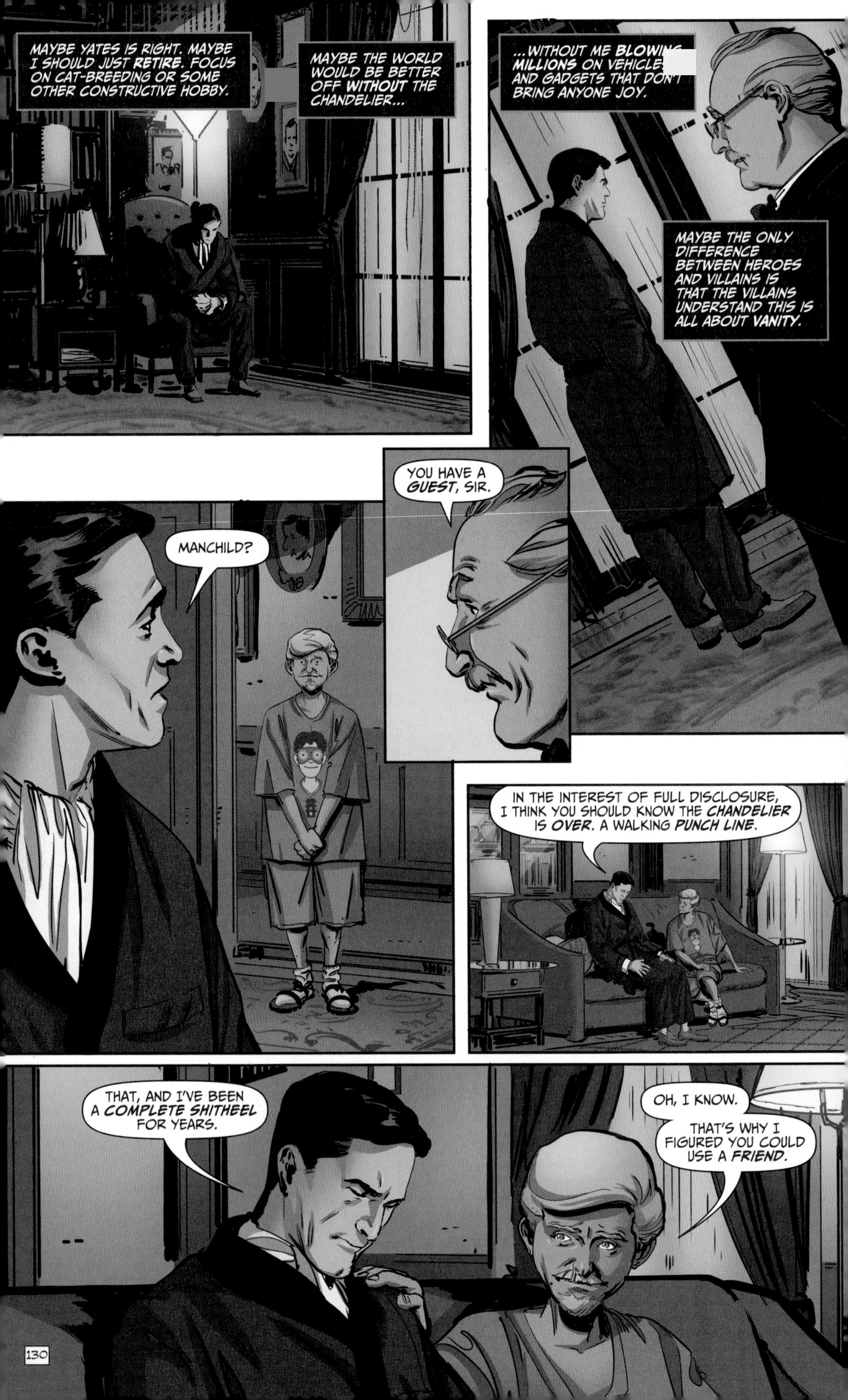
MAYBE YATES IS RIGHT. MAYBE I SHOULD JUST RETIRE. FOCUS ON CAT-BREEDING OR SOME OTHER CONSTRUCTIVE HOBBY.
MAYBE THE WORLD WOULD BE BETTER OFF WITHOUT THE CHANDELIER...
...WITHOUT ME BLOWING MILLIONS ON VEHICLES AND GADGETS THAT DON'T BRING ANYONE JOY.
MAYBE THE ONLY DIFFERENCE BETWEEN HEROES AND VILLAINS IS THAT THE VILLAINS UNDERSTAND THIS IS ALL ABOUT VANITY.
MANCHILD?
YOU HAVE A GUEST, SIR.
IN THE INTEREST OF FULL DISCLOSURE, I THINK YOU SHOULD KNOW THE CHANDELIER IS OVER. A WALKING PUNCH LINE.
THAT, AND I'VE BEEN A COMPLETE SHITHEEL FOR YEARS.
OH, I KNOW.
THAT'S WHY I FIGURED YOU COULD USE A FRIEND.

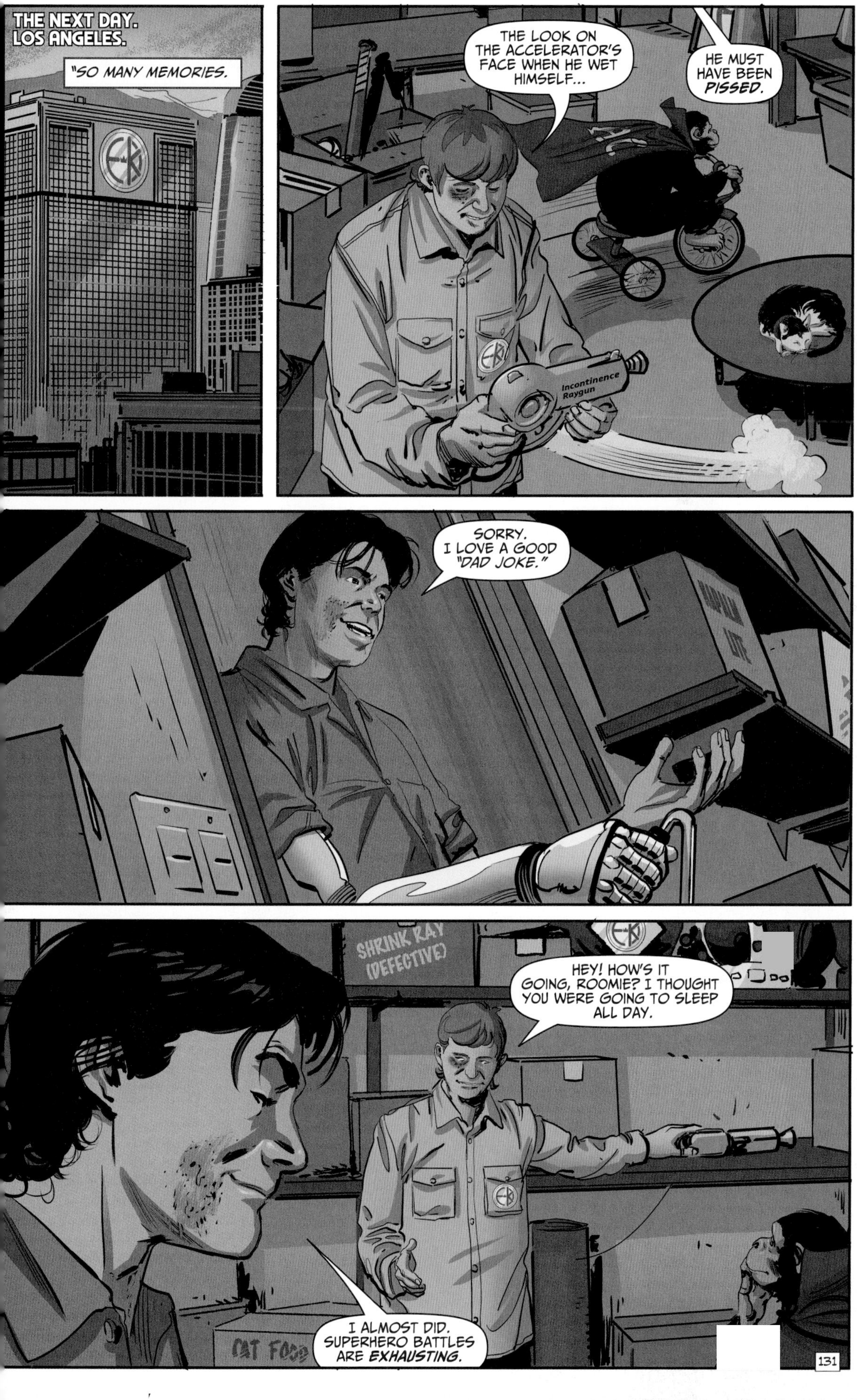
THE NEXT DAY. LOS ANGELES.
"SO MANY MEMORIES.
THE LOOK ON THE ACCELERATOR'S FACE WHEN HE WET HIMSELF...
HE MUST HAVE BEEN *PISSED*.
Incontinence Raygun
SORRY. I LOVE A GOOD "DAD JOKE."
SHRINK RAY (DEFECTIVE)
HEY! HOW'S IT GOING, ROOMIE? I THOUGHT YOU WERE GOING TO SLEEP ALL DAY.
I ALMOST DID. SUPERHERO BATTLES ARE *EXHAUSTING*.
CAT FOOD

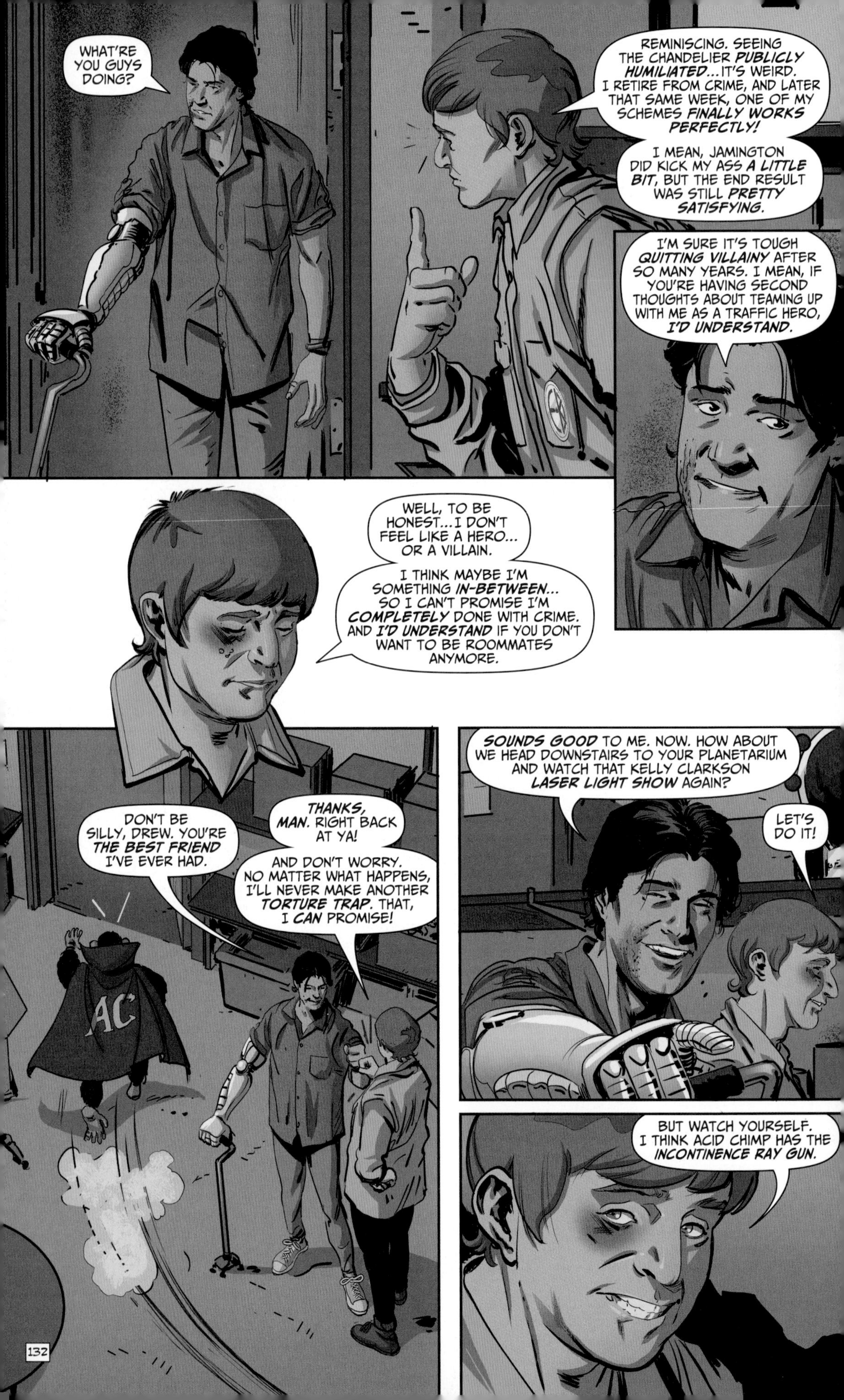
WHAT'RE YOU GUYS DOING?
REMINISCING. SEEING THE CHANDELIER PUBLICLY HUMILIATED... IT'S WEIRD. I RETIRE FROM CRIME, AND LATER THAT SAME WEEK, ONE OF MY SCHEMES FINALLY WORKS PERFECTLY!
I MEAN, JAMINGTON DID KICK MY ASS A LITTLE BIT, BUT THE END RESULT WAS STILL PRETTY SATISFYING.
I'M SURE IT'S TOUGH QUITTING VILLAINY AFTER SO MANY YEARS. I MEAN, IF YOU'RE HAVING SECOND THOUGHTS ABOUT TEAMING UP WITH ME AS A TRAFFIC HERO, I'D UNDERSTAND.
WELL, TO BE HONEST... I DON'T FEEL LIKE A HERO... OR A VILLAIN.
I THINK MAYBE I'M SOMETHING IN-BETWEEN... SO I CAN'T PROMISE I'M COMPLETELY DONE WITH CRIME. AND I'D UNDERSTAND IF YOU DON'T WANT TO BE ROOMMATES ANYMORE.
DON'T BE SILLY, DREW. YOU'RE THE BEST FRIEND I'VE EVER HAD.
THANKS, MAN. RIGHT BACK AT YA!
AND DON'T WORRY. NO MATTER WHAT HAPPENS, I'LL NEVER MAKE ANOTHER TORTURE TRAP. THAT, I CAN PROMISE!
AC
SOUNDS GOOD TO ME. NOW. HOW ABOUT WE HEAD DOWNSTAIRS TO YOUR PLANETARIUM AND WATCH THAT KELLY CLARKSON LASER LIGHT SHOW AGAIN?
LET'S DO IT!
BUT WATCH YOURSELF. I THINK ACID CHIMP HAS THE INCONTINENCE RAY GUN.

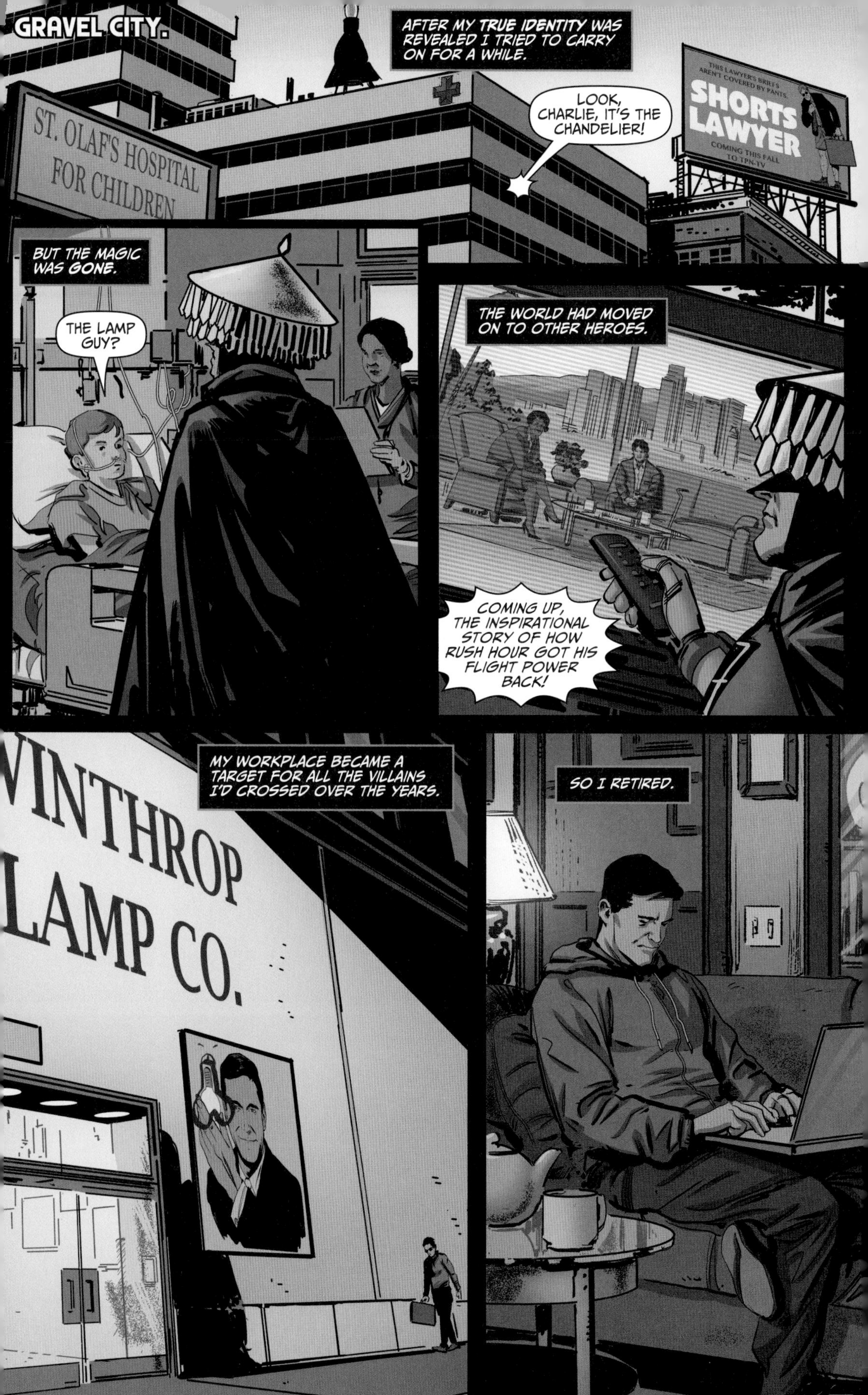
GRAVEL CITY.
AFTER MY TRUE IDENTITY WAS REVEALED I TRIED TO CARRY ON FOR A WHILE.
ST. OLAF'S HOSPITAL FOR CHILDREN
LOOK, CHARLIE, IT'S THE CHANDELIER!
THIS LAWYER'S BRIEFS AREN'T COVERED BY PANTS.
SHORTS LAWYER
COMING THIS FALL TO TPN-TV
BUT THE MAGIC WAS GONE.
THE LAMP GUY?
THE WORLD HAD MOVED ON TO OTHER HEROES.
COMING UP, THE INSPIRATIONAL STORY OF HOW RUSH HOUR GOT HIS FLIGHT POWER BACK!
MY WORKPLACE BECAME A TARGET FOR ALL THE VILLAINS I'D CROSSED OVER THE YEARS.
WINTHROP LAMP CO.
SO I RETIRED.

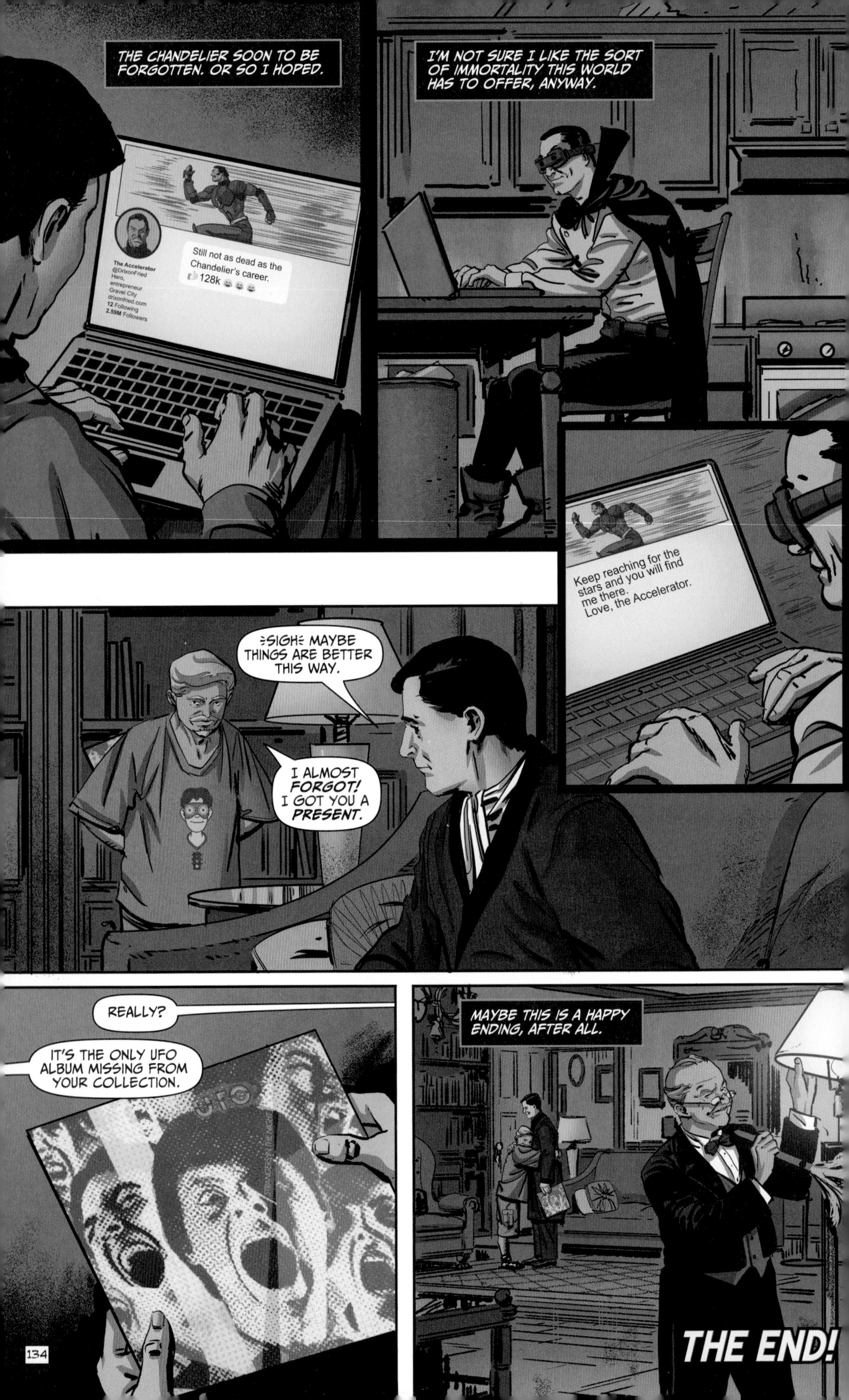
THE CHANDELIER SOON TO BE FORGOTTEN. OR SO I HOPED.
The Accelerator
@DrixonFried
Hero, entrepreneur
Gravel City
drixonfried.com
12 Following
2.59M Followers
Still not as dead as the Chandelier's career.
128k
I'M NOT SURE I LIKE THE SORT OF IMMORTALITY THIS WORLD HAS TO OFFER, ANYWAY.
Keep reaching for the stars and you will find me there.
Love, the Accelerator.
=SIGH= MAYBE THINGS ARE BETTER THIS WAY.
I ALMOST *FORGOT!* I GOT YOU A *PRESENT.*
REALLY?
IT'S THE ONLY UFO ALBUM MISSING FROM YOUR COLLECTION.
UFO
MAYBE THIS IS A HAPPY ENDING, AFTER ALL.
THE END!

Modern Warfare Set! 100 Pieces for $1.00!

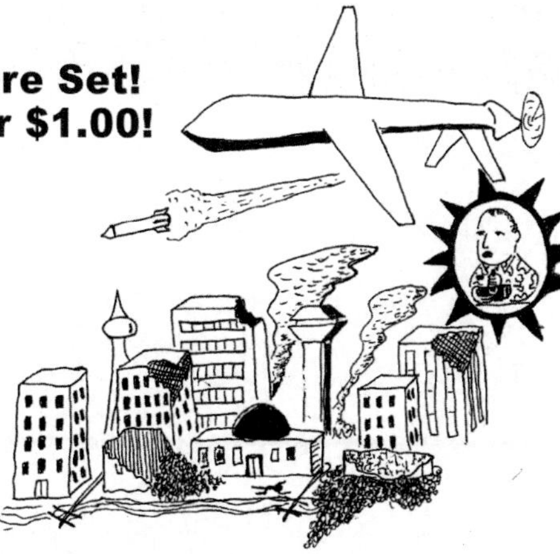

Each piece designed for realism, made in durable plastic. Set includes: 10 American drones armed with Hellfire Missiles. 1 Drone Operator (seated in office chair). 1 Drone Operator (selecting candy bar at vending machine). 50 "Action Corpses". 5 Old Men Walking Aimlessly Through Rubble. 10 shell-shocked children. 5 Grieving Widows/Mothers. 18 Survivors Who Will Never Have A Decent Night of Sleep Again. Send $1 to Devil's Playground. Quincy, MA

Sell GRIT! America's Favorite Magazine! Make $$$! Meet questionable strangers going door-to-door. Learn valuable lessons about answering ads in comic books. Sell GRIT!

Defend GRIT! Work from home! All you need is a phone! Pretend to be a lawyer or a customer service rep. Deflect spurious lawsuits and complaints away from GRIT main office. Defend GRIT!

Become GRIT! For complicated legal reasons, GRIT now claims that all sales reps were independent contractors not acting under instructions from GRIT parent company. This means you're the boss now! Become GRIT!

MAGIC HOLE!

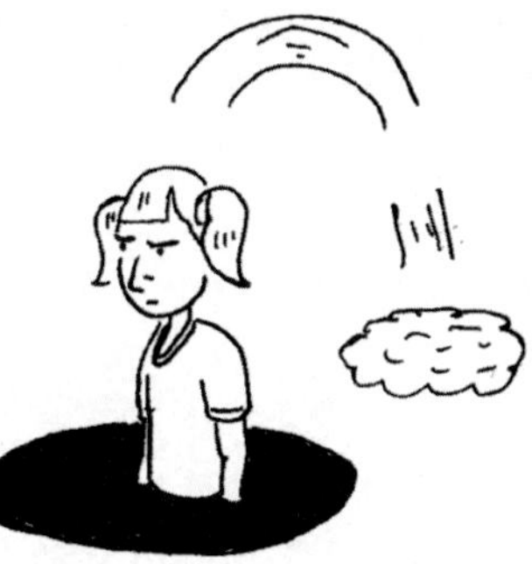

Place this black circular hole anywhere on the ground. Jump in to escape this reality (and possibly every other), or just stare into the black abyss to conceptualize your own non-existence. Works best on flat surfaces. Send $1 to Anywhere But Here Toys & Gags. Yashua, VT.

Become a Ventriloquist!

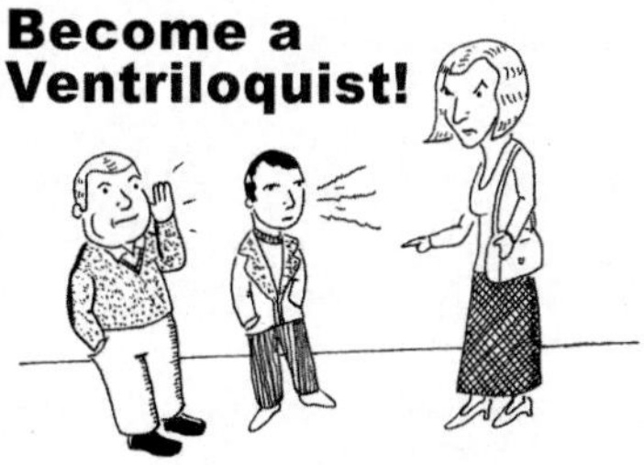

Throw your voice. Share hot-takes anonymously. Be a straight white man pretending to be a gay black woman. Toxify discourse while maintaining deniability. Accountability is for others. Send $2 to Troll Farm. Pocatello, ID.

Copper Lincoln Bust. Bust commemorating America's greatest president, forged in valuable copper and mounted on circular base. Comes stamped with year and official motto of US Treasury. Send $1 to Hoodwink LLC. Lexington, KY.

DYING INSIDE

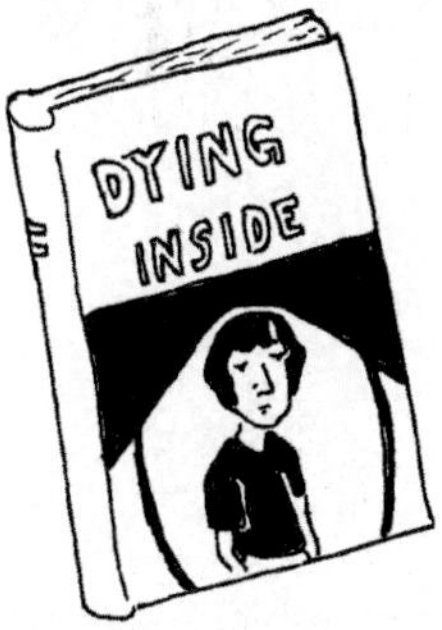
DYING INSIDE

(Book) Living in a small American town? Learn how to not get murders pinned on you despite looking vaguely satanic. Ten easy tips for keeping your mouth shut and killing time until the day when you can leave forever. Send $5.99 to Books Your Parents Will Probably Just Throw Away When They Arrive in the Mail. Seattle, WA.

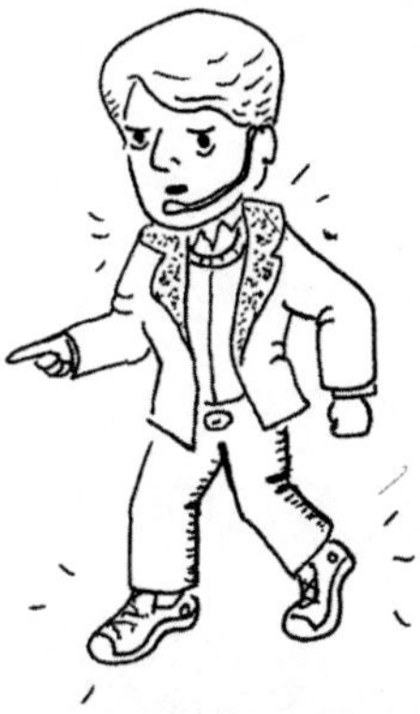

LIL MEGACHURCH PASTOR.

Comes with hair, make-up, and bluetooth headset. Look vibrant and trustworthy to the untrained eyes of an 80 year-old with dementia. Earn Big $$$ without really making anything or paying any taxes. Somehow totally legal. Send $5 to Holy Crap Industries. Amarillo, TX

BEACH BODY WORKOUT KIT!

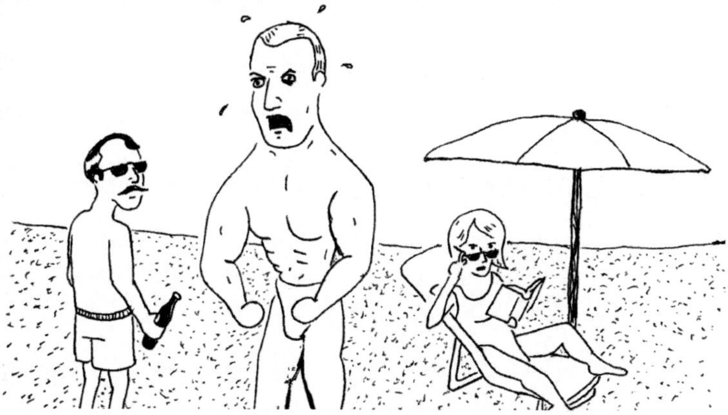

Tired of being a despised weakling? Become an insufferable bully instead! Impress all the girls until the inevitable moment when your emotional bankruptcy is discovered. Good for shaping, toning, or wondering why you are alone despite being so muscular. Send $10.99 to Poorly Conceived Solutions, Ogden UT.

BAD WORDS

Thanks for dropping by BAD WORDS. I'm Bouncing Baby Bryce, co-creator of MY BAD and your host for the next page and a third. Right here at the top, I want to let you in on some exciting news. AHOY has offered me the opportunity to continue answering your MY BAD email and letters in **BAD WORDS SEASON TWO!** And, speaking of MY BAD, hopefully the comic book itself will **also** be receiving a season two pick-up. It would be really strange to do this column without a book for it to be published in, but if that's what I'm asked to do, dammit, I'll do my level best.

Bryce and Mark,

I'm not normally a hot-headed type person, but when I saw what you did to my favorite character, the Accelerator, I'll admit, I overreacted a bit. My hero ripped in half by giant lizard men?! I was outraged. "What kind of crappy writing is this?" I said to my Guinea pig Gus. And then I began to plot my revenge against you both.

But later that night, after my bubble bath, I started to see things differently. As much as I hate it when superheroes die, I absolutely love it when they come back from the dead! It's so cool. Remember when Superman came back from the dead? And Spider-Man? And Wolverine? And Hulk? And Flash? And Human Torch? And Scarlet Witch? And Bucky? And Robin? And—

Pat
Seattle, WA

My apologies, Pat, but I had to edit out your last 347 examples of superhero resurrections. We just don't have the space to print them all. Also, you seem to be implying that the Accelerator will return from the dead in some future Important New Superhero Universe story, but I have to let you know that such a return looks very unlikely. The average superhero resurrection runs somewhere in the mid-to-upper six figures. It's no surprise that all of the 356 resurrected characters you mention are published by Marvel or DC. Perhaps when AHOY is purchased by a multi-billion dollar corporation we'll have the cash flow to afford an Accelerator resurrection. Until then, we'll all have to keep his memory alive in our hearts. Or brains. Our brains would probably be better with the memory thing.

Bryce Ingman,

This is a friendly reminder that your student loan payment is seriously past due. Make a payment today to get your account back on track!

If your loans remain in past due status we will be forced to punish you.

Dawn Garfield
Bavient Loan Servicing

Why do people keep sending private correspondence to me here at BAD WORDS? It's not cool, folks. The fact that I never respond to personal phone calls, texts, DMs, or email gives you no right to bother me here at work. Knock it off.

Papa,

Mommy said you are coming home after you finish working on this comic book. Will you be home next weekend for my birthday party?

Mommy has pictures of you on her phone and she shows them to me. I miss you so much, Papa. I'm very hungry and Mommy says you will bring food.

Love,
Bryce Jr.
Drain, OR

Okay. I just warned you guys about private correspondence! I'm tempted to ignore this, but since you're my son, I'll respond.

I'm sorry, Bryce Jr., but I won't be able to make it home for your birthday. The other day, as I was watching the sunset out on the AHOY Tower penthouse balcony here in Honolulu, Hawaii, I was visited by a charming little bird named Mayzie. And guess what! Mayzie laid an egg right there on the balcony. Mayzie is one of those talking birds and she asked me to sit on the egg and keep it warm until she came back from an important trip. Of course, I told her I would.

And although I'm constantly getting teased about the egg-sitting by Mark, Tom, and the whole AHOY crew, I'm not going to break my promise to Mayzie. She needs my help with this egg and I'm not going to let her down. I meant what I said and I said what I meant. Bouncing Baby Bryce is faithful. One hundred percent.

Say "hi" to your mom for me!

Mark, Bryce, and Peter,

MY BAD is so delightfully funny that I decided to stop pretending I'm dead so I could send you this letter. Keep up the good work!

Andy Kaufman
NYC, NY

Thanks, Andy! I loved you in Heartbeeps. Any chance of a sequel?

Peter, Mark, and Bryce,

Was I dreaming or did I see a copy of MY BAD #4 being awarded the silver medal in Men's Short Track Speed Skating at the recent Winter Olympics?

Violet
Austin, TX

No, Violet, you weren't dreaming. Honestly, I wasn't even going to bring this subject up, because I think he should have won gold. Why dwell on failure? Get this, Violet. Mark, my MY BAD co-writer, is actually going to throw MY BAD #4 a big party because "it defies both the laws of physics and common sense that a paper-and-ink comic book glued to a pair of ice skates could medal in the Olympics and this must be celebrated." (I maintain that it's pretty silly to get all worked up over nothing but I'll probably go to the party anyway because Mark said there's going to be pizza.)

And now it's time for another enlightening edition of Tom's Toolbox!

TOM'S TOOLBOX!

Oh. It's you. Greetings, AHOYniks.

As you read these remarks, you may detect a more somber tone than usual. That's because I've been going through some very heavy personal changes. I'll get to those, but first a little backstory. The eagle-eyed among you probably saw the warning from the Comics Code Authority that we featured on the first interior page of this ish. Maybe you figured that we were required by the censors to run it. Well, nothing could be further from the truth.

When I initially read the piece, I was blown away by its honesty, its insight, its Manchild-like eagerness to shatter the barriers between a life spent reading comics and one well-lived. You read that right, AHOYniks. The warning convinced me. I'm still going to show up for work every day, still going to produce the junk we've addicted you to, but consider this your notice that my heart won't be in it at all.

I now see that the joy I felt putting together these devilish pamphlets was really nothing more than the thrill of dominance. Dominance over you, my unwitting victims. And for that, I can never apologize enough.

Believe me, I could go on and on about all the ways AHOY comics—indeed, *all* comics—are so toxic, so ruinous, so catastrophically devastating, but I just don't feel up to it. Not today. Besides, they say a picture's worth a thousand words—so take it away, Joe Orsak.

Occupare omnes terras,

Tom

COMING AHOY-TRACTIONS

EDGAR ALLAN POE'S SNIFTER OF DEATH #6—Last issue! Our anthology theme this month is, "Complaining and Whining About How Terribly Public Life is Going!" First, a demon drags Poe through the hellish nightmare landscape we call the Internet, in "Silence - A Fable" by Paul Constant and John Lucas! THEN! The American people elect a new President—Death itself, in "Putting the D in DC" by Brian Schirmer and Ryan Kelly!—***March 30!***

G.I.L.T. #1—Meet Hildy Winters, a tough, outspoken survivor of New York City's Upper West Side—with her very own time-travel portal. For Hildy belongs to G.I.L.T., the Guild of Independent Lady Temporalists. Their prime directive: Do not alter the past without co-op board approval! A snappy, stylish urban fantasy by novelist/comics writer Alisa Kwitney (*Rogue: Untouched, The Sandman Presents*) and artist Mauricet (*Star Wars Adventures, Dastardly & Muttley*). Variant cover by Jill Thompson!—***April 6!***

THE WRONG EARTH: FAME & FORTUNE #1—A satirical one-shot from *MY BAD*'s own Mark Russell, featuring the gritty vigilante Dragonfly and his campy counterpart, Dragonflyman! On Earth-Alpha, Dragonflyman and his billionaire alter-ego Richard Fame work to bring citizens together. On Earth-Omega, the Dragonfly busts heads and breaks unions with a savage intensity. But they both share one goal: build a new sports stadium with Richard Fame's name on it! Art by Michael Montenat (*Happy Hour*). Cover by Jamal Igle; variants by Michael Montenat and Gene Ha!—***April 13!***

NEXT: After reading the Toolbox, I gotta say: What's the use? What good is any of this? It's a lot of effort, sure—but to what end? Can anyone answer me? Anyone? —Bryce

Write to MY BAD—or any AHOY mag—at letters@comicsahoy.com. Snail mail: PO Box 189, DeWitt, NY 13214. Mark "OK to print" if it is.

If you don't see your letter here, it might show up in the free, funny-as-anything AHOY Comics Newsletter! Subscribe at the case-sensitive bit.ly/newsahoy.

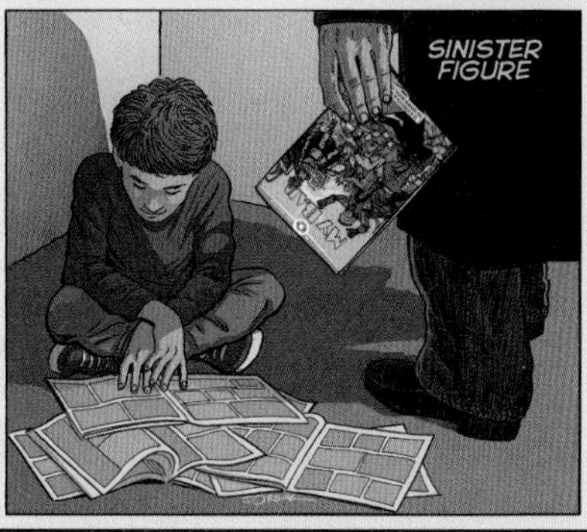
SINISTER FIGURE

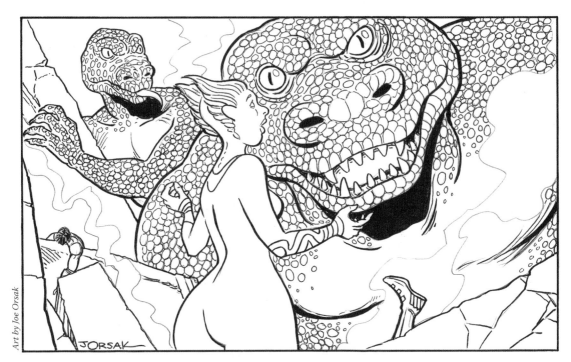

Art by Joe Orsak

FINITE CRISIS
AN UNTOLD TALE OF THE ACCELERATOR

by BRYCE INGMAN

"Mom, are the Giant Lizard Men going to hurt us?"

Dumile looked again at the insanity occurring outside of her 15th-story apartment. Three Giant Lizard Men were knocking down buildings and crushing pedestrians under their immense feet. The massive nostril of one of the vicious lizard creatures was so close that she could have opened the window and thrown the family rail-cat into it. But she didn't need to take that kind of risk. The Accelerator had arrived to save the day. He'd make short work of the Giant Lizard Men. Dumile reassured her daughter. "Don't worry, honey. The Accelerator is here."

The Accelerator was the hero of two worlds: Dumile's home planet of Drixon and a far-away planet called Earth. He was often referred to as the "fastest man in the universe." (Although the Accelerator was certainly the fastest person on Drixon, Dumile was unsure how such a universal distinction could have possibly been proven.) But lately Drixon didn't see much of the Accelerator. The hero was spending most of his time on Earth. There were even rumors that he was cheating on his Drixonian wife by mating with an Earth human. Dumile personally didn't care what the Accelerator did with his free time. She was just happy he was back on Drixon to take care of the Giant Lizard Men.

Through her window, Dumile observed the confrontation. The Accelerator was saying something to one of the Giant Lizard Men. He was wagging a finger at the creature, as if sternly warning him. The angry Lizard Man tried to step on the Accelerator, but the hero easily evaded the beast's foot. As the Accelerator laughed at the monster's ineffective attempt to crush him, another Lizard Man,

who was positioned behind the Drixonian hero, reached down to grab him. Dumile began opening her window to scream a warning, but it was too late. This second Lizard Man swiftly scooped up the surprised Accelerator, ripped his body in half, and tossed the two chunks of hero over its shoulders. For a few seconds, his legs and lower torso ran around like a beheaded kurdle-bird. Then the legs fell over, unmoving. The Accelerator was dead.

"Mom, I thought you said the Accelerator would save us."

Dumile sighed. Parenting was hard. And on top of it, the family rail-cat was nowhere to be found. She'd have to think of another solution. "I know, honey. I thought he would. Stay here. I better go talk to the Giant Lizard Men."

****

Five minutes later, Dumile stood in the street looking up at one of three Giant Lizard Men who were destroying her neighborhood. So far, it hadn't even noticed her. "Hey! Asshole! Down here!"

The Giant Lizard Man stopped trying to knock over a building with a fancy towering spire and looked down at Dumile. "What?" he growled. His voice shook the street like thunder.

"What are you doing?"

"What do you mean 'what are you doing?' Isn't it obvious, little ape? We're the Lizard Boys and we're destroying your stupid planet. Hahahaha!"

"Why? For what purpose?"

The creature shook its head in disgust. "Come on. Everyone knows that the Lizard Boys travel from planet to planet in search of salt. Once we subjugate the population of a planet, we use our machines to drain their oceans. Then we gather all the planet's salt and leave. You seriously haven't heard this about us? Seems hard to believe. We do it all the time. It's, like, common knowledge."

Of course, Dumile did know all of this. The Lizard Boys were intergalactically infamous for their murderous, destructive, thieving behavior. She'd only wanted to get the Lizard Boy's attention. Dumile pictured Drixon's majestic oceans looking drained and lifeless. It pissed her off and she wasn't going to let it happen. The Drixonian didn't have any super powers like the Accelerator, but she was a *very* convincing liar. Dumile could lie like a pro. She lied to her mate, Mago, regularly. It helped her avoid needless drama. Mago could be a bit much at times.

Dumile looked into the Giant Lizard Man's immense eyes and manufactured a sincere tone. "You know Drixon has fresh-water oceans, don't you? No salt at all." This was nonsense. Drixon's oceans contained plenty of salt.

A second Lizard Brother, who had been busy throwing magno-cars at military defense planes, overheard Dumile and stamped over to stand next to the first lizard man. "Hey. Bondar! Did I hear that little ape say there's no salt in Drixon's oceans?"

"Yep. You heard right. That's what it said."

They were taking the bait. Dumile pressed on. "What gave you the idea that we have salt in our oceans anyway?"

Bondar kicked a magno-bus that was foolishly attempting to drive between his massive legs. The bus rocketed through the air, its passengers screaming in horror. "My super-smart cousin Slyzzyx told me about how Drixon's oceans contain 37 quadrillion tons of delicious salt."

Dumile doubled down on her heroic lie. "Ha! More like 37 ounces. Your cousin screwed up. But if you don't believe me, go check. There's an ocean about fifty miles from here."

The two Lizard Brothers looked at each other. Bondar scratched his head. "Do you want to go check, Zurgy?"

"I'm actually pretty tired from the trip here. You know I don't sleep well on space planes. Do you want to?"

"Not really." Bondar dejectedly dropped the military jet he held in his hands.

Zurgy began walking up the road toward the third Lizard Boy, who was tearing apart the local hospital with apparent delight. "Lairee is going to be really disappointed. I haven't seen him this happy in months. He's really been looking forward to all that salt."

Bondar addressed the helpful little ape beneath him. "I don't suppose you know of a nearby planet with lots of salt in their oceans do you?"

****

Dumile knew little about Earth. She'd never been there. Few Drixonians had. After first contact, the leadership of her planet had decided Earth was too primitive and violent to regularly interact with. Aside from The Accelerator, Drixonians kept Earth at arm's length. It was safer that way, and since Earth hadn't developed the sort of intergalactic travel methods Drixon had, there was little chance of hotheaded, ignorant Earthlings bothering Drixonians anytime soon.

But Dumile did know one thing about Earth. They had salt. Apparently they had a lot of it. Six years ago, the Accelerator had started an "Earth Food Lottery." The Accelerator was a big fan of Earth food and wanted to popularize their recipes on Drixon. He used a transport freighter to bring back tons of Earth food whenever he returned to Drixon. But the stuff was so salty it was barely edible. And if you did force it down your throat, you were thirstier than a blood-bat.

Dumile and her mate knew this from personal experience. They'd been among the winners of the Accelerator's annual Earth Food Lottery twice now. (All Drixonians were automatically enrolled.) The first time, in 35,890, the couple had been gifted a can of food-like items called *Pringles*. They'd made Dumile violently ill. (Although her mate seemed to enjoy them.) Then, in 35,893, they won a food item described as "tomato soup." It was liquid and better than *Pringles*, but the fact that she was terribly thirsty for days afterward made Dumile certain it was just another Earthling salt-delivery device. What sort of palates did Earthlings have?

Still, even if they did eat shitty food, she doubted Earthlings were all bad. Dumile could have just made up a fake planet. But, as an expert liar, she knew it was much easier to lie convincingly if the lie contained some truth. And she'd needed to be sure the Lizard Boys would believe her deception about Drixon's oceans; she had a daughter to protect. There had been no choice but to point them toward Earth.

Dumile considered sending a warning message to Earth. But she didn't know how to contact the distant planet. She consoled herself with the well-known fact that the Lizard Boys were extremely poor navigators. Slyzzyx had almost certainly helped them locate Drixon. And Dumile had given the massive creatures only the vaguest of directions to Earth's solar system. It was unlikely that they could find it on their own. And even if they asked Slyzzyx, there was no reason to think that Bondar's cousin even knew about the existence of Earth, let alone its location.

Dumile decided to let it go and think about warning Earth tomorrow. After all, she had already saved one planet from destruction this afternoon. That was pretty good for a Flurzday.

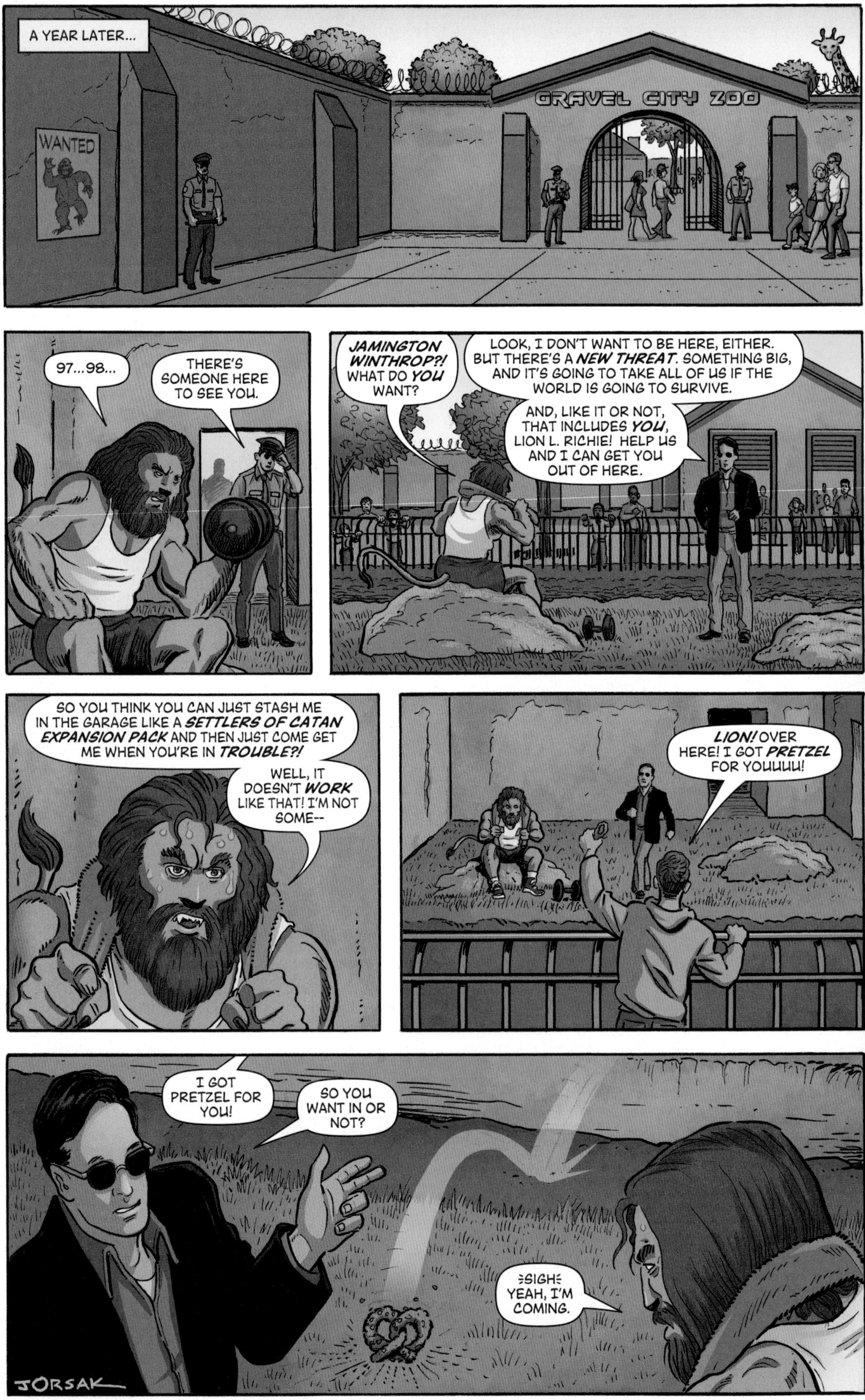
A YEAR LATER...
WANTED
GRAVEL CITY ZOO
97...98...
THERE'S SOMEONE HERE TO SEE YOU.
JAMINGTON WINTHROP?! WHAT DO YOU WANT?
LOOK, I DON'T WANT TO BE HERE, EITHER. BUT THERE'S A NEW THREAT. SOMETHING BIG, AND IT'S GOING TO TAKE ALL OF US IF THE WORLD IS GOING TO SURVIVE.
AND, LIKE IT OR NOT, THAT INCLUDES YOU, LION L. RICHIE! HELP US AND I CAN GET YOU OUT OF HERE.
SO YOU THINK YOU CAN JUST STASH ME IN THE GARAGE LIKE A SETTLERS OF CATAN EXPANSION PACK AND THEN JUST COME GET ME WHEN YOU'RE IN TROUBLE?!
WELL, IT DOESN'T WORK LIKE THAT! I'M NOT SOME--
LION! OVER HERE! I GOT PRETZEL FOR YOUUUU!
I GOT PRETZEL FOR YOU!
SO YOU WANT IN OR NOT?
SIGH
YEAH, I'M COMING.
JORSAK

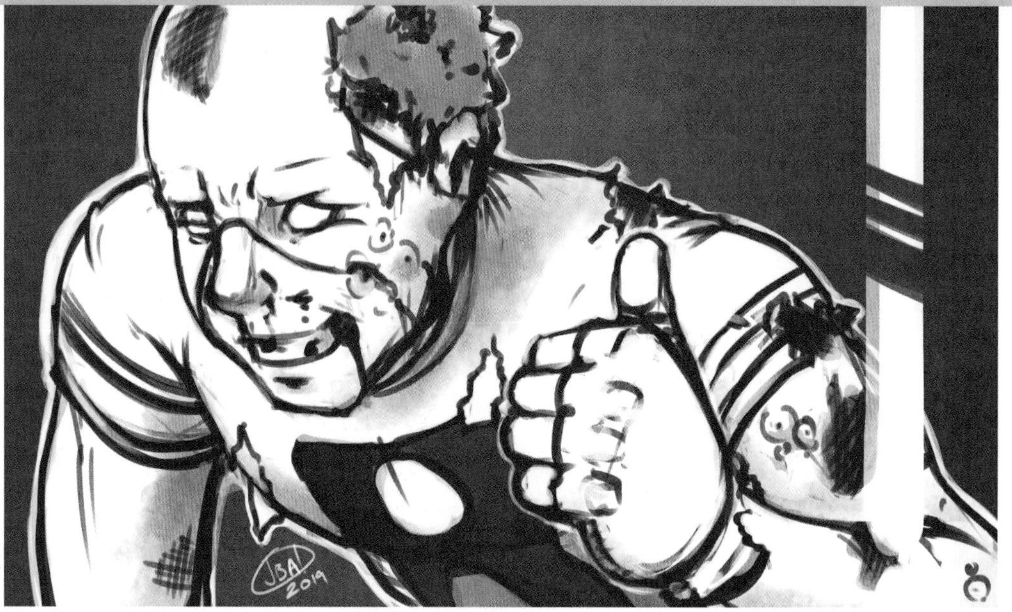
JBAD 2019

Art by Justin Addison

MY BAD

by BRYCE INGMAN

When the alarm sounded at 3:00 a.m. to alert him that his trap had finally sprung, Emperor King was deep in the embrace of a lovely dream wherein the entire population of Los Angeles, California, had gathered outside his window to listen to him sing karaoke. His annoyance at the interruption quickly evaporated as he realized the alarm's meaning. He had captured his archenemy, the Accelerator. If he wanted to watch that arrogant jerk be tortured to death, he needed to get up to the roof. He threw on a robe and affixed a solid gold crown atop his balding head. The fun was about to start.

"Not fast enough this time, were you, Accelerator? You never should have returned to Earth. This is my planet, alien. I am destined to be its emperor. And with your death, nothing will—"

It was hard to see. The moon was new and partially blocked by clouds.

"Wait. Hold on a second."

Emperor King flipped on the floodlights and took a good look at the figure ensnared behind the airtight, bulletproof glass of the eight-foot-tall cylinder.

"Shit."

It wasn't the Accelerator. It was some guy in a reflective orange leotard with the image of a green traffic signal on his chest. It was the ugliest costume Emperor King had ever seen. "Who the hell are you?"

The man cleared his throat. "Rush Hour."

"I've never heard of you."

Rush Hour sighed. "Yeah. Not surprised. I'm kind of new. I need a viral video or something."

At that moment, a bell rang, signaling the first stage of torture was about to begin. A light mist began to fill the chamber. Rush Hour recoiled. "What is it? Poison?"

"No. It's Drixonite gas from the Forbidden Continent on Drixon, home planet of the Accelerator. It's harmless to humans, but it causes excruciating pain for Drixonians."

Rush Hour cautiously sniffed the air. "Hey . . . it smells like barbecue!"

Emperor King laughed. "It does, doesn't it? Like burgers!"

"Yeah, *exactly* like a burger . . . Look, man. This was all a mix-up. I'm a traffic-based hero. I fly around and help motorists when there's an accident, blow debris off roadways with my breath blasts, and give tailgaters spankings."

"Nice! I hate tailgaters."

"Right? Anyway, I guess the message I read on reddit/villainboasts was meant for the Accelerator. It's the one about how you're going to 'slow down the world' with a device on this rooftop. See, I recently fought a guy calling himself the Snarl. His whole deal is creating traffic jams, so the 'slow down the world' bit fits his MO, but when I got here, and your trap materialized around me, I realized it wasn't the Snarl who posted the message."

"How?"

Rush Hour pointed up. "You've got your Emperor King logo up here on the ceiling."

Emperor King palm-slapped his forehead. "Of course. I totally forgot I did that."

"It's a cool logo."

"Thanks."

"Look. If you let me out, I'll just be on my way. This doesn't seem to be a traffic-related scheme, so it doesn't really concern me."

Emperor King hesitated. He'd set a rat trap and snared a bird. This was embarrassing. "Look. I'd love to. You seem like a great guy. But. The trap won't open until the torture sequence is complete. That Accelerator's got a silver tongue, and he always tricks me into setting him free with his fancy talk. So, this time, I just did away with the 'off' switch."

The bell rang again.

Rush Hour's eyes grew wide. "More harmless-to-humans stuff?"

"Well, that depends . . . how are you with fire?"

Rush Hour, it turned out, was not too great with fire. Over the two-minute span of stage two, he was repeatedly burned by the seven blowtorches built into the chamber. He attempted to dodge the fiery bursts, but the trap was designed to counteract the lightning-quick movements of the Accelerator, so his attempts to avoid them were pitifully inadequate. Emperor King couldn't watch. After what seemed like an eternity of listening to the man's howls of pain, stage two ended. Rush Hour collapsed to the floor of the trap, third degree burns covering 40 percent of his body, his uniform largely melted into his skin.

Emperor King tried to contain his horror as he assessed the damage. He offered Rush Hour an apologetic smile. "Sorry about that."

The hero sat up, wincing with pain. "Don't stress, man. It's all a misunderstanding. No one's at fault here."

"Wow. That's really understanding of you."

The bell rang. Stage three began. A large metal thermos labeled "WATER" was lowered to the floor near Rush Hour. He immediately grabbed for it and began to unscrew the lid. "Thank God. So thirsty."

"Wait!"

But Emperor King's warning came too late. Hundreds of angry Africanized bees burst forth from the open thermos, and began to sting Rush Hour, oftentimes in the same places as his terrible burns. He jumped around, slapping at the bees. "No! No! Why? Why would you put bees in a thermos?!"

Emperor King wrapped his robe tightly around his body. It was a good question. He attempted to explain his hatred of the Accelerator and how much fun he had imagined the bee trick would be to watch. But seeing it play out with Rush Hour only made him feel queasy.

Finally, a vacuum device in the trap's ceiling began sucking the killer bees out of the chamber. Rush Hour stood in the center of his prison, breathing heavily, looking around for bees.

"They're gone. You can relax. I'm so, so sorry. This whole thing is my bad. My real name's Drew King, by the way. What's your name, buddy?"

Rush Hour's voice was weak. "Aaron Lanebo."

"Lanebo? I went to prep school with a Brad Lanebo. Any relation?"

"Cousin."

"Brad's your cousin?! Holy shit. Braddy and I were on the water polo team together! How's he doing?"

"Good. Wife . . . just had . . . baby."

"Really? That's awesome. I should give him a call. Do you have his number?"

The bell rang again. Rush Hour began to cry.

Stage four consisted of drone-powered metal arms flying around the cylinder and repeatedly punching Rush Hour in the face and groin. Several of his teeth now littered the floor of the trap. His face barely resembled a human visage. The blood and swelling obliterated his normal features. He attempted to speak. "Iz dat ul?"

"Sorry? What was that? I couldn't—"

"Iz dat ul?"

"I'm not catching it. Isabel?"

"No. Iz et ofer?"

"Oh! 'Is it over?' Is that it, Aaron? Are you asking if it's over?"

Rush Hour attempted to smile, nodding. And then the bell rang.

Later, Emperor King decided that the acid stage was the worst. (It certainly did the most damage, completely dissolving Rush Hour's left foot.) But he had to admit that the stabbing sequence was also particularly brutal.

By the sixteenth, and final, stage Rush Hour was unconscious on the floor of the trap, slowly bleeding to death, and so he missed the holograms of beautiful Drixonian women mocking the Accelerator's diminished manhood. (The stabbing stage, like the punching stage, had largely been focused on the groin area.) Emperor King questioned why he had included the mockery stage at all. He had expected the Accelerator would be dead by this point anyway. He just hated the Accelerator *so much*. For the first time in his life, Emperor King realized he may have "anger issues."

As the last hologram faded away, *Blurred Lines* by Robin Thicke began to play from the rooftop sound system, and the cylinder cracked open.

Emperor King called 9-1-1.

Skin grafts. Dental reconstruction. Genital reconstruction. Hair implants. Kidney transplant. Metal plate in skull. Bionic foot. Slowly, Rush Hour healed. And Emperor King paid for it all. It was a miracle that Rush Hour had survived the torture, and an even greater miracle that he declined to press charges against the man responsible. Aaron Lanebo was *extremely* affable. Emperor King was determined to see to it that the young hero fully recovered.

After Rush Hour was released from the hospital, Emperor King visited his home every night to make sure the recovering hero had everything he needed. And four months later, when Emperor King confessed he was having financial troubles because the combination of medical bills and torture chamber construction had drained away nearly all of his trust fund, Rush Hour offered to let the villain move into his spare room.

On the one-year anniversary of the night they met, the two friends sat in their apartment, eating pizza and watching on cable. Emperor King felt better than he had in years. And it wasn't just the delightful antics of Richard Pryor and John Candy that were making him feel so good. Over the last year, his anger had faded away. Maybe all he had ever needed was a friend.

Suddenly, a breaking news report appeared on the television. A sad-eyed reporter shared the news that the Accelerator, a hero admired by freedom-loving people throughout the universe, had been ripped in half and died while protecting his home planet from an alien invasion.

Emperor King smiled. What a perfect day.

BIOGRAPHIES

MARK RUSSELL is the author of not one, but two, books about the Bible: *God Is Disappointed in You* and *Apocrypha Now*. In addition, he is the writer behind AHOY's *SECOND COMING*, *BILLIONAIRE ISLAND* and "The Monster Serials" in *EDGAR ALLAN POE'S SNIFTER OF TERROR*, as well as various DC comic books including *Prez*, *The Flintstones*, and *Exit Stage Left: The Snagglepuss Chronicles*. He lives in obscurity with his family in Portland, Oregon.

Writer/actor/director **BRYCE INGMAN** is the only male writer living in Portland, Oregon without a beard. And it's not because he can't grow one. Because he totally can.

PETER KRAUSE has worked as an artist in comics for over thirty years. Past credits include *Power of Shazam!*, *Metropolis S.C.U.* and *Star Trek: The Next Generation* for DC. His work with writer Mark Waid on *Irredeemable* (Boom Studios) and *Daredevil: Road Warrior* (Marvel) garnered several Eisner nominations. Most recently, he helped reimagine the Archie gang as teens during World War II in *Archie: 1941*.

KELLY FITZPATRICK is a Hugo-nominated comic book colorist and illustrator. She emigrated to Calgary, AB with her Boston Terrier mix, Archie and drinks too much coffee. In her free time, she creates illustrations, self-publishes books, and does aerial acrobatics and yoga. Kelly is also outspoken and committed to educating others on topics such as kink, fibromyalgia/ME/CFS, asexuality, and anxiety/depression.

ROB STEEN is the illustrator of *Flanimals*, the best-selling series of children's books written by Ricky Gervais, and *Erf*, a children's book written by Garth Ennis.

JOE ORSAK was inspired to pursue a life in comics at the age of eleven by the artwork of Joe Sinnott. In 1982, Orsak launched *The Adventures of Captain 'Cuse* comic strip that ran in Syracuse, NY, newspapers for nearly a decade. Joe turned to sports comics in the 1990s, working on comic biographies of Mickey Mantle, Brooks Robinson, and Duke Snider for Magnum Comics—inked by no less than Joe Sinnott! In 2008, Orsak returned to comic strips with *Salt City*, another series about his hometown, written by Douglas Brode. Joe and Doug have also collaborated on the graphic novels *Yellow Rose of Texas: The Myth of Emily Morgan* and *Virgin Vampires*.

PAUL LITTLE is a Canadian colorist who has contributed hues to a bevy of titles from publishers including Image Comics (*Morning Glories*, *Five Weapons*), BOOM! Studios (*Sons of Anarchy*, *Palmiotti and Brady's The Big Con Job*), Joe Books (*Darkwing Duck*, *Disney Princess*), and many more. He lives in the honeymoon capital of the world and is one of the few people who can honestly claim to see Niagara Falls from his living room.

JERRY ORDWAY has written and illustrated comics since the early 1980s, earning acclaim as one of the defining Superman creators of his generation. His groundbreaking work includes the "Death of Superman" storyline and Clark Kent's proposal to Lois Lane. Ordway also reintroduced Captain Marvel in *The Power of Shazam!* and illustrated the adaptation of the blockbuster 1989 *Batman* film.

LEE LOUGHRIDGE is a color artist who has created award-winning work for Marvel, DC, Dark Horse and Image Comics throughout his 25-year career.

JONATHAN CASE hails from the great Pacific Northwest where he loves to make art, write stories, and go on adventures with loved ones—especially if there's a hammock involved. (Daddy's sleepy.) His work includes *Dear Creature*, the crime graphic novel *The New Deal* and the Eisner-award winning *Green River Killer: A True Detective Story* as well as *Batman '66* and *Superman: American Alien*. Case has also contributed to the *Over the Garden Wall* series and created *Little Monarchs*, a joyful post-apocalyptic adventure book for kids. In addition to comics, he creates book covers, illustrates for print and paints murals. You can find some of that up on walls around his current home base of Portland, Oregon.